Catherine Coucom

Cambridge IGCSE™ and O Level
Accounting
Coursebook

Second edition

CAMBRIDGE
UNIVERSITY PRESS

Shaftesbury Road, Cambridge CB2 8EA, United Kingdom

One Liberty Plaza, 20th Floor, New York, NY 10006, USA

477 Williamstown Road, Port Melbourne, VIC 3207, Australia

314–321, 3rd Floor, Plot 3, Splendor Forum, Jasola District Centre, New Delhi – 110025, India

103 Penang Road, #05-06/07, Visioncrest Commercial, Singapore 238467

Cambridge University Press is part of the University of Cambridge.

It furthers the University's mission by disseminating knowledge in the pursuit of education, learning and research at the highest international levels of excellence.

www.cambridge.org
Information on this title: www.cambridge.org/9781316502778

© Cambridge University Press & Assessment 2018

This publication is in copyright. Subject to statutory exception and to the provisions of relevant collective licensing agreements, no reproduction of any part may take place without the written permission of Cambridge University Press.

First published 2018

30 29 28 27 26 25 24 23 22

Printed in Poland by Opolgraf

A catalogue record for this publication is available from the British Library

ISBN 978-1-108-71241-5 Paperback
ISBN 978-1-108-43901-5 Cambridge Elevate enhanced edition (2 years)
ISBN 978-1-108-33917-9 Paperback + Cambridge Elevate enhanced edition (2 years)

Additional resources for this publication at cambridge.org/9781108339179

Cambridge University Press has no responsibility for the persistence or accuracy of URLs for external or third-party internet websites referred to in this publication, and does not guarantee that any content on such websites is, or will remain, accurate or appropriate. Information regarding prices, travel timetables, and other factual information given in this work is correct at the time of first printing but Cambridge University Press does not guarantee the accuracy of such information thereafter.

....

NOTICE TO TEACHERS IN THE UK
It is illegal to reproduce any part of this work in material form (including photocopying and electronic storage) except under the following circumstances:
(i) where you are abiding by a licence granted to your school or institution by the Copyright Licensing Agency;
(ii) where no such licence exists, or where you wish to exceed the terms of a licence, and you have gained the written permission of Cambridge University Press;
(iii) where you are allowed to reproduce without permission under the provisions of Chapter 3 of the Copyright, Designs and Patents Act 1988, which covers, for example, the reproduction of short passages within certain types of educational anthology and reproduction for the purposes of setting examination questions.

....

Example answers and all other end-of-chapter questions were written by the author.

IGCSE™ is the registered trademark of Cambridge Assessment International Education.

Contents

Introduction	iv
Where to find each section of the syllabus	v
How to use this book	vi
Acknowledgements	iix

Section 1		1
1	Introduction to accounting	2
2	Double entry book-keeping – Part A	10
3	The trial balance	29
4	Double entry book-keeping – Part B	38
5	Petty cash books	52
	Section 1: Practice questions	61
Section 2		66
6	Business documents	67
7	Books of prime entry	78
	Section 2: Practice questions	89
Section 3		93
8	Financial statements – Part A	94
9	Financial statements – Part B	110
10	Accounting rules	120
11	Other payables and other receivables	132
12	Accounting for depreciation and disposal of non-current assets	153
13	Irrecoverable debts and provisions for doubtful debts	171
	Section 3: Practice questions	185
Section 4		193
14	Bank reconciliation statements	194
15	Journal entries and correction of errors	206
16	Control accounts	228
17	Incomplete records	241
18	Accounts of clubs and societies	261
19	Partnerships	277
20	Manufacturing accounts	290
21	Limited companies	302
22	Analysis and interpretation	312
	Section 4: Practice questions	331
Glossary		345
Index		349

Introduction

The aim of this book is to provide an up-to-date text covering the Cambridge IGCSE and O Level Accounting syllabuses (0452 and 7707).

This book covers all the topics included on the latest syllabuses for IGCSE Accounting and O Level Accounting. The topics are not necessarily included in the order in which they appear in the syllabus. They have been presented in what the author's long teaching experience has shown to be a suitable order for an accounting student commencing a course at this level. However, there is some flexibility in the sequence in which the topics are studied. Whichever the order in which the topics are studied, it is essential that the whole of the syllabus is covered. The table on page v shows the chapter(s) of the book in which each section of the syllabus may be found. The learning objectives at the beginning of each chapter are exactly the same as the syllabus topics with the following exceptions. The syllabus topics (4.3) '*prepare ledger accounts and journal entries to record accrued and prepaid expenses*' and '*prepare ledger accounts and journal entries to record accrued and prepaid incomes*' have each been split into two learning objectives across two separate chapters. Chapter 11 contains '*prepare ledger accounts to record accrued and prepaid expenses*' and '*prepare ledger accounts to record accrued and prepaid incomes.*' Chapter 15 contains '*prepare journal entries to record accrued and prepaid expenses*' and '*prepare journal entries to record accrued and prepaid incomes.*'

No prior knowledge of accounting is required as this book provides an introduction to accounting and covers all the topics on the syllabus. Each chapter is complete in itself and contains appropriate walkthroughs. There are also short-answer questions at regular intervals which students can use to test their understanding of each section. There are exam-style questions at the end of each chapter and also at the end of each section. Answers to all questions in this Coursebook are provided on the accompanying Teacher's Resource.

In common with most accounting textbooks, dates used in the examples, walkthroughs and questions throughout this book are expressed as 20–0, 20–1, 20–2, and so on.

Where to find each section of the syllabus

Chapter	Syllabus 1		2			3				4					5						6					7	
	1	2	1	2	3	1	2	3	4	1	2	3	4	5	1	2	3	4	5	6	1	2	3	4	5	1	2
One	✓	✓																									
Two			✓																								
Three						✓																					
Four			✓		✓																						
Five					✓																						
Six				✓	✓																						
Seven				✓	✓																						
Eight			✓																								
Nine																											
Ten										✓				✓												✓	✓
Eleven										✓																	
Twelve										✓	✓	✓															
Thirteen								✓					✓														
Fourteen					✓										✓												
Fifteen							✓			✓																	
Sixteen									✓																		
Seventeen															✓					✓							
Eighteen															✓			✓									
Nineteen															✓	✓			✓								
Twenty															✓		✓										
Twenty one															✓				✓								
Twenty two																					✓	✓	✓	✓	✓		

How to use this book

The book is designed to be a practical guide to help build knowledge and understanding of accounting terms, principles and procedures and assumes no prior knowledge of the topics. The book is aligned to the syllabus and will enable you to analyse and present information in the appropriate accounting form as well as interpret and evaluate accounting data so you can draw reasoned conclusions.

Each chapter focuses on developing knowledge and understanding using easy-to-follow walkthroughs that explain accounting concepts. Key terms are highlighted and there are regular opportunities to check progress, test understanding and practice accounting skills.

Learning objectives

In this chapter you will learn to:

- understand and explain the difference between book-keeping and accounting   1.1
- state the purposes of measuring business profit and loss   1.1
- explain the role of accounting in providing information for monitoring progress and decision-making   1.1
- explain the meaning of assets, liabilities and owner's equity   1.2
- explain and apply the accounting equation   1.2
- understand that statements of financial position record assets and liabilities on a specified date.   5.5

Learning objectives – Each chapter begins with the key accounting concepts that you will learn to help you navigate your way through the book and remind you what is important about each topic for your revision. The number after each learning objective refers to the topic number in the syllabus.

LINK

You will learn more about double entry book-keeping in Chapter 4.

Link – Links show you where you can find additional information about related topics.

Walkthrough 22.9

Using the financial statements shown in **Walkthrough 22.1**, calculate (to the nearest whole day) Arun's trade payables turnover.

$$\frac{\$12\,500}{\$97\,000} \times \frac{365}{1} = 47.04 \text{ days} = 48 \text{ days}$$

Walkthrough – Walkthroughs guide you step-by-step through different accounting processes, helping to build your knowledge and skills.

TIP

If you know two elements of the accounting equation you can easily calculate the third element.

Tip – Tips provide additional context, reminders and useful information about key points.

KEY TERMS

Carriage is the cost of transporting goods.
Carriage inwards is the cost of bringing the goods to the business and **carriage outwards** is the cost of delivering the goods to the customer.

Key terms – Definitions help you identify and understand important accounting terminology and concepts.

TEST YOURSELF 2.1

1. Explain why it is necessary to make a double entry in the ledger for each transaction.
2. Explain the use of the folio column in a ledger account.

Test yourself – Test yourself questions aid self-assessment and reinforce knowledge and understanding.

Revision checklist

- A trial balance is a list of the balances on the accounts in the ledger at a certain date.
- A trial balance is prepared to check the arithmetical accuracy of the double entry book-keeping.
- If a trial balance fails to balance, it indicates that an error has been made.
- There are six types of error which are not revealed by a trial balance.

Revision checklist – Checklists at the end of each unit provide a useful summary of the learning points covered.

Exam-style questions

1. Which account will appear in the sales ledger?
   - A Dan, a credit supplier
   - B Gill, a credit customer
   - C Sales
   - D Sales returns

2. Mariam is a trader. On 1 March 20–2 the balances in her cash book were:

   Cash $100 debit
   Bank $494 credit

   The following transactions took place in March 20–2:

   March 4   Paid for repairs to office equipment by cheque, $293
   7   Received a cheque from Nawaz, $110
   11 Purchased motor vehicle paying by credit transfer, $5 130
   13 Took $1 500 from the bank for personal use
   19 Paid $286 to Anwar by credit transfer
   21 Paid office expenses in cash, $67
   27 Cash sales, $2 150
   28 Paid wages in cash, $953
   31 Paid all cash into bank except $150

   a Prepare Mariam's cash book for March 20–2. Balance the book and bring down the balances on 1 April 20–2.
   b Explain the significance of the credit balance on the bank column on 1 March 20–2.
   c Explain why it is not possible to have a credit balance on the cash column.
   d Explain the term 'contra'. Illustrate your answer with reference to an appropriate entry in the cash book in **a**.

3. Raminder paid a cheque, $975, to Kumar in full settlement of a debt of $1 000.
   How did Kumar record this?

	Debit	$	Credit	$
A	bank discount allowed	975 25	Raminder	1 000
B	bank discount received	975 25	Raminder	1 000
C	Raminder	1 000	bank discount allowed	975 25
D	Raminder	1 000	bank discount received	975 25

Section 4: Practice questions

1. A trader's cash book had a credit balance of $480. On the same date, his bank statement showed a credit balance of $389. The difference in the balances was caused by bank charges, $25, which appeared only on the bank statement, and a cheque not yet presented.
   What was the amount of the unpresented cheque?
   - A $66
   - B $116
   - C $848
   - D $894

2. Goods returned by Zeena, $100, were debited to her account as $1 000.
   What entries are required to correct this error?

	Account to be debited	$	Account to be credited	$
A	suspense	900	Zeena	900
B	suspense	1 100	Zeena	1 100
C	Zeena	900	suspense	900
D	Zeena	1 100	suspense	1 100

3. Gary is both a customer and a supplier to Leroy. On 28 June Leroy's account in Gary's purchases ledger had a credit balance of $275, and his account in Gary's sales ledger had a debit balance of $140. A contra entry was made to set the balance of one account against the balance of the other account.
   What entry will be made in the control accounts prepared on 30 June?

	Debited	$	Credited	$
A	purchases ledger control account	135	sales ledger control account	135
B	purchases ledger control account	140	sales ledger control account	140
C	sales ledger control account	135	purchases ledger control account	135
D	sales ledger control account	140	purchases ledger control account	140

4. A sports club provided the following information at the end of its first financial year:

	$
Subscriptions received for the current year	9 750
Subscriptions received in advance for the following year	150
Expenses of sports competition	2 040
Rates and insurance	1 986
General expenses	787
General expenses accrued at the end of the year	103
Balance at bank at the end of the year	7 403
Receipts from sports competition entry fees	?

   How much was received from the sports competition entry fees?
   - A $2 316
   - B $2 466
   - C $3 103
   - D $3 253

Acknowledgements

Thanks to the following for permission to reproduce images:

Cover image: Sudarshan v/Getty Images

Chapter Opener 1 Atomic Imagery/The Image Bank/Getty Images; Chapter Opener 2 Marekuliasz/iStock/Getty Images Plus; Chapter Opener 3 Vasily Nesterov/Hemera/Getty Images Plus; Chapter Opener 4 Peter Kirillov/Hemera/Getty Images Plus; Chapter Opener 5 Marina Datsenko/Hemera/Getty Images Plus; Chapter Opener 6 Lite Productions/Lite Productions/Getty Images Plus; Chapter Opener 7 Inok/iStock/Getty Images Plus; Chapter Opener 8 Deepblue4you/E+/Getty Images; Chapter Opener 9 Chris Cheadle/All Canada Photos/Getty Images; Chapter Opener 10 Pixel_dreams/iStock/Getty Images Plus; Chapter Opener 11 3dts/iStock /Getty Images Plus; Chapter Opener 12 Alzay/iStock/Getty Images Plus; Chapter Opener 13 Valeriya/iStock/Getty Images Plus; Chapter Opener 14 Ekapol/iStock/Getty Images Plus; Chapter Opener 15 Aslan Alphan/iStock/Getty Images Plus; Chapter Opener 16 Maciek905/iStock/Getty Images Plus; Chapter Opener 17 Gam1983/iStock/Getty Images Plus; Chapter Opener 18 Srisakorn/iStock/Getty Images Plus; Chapter Opener 19 Baona/iStock/Getty Images Plus; Chapter Opener 20 Monsitj/iStock/Getty Images Plus; Chapter Opener 21 Evgeny_Kozhevnikov/iStock/Getty Images Plus; Chapter Opener 22 Monsitj/iStock/Getty Images Plus.

Section 1

Chapter 1
Introduction to accounting

Learning objectives

In this chapter you will learn to:

- understand and explain the difference between book-keeping and accounting 1.1
- state the purposes of measuring business profit and loss 1.1
- explain the role of accounting in providing information for monitoring progress and decision-making 1.1
- explain the meaning of assets, liabilities and owner's equity 1.2
- explain and apply the accounting equation 1.2
- understand that statements of financial position record assets and liabilities on a specified date. 5.5

Chapter 1: Introduction to accounting

1.1 Introduction

Accounting is regarded as the language of business. Accounting can be divided into two sections:

Book-keeping

Book-keeping is a process of **detailed recording of all the financial transactions of a business**. It is necessary for even the smallest business to make a record of every transaction which affects the business. If the records are not maintained, it is likely that something will be forgotten or overlooked. The basis of maintaining these detailed records is **double entry book-keeping**. The actual records maintained by one business may vary from those maintained by another business because each business is different. However, all businesses apply the same principles while maintaining double entry records.

Accounting

Accounting uses the book-keeping records to prepare financial statements at regular intervals. The owner of a business needs to know whether the business is making a profit or a loss. Periodically (often at yearly intervals), **an income statement** is drawn up. This shows the calculation of the profit or loss earned by the business. If the business has earned a profit then the owner is receiving a return on his investment and funds are available for expanding or improving the business. However, if the business has made a loss then it may eventually close down as the owner is not receiving any return on his investment and funds are not available for running or maintaining the business.

You can now answer Question 1 at the end of this chapter.

The owner of the business also needs to know the financial position at regular intervals so a **statement of financial position** is prepared. This shows what the business owns and what is owing to it, its **assets**; and what the business owes, its **liabilities**. The term **financial statements** is often used as a collective name for an income statement and a statement of financial position.

The progress of the business can be measured by comparing the financial statements of one year with those of previous years, or with those of other similar businesses. The calculation of various accounting ratios is used to measure the relationship between figures within a set of financial statements. These are also useful for comparison purposes.

The information provided by the financial statements shows the owner of the business what has happened during a certain period of time and helps in monitoring the progress of the business. The plans for the future development of the business are also based on these financial statements.

KEY TERMS

Book-keeping is the detailed recording of all the financial transactions of a business.

Accounting is using book-keeping records to prepare financial statements and to assist in decision-making.

A **statement of financial position** shows the assets and liabilities of a business on a certain date.

LINK

You will learn more about financial statements in Chapters 8 and 9.

TEST YOURSELF 1.1

1. Define the term book-keeping.
2. Define the term accounting.
3. State **two** reasons why it is necessary to prepare financial statements at regular intervals.
4. State what is included in the term financial statements.

Cambridge IGCSE and O Level Accounting

LINK

You will learn more about assets and liabilities in Chapter 9.

KEY TERMS

Capital is the total resources provided by the owner and represents what the business owes the owner.

Assets represent anything owed by or owing to the business.

Liabilities represent anything owed by the business.

1.2 Assets, liabilities and capital

It is important to remember that the accounting records of a business relate only to the business. From an accounting viewpoint, the owner of that business is regarded as being completely separate from the business.

When a person decides to start a business he will have to provide the necessary funds (resources). This is often in the form of monetary funds, but may consist of buildings, motors, goods and so on. Any resources provided by the owner of the business are known as **capital**. This represents the amount owed by the business to the owner of that business.

Once the business is formed and capital introduced, the business will own the money or other items provided by the owner. Things owned by the business (or owed to the business) are regarded as the resources of the business or the **assets** of the business.

In addition to the owner, other people may also provide assets to the business. The amount owed by the business to these people is known as **liabilities**.

> **TIP**
> Anything provided for a business by the owner represents capital. This is not necessarily in the form of money.

Many businesses are set up and operated by one person. These are known as **sole traders**. The early chapters in this book cover accounts maintained by sole traders.

LINK

You will learn about the accounting records of partnerships and limited companies in Chapters 19 and 21.

> **TEST YOURSELF 1.2**
>
> 1 Define **each** of the following terms.
>   **a** assets   **b** liabilities   **c** capital

1.3 The accounting equation

Like any other mathematical equation, the two sides of the equation will always be equal. The formula for this equation is:

   Assets = Capital + Liabilities.

Capital is sometimes referred to as **owner's equity**. So the previous equation can also be written as:

   Assets = Owner's equity + Liabilities.

Like any mathematical equation, the accounting equation can be used to find any one of the three elements if the other two are present.

This equation illustrates that the assets of a business (the resources used by a business) are always equal to the liabilities and capital of a business (the resources provided for the business by others). The assets represent how the resources are used by the business and the liabilities and capital represent where these resources come from.

> **TIP**
> If you know two elements of the accounting equation you can easily calculate the third element.

Walkthrough 1.1

20–7

January 1 Leena set up a business to trade under the name of The Dress Shop. She opened a business bank account and paid in $20 000 as capital.

2 The business purchased premises, $15 000, and paid by cheque.

3 The business purchased goods, $3 000, on credit.

4 The business sold goods, at the cost price of $1 000, on credit.

Show the accounting equation after **each** of the above transactions.

Date	Assets		=	Capital	+	Liabilities	
1 January	Bank	$20 000		$20 000		Nil	
2 January	Premises	15 000					
	Bank	5 000					
		$20 000		$20 000		Nil	
3 January	Premises	15 000					
	Inventory	3 000					
	Bank	5 000					
		$23 000		$20 000		Trade payable	$3 000
4 January	Premises	15 000					
	Inventory	2 000					
	Trade receivable	1 000					
	Bank	5 000					
		$23 000		$20 000		Trade payable	$3 000

- 1 January   The assets of the business are equal to the capital of the business.
- 2 January   The money in the bank has decreased because a new asset has been bought. The total assets are equal to the capital.
- 3 January   Purchasing on credit means that the business does not pay immediately. A new asset **inventory** has been acquired, but the business has also acquired a liability as it owes money to the supplier (who is known as a creditor). In a statement of financial position this is described as a **trade payable**. The total assets are equal to the capital plus the liabilities.
- 4 January   Selling on credit means that the business does not immediately receive the money. The inventory has decreased but a new asset has been acquired in the form of money owing to the business by a customer (who is known as a **debtor**). In a statement of financial position this is described as a **trade receivable**. The total assets are equal to the capital plus the liabilities. (For the sake of simplicity, the goods were sold to the customer at cost price. In practice, they need to be sold at a price above cost price to enable the business to make a profit.)

LINK

You will learn more about buying and selling on credit in Chapter 2.

KEY TERMS

Inventory is the goods a business has available for resale.

Trade payables represent the amount the business owes to the credit suppliers of goods (the trade creditors).

Trade receivables represent the amount owed to the business by its credit customers (the trade debtors).

TEST YOURSELF 1.3

1 Fill in the missing figures in the following table.

	Assets $	Capital $	Liabilities $
a	35 000	?	12 500
b	?	44 400	19 300
c	67 300	55 000	?

You can now answer Question 2 at the end of this chapter.

1.4 The statement of financial position

The accounting equation may be shown in the form of a statement of financial position. This shows the three elements of the accounting equation – the assets, the capital and the liabilities. The statement of financial position will be affected every time the business makes changes to the assets, liabilities or capital.

Walkthrough 1.2

Prepare the statement of financial position of The Dress Shop after **each** of the transactions shown in **Walkthrough 1.1**.

The Dress Shop
Statement of financial position at 1 January 20–7

Assets	$	Liabilities	$
Bank	20 000	Capital	20 000
	20 000		20 000

The Dress Shop
Statement of financial position at 2 January 20–7

Assets	$	Liabilities	$
Premises	15 000	Capital	20 000
Bank	5 000		
	20 000		20 000

The Dress Shop
Statement of financial position at 3 January 20–7

Assets	$	Liabilities	$
Premises	15 000	Capital	20 000
Inventory	3 000	Trade payable	3 000
Bank	5 000		
	23 000		23 000

Chapter 1: Introduction to accounting

The Dress Shop			
Statement of financial position at 4 January 20–7			
Assets	$	Liabilities	$
Premises	15 000	Capital	20 000
Inventory	2 000	Trade payable	3 000
Trade receivable	1 000		
Bank	5 000		
	23 000		23 000

TEST YOURSELF 1.4

1. Give **two** examples of **each** of the following (excluding those shown in **Walkthrough 1.1** and **1.2**):
   a. asset
   b. liability.
2. Explain the meaning of **each** of the following terms:
   a. trade payable
   b. trade receivable

LINK

You will learn more about statements of financial position in Chapter 9.

The statements of financial position shown in **Walkthrough 1.2** were presented in a horizontal format. There are different ways to present a statement of financial position and these are explained in Chapter 9 . A statement of financial position is also more useful if the assets and liabilities are divided into different types (see Chapter 9).

Walkthrough 1.1 showed that every single transaction involves a change to the assets and/or the liabilities and/or the capital. This means that it is necessary to prepare a statement of financial position after every single transaction, as shown in **Walkthrough 1.2**. However, this is not possible in practice as many transactions can take place every hour of each working day. In practice, the day-to-day business transactions are recorded using **double entry book-keeping** and a statement of financial position is prepared only periodically. This is usually done at the closing of a business on the last day of the financial year as part of the **financial statements**. As the business can be started on any day of the year, its financial year may not necessarily match the calendar year (i.e. from 1 January to 31 December). The financial statements are prepared for 12 month periods from the date the business started.

TIP

The totals of a statement of financial position must always agree: if they do not you know that there is an error.

LINK

You will learn more about double entry book-keeping in Chapters 2 and 4.

You can now answer Questions 3–6 at the end of this chapter.

Revision checklist

- Book-keeping is the detailed recording of all the financial transactions of a business. Accounting uses these book-keeping records to prepare financial statements.
- It is necessary to prepare financial statements to show the profit or loss of the business and the financial position of the business and to help in decision-making.
- The accounting equation shows that the assets are always equal to the capital plus the liabilities of the business.
- A statement of financial position shows the assets and liabilities of a business on a certain date.

Exam-style questions

1 Which task is performed by a book-keeper?
   A analysing the trading results
   B entering transactions in the ledger
   C preparing year-end financial statements
   D providing information for decision-making

2 A trader provided the following information:

	$
Premises	180 000
Inventory	23 420
Trade payables	26 180
Trade receivables	21 710
Office fixtures and fittings	32 600
Loan from bank	80 000
Cash at bank	2 550
Motor vehicles	15 900

   a Calculate the value of the assets.
   b Calculate the value of the liabilities.
   c Use the accounting equation to calculate the trader's capital.

3 What is a statement of financial position?
   A a calculation of the amount owed to the owner of the business
   B a list of assets and liabilities of a business on a certain date
   C a list of everything owned by and owed to a business
   D a summary of money paid to and received by a business

4 A business had $9 420 in its bank account. The following transactions took place:

	$
Bought goods on credit	250
Sold goods on credit	1 100
Repaid a loan by cheque	5 000

   How much was there in the bank after these transactions?
   A $3 570   B $4 420   C $4 670   D $5 270

5 Complete the following table to show the effect of each of the following transactions. The first one has been completed as an example.

a Bought a motor vehicle and paid by cheque
b Bought goods on credit from a credit supplier
c Received a cheque from a credit customer
d Sold goods on credit
e Paid off a loan in cash

	Effect on assets	$	Effect on liabilities	$
a	Motor vehicles Bank	Increase Decrease	No effect	
b				
c				
d				
e				

6 The statement of financial position of Bharwani Traders on 31 October 20–4 is shown below.

Bharwani Traders

Statement of financial position at 31 October 20–4

Assets	$	Liabilities	$
Machinery	19 000	Capital	35 000
Motor vehicles	6 000	Trade payables	8 000
Inventory	4 900		
Trade receivables	3 000		
Bank	10 100		
	43 000		43 000

On 1 November 20–4 the following transactions took place:
   A cheque for $3 000 was paid to a credit supplier.
   A credit customer paid $500 in cash.
   A loan for $8 000, which was paid into the bank, was received from Lenders Limited.
   A cheque for $7 000 was paid for an additional machine.

Prepare the statement of financial position of Bharwani Traders on 1 November 20–4 after the above transactions have taken place.

Chapter 2
Double entry book-keeping – Part A

Learning objectives

In this chapter you will learn to:

- outline the double entry system of book-keeping   2.1
- process accounting data using the double entry system   2.1
- prepare ledger accounts   2.1
- post transactions to the ledger accounts   2.1
- balance ledger accounts as required   2.1
- interpret ledger accounts and their balances.   2.1

Chapter 2: Double entry book-keeping – Part A

2.1 Introduction

A business would find it impossible to prepare a statement of financial position after every single transaction. The day-to-day transactions are recorded in the books of a business using the **double entry system of book-keeping**. The term **double entry** is used because the two effects of a transaction (a **giving** and a **receiving**) are both recorded in the ledger.

A business maintains a separate ledger account for each type of asset, expense, liability and income and also for each individual debtor and creditor. Every transaction is recorded in the ledger account relating to that particular item or person.

A **ledger** is traditionally a bound book where each account appears on a separate page. Over the years, the ledger has developed into a looseleaf folder with separate sheets, each containing a ledger account. Recent developments have seen the introduction of a computer file divided into separate ledger accounts.

The layout of a ledger account is as follows:

KEY TERM

Double entry book-keeping is the process of making a debit entry and a credit entry for each transaction.

TIP
The debit side of a ledger account is the side which is receiving or gaining value and the credit side of a ledger account is the side which is giving value.

		Account name						
Debit								Credit
Date	Details	Folio	$	Date	Details	Folio		$

Ledger accounts are divided into two sections, this can be shown by a central vertical line, in this text book the central vertical line is not shown. The left-hand-side is known as the **debit** side and the right-hand-side is known as the **credit** side. The term debit is usually abbreviated to '**dr**' and the term credit is usually abbreviated to '**cr**'. On either side of the account there are columns to record the date, details and amount of each transaction.

A folio number column is used for reference purposes. The use of folio numbers is not required when answering questions. However, folio numbers have been included in examples present up to Chapter 7 so that you can appreciate their use and purpose.

In order to record the two aspects of every transaction, every transaction is entered twice – on the debit side of one account and on the credit side of another account. The account which is receiving or gaining the value is debited and the account which is giving the value is credited.

Walkthrough 2.1

20–7

January 1 Ajay began business. He opened a business bank account and invested $80 000 as capital **a**

  2 Fixtures and equipment costing $30 000 were bought and paid for by cheque **b**

Enter these transactions in Ajay's ledger.

Ajay

Bank account — Page 1

Date 20–7	Details	Folio	$	Date 20–7	Details	Folio	$
Jan 1 **a**	Capital	2	80 000	Jan 2 **b**	Fixtures and equipment	3	30 000

Capital account — Page 2

Date	Details	Folio	$	Date 20–7	Details	Folio	$
				Jan 1 **a**	Bank	1	80 000

Fixtures and equipment account — Page 3

Date 20–7	Details	Folio	$	Date	Details	Folio	$
Jan 2 **b**	Bank	1	30 000				

- The first transaction **a** is debited in the bank account, as this is the account which is receiving the money, and credited in the capital account, as this is where the money is coming from.
- The second transaction **b** is debited in the fixtures and equipment, to show the value being received, and credited in the bank account, as this is where the money is coming from.
- In each transaction, the details column shows the name of the account in which the other half of the double entry is made.
- The folio number is used for reference purposes and shows the page of the ledger on which the account named in the details column appears.

It is important that a double entry is made for every transaction.

TIP

It is important to ensure that every transaction is entered twice, once on the debit side and once on the credit side.

LINK

You will learn more about business documents in Chapter 6.

In practice, the information entered in the accounting records is obtained from business documents.

In practice, each ledger account has its own page or sheet.

> **TEST YOURSELF 2.1**
>
> 1 Explain why it is necessary to make a double entry in the ledger for each transaction.
> 2 Explain the use of the folio column in a ledger account.

2.2 Double entry records for assets and liabilities

A ledger account is opened for each type of asset and liability. Applying the double entry principles, every transaction is entered twice. The account which is receiving the money is debited and the account which is giving the money is credited.

Walkthrough 2.2

20–7

January 1 Ajay began business. He opened a business bank account and invested $80 000 as capital

2 Fixtures and equipment costing $30 000 were bought and paid for by cheque

3 A short-term loan of $10 000 was received from AB Loans

5 A motor vehicle costing $9 000 was bought and paid for by cheque

6 A long-term loan of $5 000 was received from Ajay's sister Mallika

Enter these transactions in Ajay's ledger.

Ajay

Bank account — Page 1

Date	Details	Folio	$	Date	Details	Folio	$
20–7				20–7			
Jan 1	Capital	2	80 000	Jan 2	Fixtures and equipment	3	30 000
3	AB Loans	4	10 000	5	Motor vehicles	5	9 000
6	Mallika loan	6	5 000				

Capital account — Page 2

Date	Details	Folio	$	Date	Details	Folio	$
				20–7			
				Jan 1	Bank	1	80 000

Fixtures and equipment account — Page 3

Date	Details	Folio	$	Date	Details	Folio	$
20–7							
Jan 2	Bank	1	30 000				

AB Loans account							Page 4
Date	Details	Folio	$	Date	Details	Folio	$
				20–7			
				Jan 3	Bank	1	10 000

Motor vehicles account							Page 5
Date	Details	Folio	$	Date	Details	Folio	$
20–7							
Jan 5	Bank	1	9 000				

Mallika loan account							Page 6
Date	Details	Folio	$	Date	Details	Folio	$
				20–7			
				Jan 6	Bank	1	5 000

2.3 Double entry records for expenses and income

A ledger account is opened for each type of expense and income. The same double entry principles applied to assets and liabilities are applied to expenses and income. The account which is receiving the money is debited and the account which is giving the money is credited.

Walkthrough 2.3

20–7

January 1 Ajay began business with a capital of $80 000 in the business bank account

1 He paid rent of premises, $400, by cheque

2 Fixtures and equipment costing $30 000 were bought and paid for by cheque

3 He paid insurance, $250, by cheque

3 A short-term loan of $10 000 was received from AB Loans

5 A motor vehicle costing $9 000 was bought and paid for by cheque

5 He paid motor expenses, $50, by cheque

6 A long-term loan of $5 000 was received from Ajay's sister Mallika

7 Part of the premises were rented out to another business and a cheque for $95 was received

Enter these transactions in Ajay's ledger.

Ajay
Bank account — Page 1

Date	Details	Folio	$	Date	Details	Folio	$
20-7				20-7			
Jan 1	Capital	2	80 000	Jan 1	Rent payable	7	400
3	AB Loans	4	10 000	2	Fixtures and equipment	3	30 000
6	Mallika loan	6	5 000	3	Insurance	8	250
7	Rent receivable	10	95	5	Motor vehicles	5	9 000
					Motor expenses	9	50

Capital account — Page 2

Date	Details	Folio	$	Date	Details	Folio	$
				20-7			
				Jan 1	Bank	1	80 000

Fixtures and equipment account — Page 3

Date	Details	Folio	$	Date	Details	Folio	$
20-7							
Jan 2	Bank	1	30 000				

AB Loans account — Page 4

Date	Details	Folio	$	Date	Details	Folio	$
				20-7			
				Jan 3	Bank	1	10 000

Motor vehicles account — Page 5

Date	Details	Folio	$	Date	Details	Folio	$
20-7							
Jan 5	Bank	1	9 000				

Mallika loan account — Page 6

Date	Details	Folio	$	Date	Details	Folio	$
				20-7			
				Jan 6	Bank	1	5 000

Rent payable account							Page 7
Date	Details	Folio	$	Date	Details	Folio	$
20–7							
Jan 1	Bank	1	400				

Insurance account							Page 8
Date	Details	Folio	$	Date	Details	Folio	$
20–7							
Jan 3	Bank	1	250				

Motor expenses account							Page 9
Date	Details	Folio	$	Date	Details	Folio	$
20–7							
Jan 5	Bank	1	50				

Rent receivable account							Page 10
Date	Details	Folio	$	Date	Details	Folio	$
				20–7			
				Jan 7	Bank	1	95

- The motor expenses such as fuel and repairs are shown in an expense account as they do not increase the value of the motor vehicle.
- The rent received from a tenant is shown in an income account and is kept separate from the expense of rent payable.
- No lines are left blank in the middle of ledger accounts as each entry is made on the next available line.
- In practice, for ease of reference, accounts of the same type (e.g. assets, expenses and so on) are kept in the same area of the ledger.

> **TIP**
> When an item such as rent is both paid and received by a business, separate accounts are maintained, one for rent payable and one for rent receivable.

TEST YOURSELF 2.2

1. For **each** of the following transactions, state the name of the account which will be debited and the name of the account which will be credited.
   a. Paid rates by cheque
   b. Bought machinery and paid by cheque
   c. Received commission by cheque for work done for another business
   d. Repaid, by cheque, money borrowed from XYZ Loan Co

2.4 Double entry records for drawings

Whenever the owner of a business takes value from the business for his/her own use this is known as **drawings**. This value may be in the form of money, non-current assets or goods from the inventory held by the business. It is usual to open a **drawings account** to record these values so that the capital account does not have a large number of entries.

Any drawings are debited in the drawings account to show the value going into that account. The credit entry will be in the account giving the value. When money is withdrawn, either the cash or bank account will be credited. When a non-current asset is withdrawn, the appropriate non-current asset account will be credited. When goods are withdrawn, the purchases account will be credited. This is because these goods were originally purchased for resale and the amount of goods available for resale is reduced when goods are taken by the owner.

At the end of the financial year, the total of the drawings account is transferred to the capital account. This reduces the amount owed by the business to the owner of the business.

> **KEY TERMS**
>
> **Drawings** represent any value taken from the business by the owner of that business.
>
> A **balance** on a ledger account is the difference between the debit side and the credit side.

> **TEST YOURSELF 2.3**
>
> 1 For **each** of the following transactions, state the name of the account which will be debited and the name of the account which will be credited.
>   a   The owner of a business invested more money in the business.
>   b   The owner of a business took an unused motor vehicle for personal use.
>   c   The owner of a business took goods for personal use.

2.5 Balancing ledger accounts

At the end of each month, it is usual to **balance** any account of assets and liabilities which contain more than one entry. The **balance is the difference between the two sides of the account** and represents the amount which is left in that account.

The steps necessary to balance a ledger account are summarised as follows:

- On a calculator or a separate sheet of paper, add up each side of the account and find the difference between the two sides.

- Enter this difference on the next available line on the side which is the smaller in money. Enter the date (usually the last day of the month) in the date column and the word 'balance' in the details column. It is usual to insert 'c/d' in the folio column. This is the abbreviation for 'carried down' and indicates where the double entry for this item will be made.

- Total each side of the account. This is done by drawing total lines and inserting the figure between these lines. It is usual to show a single line above the total and either a single or a double line below the total. The totals of an account must be on the same level and must be the same figure.

- Make the double entry for the balance carried down. On the line below the totals, write the amount of the balance on the opposite side to where the words 'Balance c/d' were written. Enter the date (usually the first day of the next month) in the date column and the word 'balance' in the details column. It is usual to insert 'b/d' in the folio column. This is the abbreviation for 'brought down' and indicates where the double entry for this item was made.

> **TIP**
>
> When balancing an account, add up each side of the account and find the difference between them before drawing total lines and before writing the word 'balance'.

Walkthrough 2.4

The bank account prepared in **Walkthrough 2.3** shows the entries made by Ajay during the first week of trading. Balance the bank account in Ajay's books on 7 January 20–7.

Ajay
Bank account   Page 1

Date 20–7	Details	Folio	$	Date 20–7	Details	Folio	$
Jan 1	Capital	2	80 000	Jan 1	Rent payable	7	400
3	AB Loans	4	10 000	2	Fixtures and equipment	3	30 000
6	Mallika loan	6	5 000	3	Insurance	8	250
7	Rent receivable	10	95	5	Motor vehicles	5	9 000
					Motor expenses	9	50
				7	Balance	c/d	55 395
			95 095				95 095
20–7							
Jan 8	Balance	b/d	55 395				

You can now answer Question 1 at the end of this chapter.

2.6 Double entry records for sales, purchases and returns

It is necessary to open an account to record goods which are purchased for resale and also an account to record goods which are sold by the business. Whilst these are actually the same goods coming into the business and going out of the business, it is necessary to record them in separate accounts as the purchases will be at cost price and the sales at selling price. A **purchases account** and a **sales account** are used rather than a goods account. An **inventory account** is only used to record the goods left at the end of the financial year and not for day-to-day transactions.

The same double entry principles applied to assets and liabilities are applied to purchases, sales and returns.

Purchases

a Goods purchased for cash or cheque

Whenever goods are purchased, the purchases account will be debited as the goods are coming into the business and the purchases account is receiving that value. The double entry will be a credit in either the cash account or the bank account depending on whether the amount was paid in cash or by cheque.

b Goods purchased on credit

It is common for businesses to buy on credit and pay for the goods at a later date rather than at the time of purchase. The purchases account will be debited in the usual way.

The credit entry will be made in the account of the supplier of the goods to show the value coming from that person. The supplier of goods is known as a **trade creditor**.

When payment is made to the supplier, the bank or cash account will be credited (to show value going out of that account) and the account of the supplier will be debited (to show value going into that account).

Walkthrough 2.5

20–7
January 9   Ajay bought goods, $650, on credit from Kolkata & Co
         10 Ajay bought goods, $150, and paid by cheque
         13 Ajay paid the amount owing to Kolkata & Co by cheque

Enter these transactions in Ajay's ledger.

Ajay

Bank account — Page 1

Date	Details	Folio	$	Date	Details	Folio	$
				20–7			
				Jan 10	Purchases	11	150
				13	Kolkata & Co	12	650

Purchases account — Page 11

Date	Details	Folio	$	Date	Details	Folio	$
20–7							
Jan 9	Kolkata & Co	12	650				
10	Bank	1	150				

Kolkata & Co account — Page 12

Date	Details	Folio	$	Date	Details	Folio	$
20–7				20–7			
Jan 13	Bank	1	650	Jan 9	Purchases	11	650
			650				650

- The account of Kolkata & Co is 'in balance' as both sides equal $650. The account has been totalled to indicate that the account is now closed.
- It is not necessary to write the month against each transaction, only when it is the first entry for the month.
- If there is more than one entry on the same side of an account on the same date, it is not necessary to write the day of the month each time.

TIP
Only goods bought for resale are entered in the purchases account.

Sales

a Goods sold for cash or cheque

Whenever goods are sold, the sales account will be credited as the goods are going out of the business and the sales account is giving out that value. The double entry will be a debit in either the cash account or the bank account depending on whether the amount was received in cash or by cheque.

b Goods sold on credit

Just as a business may purchase goods and pay for them at a later date, it may also sell goods on credit. The sales account will be credited in the usual way. The debit entry will be made in the account of the customer to whom the goods were sold to show the value going to that person. The customer who bought the goods on credit is known as a **trade debtor**. When payment is received from the debtor, the bank or cash account will be debited (to show value coming into that account) and the account of the debtor will be credited (to show value going out of that account).

Walkthrough 2.6

20–7
January 16   Ajay sold goods, $175, for cash
           17   Ajay sold goods, $770, on credit to Prerna
           20   Prerna gave Ajay a cheque for $500 on account

Enter these transactions in Ajay's ledger.

Ajay

Bank account — Page 1

Date	Details	Folio	$	Date	Details	Folio	$
20–7							
Jan 20	Prerna	15	500				

Cash account — Page 13

Date	Details	Folio	$	Date	Details	Folio	$
20–7							
Jan 16	Sales	14	175				

Sales account — Page 14

Date	Details	Folio	$	Date	Details	Folio	$
				20–7			
				Jan 16	Cash	13	175
				17	Prerna	15	770

	Prerna account						Page 15
Date	Details	Folio	$	Date	Details	Folio	$
20–7				20–7			
Jan 17	Sales	14	770	Jan 20	Bank	1	500
				20	Balance	c/d	270
			770				770
20–7							
Jan 21	Balance	b/d	270				

- The term 'on account' indicates that only part of the amount outstanding is being paid. The remainder will be paid at a later date.
- Prerna's account has been balanced following the stages mentioned previously in this chapter (though this is usually done at the end of the month).
- On 21 January, Prerna is Ajay's debtor as an amount of $270 is owing to Ajay.

TIP
When goods (originally purchased for resale) are sold they are recorded in the sales account.

Returns

Sometimes goods which have been purchased have to be returned to the supplier. They may be faulty, damaged or not what was ordered. These goods are known as **purchases returns** or **returns outward**. A special account known as a purchases returns account (or returns outward account) is opened and any returns are credited to this account to show the value going out. The debit entry will be made in the account of the supplier to whom the goods are being returned (to show the value going to that person).

Similarly, a customer may return goods to the business. These goods are known as **sales returns** or **returns inwards**. An account known as the sales returns account (or returns inwards account) is opened and any returns are debited to this account to show the value coming in. The credit entry will be made in the account of the customer who returned the goods (to show the value coming from that person).

Walkthrough 2.7

20–7
January 21 Ajay sold goods, $245, on credit to Xavier Traders
         22 Xavier Traders returned damaged goods, $55, to Ajay
         23 Ajay purchased goods, $820, on credit from Varun
         25 Xavier Traders paid their account by cheque
         27 Ajay returned faulty goods, $44, to Varun
         30 Ajay gave Varun a cheque for $700 on account

Enter these transactions in Ajay's ledger.

Ajay
Bank account — Page 1

Date	Details	Folio	$	Date	Details	Folio	$
20–7				20–7			
Jan 25	Xavier Traders	16	190	Jan 30	Varun	18	700

Purchases account — Page 11

Date	Details	Folio	$	Date	Details	Folio	$
20–7							
Jan 23	Varun	18	820				

Sales account — Page 14

Date	Details	Folio	$	Date	Details	Folio	$
				20–7			
				Jan 21	Xavier Traders	16	245

Xavier Traders account — Page 16

Date	Details	Folio	$	Date	Details	Folio	$
20–7				20–7			
Jan 21	Sales	14	245	Jan 22	Sales returns	17	55
				25	Bank	1	190
			245				245

Sales returns account — Page 17

Date	Details	Folio	$	Date	Details	Folio	$
20–7							
Jan 22	Xavier Traders	16	55				

Varun account							Page 18
Date	Details	Folio	$	Date	Details	Folio	$
20–7				20–7			
Jan 27	Purchases returns	19	44	Jan 23	Purchases	11	820
30	Bank	1	700				
31	Balance	c/d	76				
			820				820
				20–7			
				Jan 21	Balance	b/d	76

Purchases returns account							Page 19
Date	Details	Folio	$	Date	Details	Folio	$
				20–7			
				Jan 27	Varun	18	44

You can now answer Questions 2–4 at the end of this chapter.

2.7 Double entry records for carriage inwards and carriage outwards

The term **carriage** refers to the cost of carrying or transporting goods. **Carriage inwards** is part of the cost of purchasing goods as it occurs when a business has to pay for goods it has purchased to be delivered to its premises. **Carriage outwards** is a selling expense as it occurs when a business pays for goods to be delivered to the customer's premises. It is important that these two expenses are treated separately in the accounts.

Applying the double entry principle to carriage inwards, the carriage inwards account is debited as this is the account receiving the money and the cash account (or the bank account if the money is paid by cheque) is credited as the money is coming from this account. Similarly, if the payment relates to carriage outwards, the cash account or bank account is credited and the carriage outwards account is debited.

If the carriage is not actually paid for at the time, the account of the supplier of the carriage service will be credited instead of the cash account or bank account.

> **KEY TERMS**
>
> **Carriage** is the cost of transporting goods.
> **Carriage inwards** is the cost of bringing the goods to the business and **carriage outwards** is the cost of delivering the goods to the customer.

TEST YOURSELF 2.4

1. Explain how to balance a ledger account.
2. Explain the meaning of the term credit purchases.
3. State **two** reasons why it may be necessary to return goods to a supplier.
4. State an alternative name for sales returns.
5. Explain the difference between carriage inwards and carriage outwards.

LINK
You will learn more about double entry book-keeping in Chapter 4.

You can now answer Question 5 at the end of this chapter.

2.8 Three column running balance accounts

The ledger accounts presented so far have been in the traditional form. This form is also known as the 'T' account format.

There is another method of presenting ledger accounts which is commonly used on computer-generated accounts which is known as the three column running balance format. This form of presentation uses only one column each for the date, details and folio and has three money columns side-by-side – one for debit, one for credit and one for balance after each transaction. The layout of a ledger account using this format is as follows:

Date	Details	Folio	Debit $	Credit $	Balance $

The advantage of this method is that it shows the balance of the account after every transaction. When the accounts are prepared manually, it involves extra calculations which may lead to errors.

Walkthrough 2.8

20–7

January 1 Ajay began business. He opened a business bank account and invested $80 000 as capital

1 Paid rent of premises, $400, by cheque

2 Fixtures and equipment costing $30 000 were bought and paid for by cheque

3 Paid insurance, $250, by cheque

3 A short-term loan of $10 000 was received from AB Loans

5 A motor vehicle costing $9 000 was bought and paid for by cheque

5 Paid motor expenses, $50, by cheque

6 A long-term loan of $5 000 was received from Ajay's sister Mallika

7 Part of the premises were rented out to another business and a cheque for $95 was received

Enter these transactions in the bank account in Ajay's ledger using the three column running balance format.

Ajay
Bank account   Page 1

Date	Details	Folio	Debit $	Credit $	Balance $
20–7					
Jan 1	Capital		80 000		80 000 dr
	Rent payable			400	79 600 dr
2	Fixtures and equipment			30 000	49 600 dr
3	Insurance			250	49 350 dr
	AB Loans		10 000		59 350 dr
5	Motor vehicles			9 000	50 350 dr
	Motor expenses			50	50 300 dr
6	Mallika loan		5 000		55 300 dr
7	Rent receivable		95		55 395 dr

- It is common for the abbreviation 'dr' or 'cr' to appear after the figure in the balance column to indicate the nature of the balance.

2.9 Interpreting ledger accounts and their balances

It is necessary to be able to understand the entries made in a ledger account and to be able to explain those entries.

Walkthrough 2.9
The following account appeared in the ledger of Ajay.

Ajay
Xavier Traders account

Date	Details	Folio	$	Date	Details	Folio	$
20–7				20–7			
Mar 1	Balance	b/d	122	Mar 9	Cash		122
8	Sales		650	12	Returns		98
20	Sales		820	29	Bank		550
				31	Balance	c/d	822
			1 592				1 592

Explain each entry in the account of Xavier Traders and state where the double entry for each item will be found.

March 1 Xavier Traders owe Ajay $122 for goods supplied on credit in previous months
Double entry: Xavier Traders account for February 20–7 credit side

8 Ajay sold goods on credit to Xavier Traders, $650
Double entry: Sales account credit side

9 Ajay received cash, $122, from Xavier Traders
   Double entry: Cash account debit side

12 Xavier Traders returned goods, $98, to Ajay
   Double entry: Sales returns account debit side

20 Ajay sold goods on credit to Xavier Traders, $820
   Double entry: Sales account credit side

29 Xavier Traders paid Ajay $550 by cheque (or by bank transfer)
   Double entry: Bank account debit side

31 Xavier Traders owe Ajay $822
   Double entry: Xavier Traders account for April 20–7 on the debit side

You can now answer Question 6 at the end of this chapter.

As students often find the traditional form of ledger accounts easier to understand, the 'T' format is used in all ledger accounts throughout this book. However, either form of presentation is acceptable.

Revision checklist

- Every transaction must be entered twice – on the debit side of one account and on the credit side of another account.
- The debit entry is made in the account which is receiving the value and the credit entry is made in the account which is giving the value.
- Each type of asset, liability, expense and income has its own ledger account.
- Any value taken from the business by the owner of the business is known as drawings.
- At the end of the period, the accounts of assets and liabilities which contain more than one entry should be balanced.
- The entries for purchases and sales, and purchases returns and sales returns, are recorded in separate accounts.
- Carriage is the cost of transporting goods.

Exam-style questions

1 Mahela is a trader. He took goods costing $100 for his own use.
How would Mahela record this in his ledger?

	Account to be debited	Account to be credited
A	drawings	inventory
B	drawings	purchases
C	inventory	drawings
D	purchases	drawings

2 Jaswant purchased goods from Ali and paid in cash.
Which entries would Ali make in his ledger?

	Account to be debited	Account to be credited
A	cash	sales
B	Jaswant	sales
C	sales	Jaswant
D	sales	cash

3 Dinesh returned goods to his credit supplier, Thisara.
How would Dinesh record this in his ledger?

	Account to be debited	Account to be credited
A	sales returns	Thisara
B	purchases returns	Thisara
C	Thisara	sales returns
D	Thisara	purchases returns

4 On 1 July 20–6 Mumtaz started a business. The following are her transactions for the first two weeks of trading:

July 1   Mumtaz paid capital, $50 000, into the business bank account
      2   Bought premises, $25 000, and paid by cheque
      4   Bought equipment, $4 000, and paid by cheque
      6   Bought goods, $1 500, on credit from Mayur Vihar Traders
      7   Paid advertising expenses, $60, by cheque
      9   Sold goods, $200, and received a cheque

12 Sold goods, $310, on credit, to Ridhima
13 Ridhima returned damaged goods, $20
14 Paid $1 000 by cheque on account to Mayur Vihar Traders

Enter these transactions in the ledger of Mumtaz. Balance the bank account and the accounts of Mayur Vihar Traders and Ridhima on 14 July and bring down the balances on 15 July 20–6.

5 Katie is a trader. On 1 October 20–4 she had the following balances in her ledger:

	$	
Capital	15 000	
Inventory	3 400	
Fixtures and fittings	10 100	
Trade receivable – Daisy	1 110	
Trade payable – Zara	1 760	
Loan from AB Finance	2 000	
Bank	4 150	debit

a Enter these balances in the appropriate accounts.

The following transactions took place in October 20–4:

October 2 Bought goods on credit from Zara, $1 500
7 Returned goods to Zara, $80
10 Repaid the loan by cheque
14 Paid Zara a cheque for the amount owing on 1 October 20–4
21 Cash received from sales of goods, paid directly into the bank, $940
28 Katie took goods for her own use, $140
30 Daisy paid the amount due by cheque

b Enter these transactions in Katie's ledger. Balance the bank account and Zara's account and bring down the balances on 1 November 20–4.

6 The following account appeared in the ledger of Marine Drive Stores:

Central Wholesalers account							
Date	Details	Folio	$	Date	Details	Folio	$
20–4				20–4			
May 17	Returns		120	May 1	Balance	b/d	180
20	Bank		300	10	Purchases		410
31	Balance	c/d	170				
			590				590

Explain **each** entry in this account and also state where the double entry for **each** entry will be found.

Chapter 3
The trial balance

Learning objectives

In this chapter you will learn to:

- understand that a trial balance is a statement of ledger balances on a particular date   3.1
- outline the uses and limitations of a trial balance   3.1
- prepare a trial balance from a given list of balances and amend a trial balance which contains errors   3.1
- identify and explain those errors which do not affect the trial balance – commission, compensating, complete reversal, omission, original entry, principle.   3.1

> **KEY TERM**
>
> A **trial balance** is a list of balances on the accounts in the ledger at a certain date.

> **TIP**
>
> A trial balance is a list of balances: it is not part of the double entry system.

> **TIP**
>
> A trial balance is a useful list from which to prepare a set of financial statements.

> **LINK**
>
> You will learn about financial statements in Chapters 8 and 9.

3.1 Introduction

A **trial balance** is a list of the balances on the accounts in the ledger at a certain date. A trial balance is prepared to check the arithmetical accuracy of the double entry book-keeping. The name of each account is listed in the trial balance. The balance on each account is shown according to whether it is a debit balance or a credit balance. The trial balance will show if the total of the debit balances is equal to the total credit balances.

It is important to remember that the trial balance is **not** a part of the double entry system of book-keeping as it is simply a list of balances. If the ledger accounts are balanced monthly then a trial balance may also be drawn up at the end of each month.

The trial balance should be headed with the term 'trial balance' along with the date on which it was prepared.

The layout of a trial balance is as follows:

Trial balance at .... *			
Details	Folio	Debit $	Credit $

*The date at which it is prepared.

3.2 The purpose of a trial balance

1. The trial balance can help in locating arithmetical errors. However, the balancing of the trial balance is not proof that the entries in the ledger accounts are completely free from errors.
2. A trial balance is useful in preparing financial statements.

3.3 The preparation of a trial balance

All the ledger accounts which are 'open' (those which still have an amount of money showing in the account) are listed together with the balance on each account. If the debit side of the account is larger in money than the credit side then that account has a debit balance and the amount of the balance (or difference) is entered in the debit column of the trial balance. If the credit side of the account has more money than the debit side then that account has a credit balance and the amount of the balance (or difference) is entered in the credit column of the trial balance.

The debit column and the credit column are totalled. If the totals agree, it indicates that the double entry book-keeping is arithmetically correct.

Walkthrough 3.1

Ajay started his business on 1 January 20–7. His transactions for his first week of trading were shown in the solution to **Walkthrough 2.3** in Chapter 2.

Prepare a trial balance for Ajay on 7 January 20–7.

Chapter 3: The trial balance

Ajay			
Trial balance at 7 January 20–7			
	Folio	Debit $	Credit $
Bank	1	55 395	
Capital	2		80 000
Fixtures and equipment	3	30 000	
AB Loans	4		10 000
Motor vehicles	5	9 000	
Mallika loan	6		5 000
Rent payable	7	400	
Insurance	8	250	
Motor expenses	9	50	
Rent receivable	10		95
		95 095	95 095

- Folio numbers do not always appear in a trial balance.
- It is common to find the words 'debit' and 'credit' abbreviated to 'dr' and 'cr'.
- In this particular example, the totals of the trial balance are same as the totals of the bank account. This will not always be the case. It occurred in this example as all the transactions passed through the bank account.

TEST YOURSELF 3.1

1. Explain what a trial balance is.
2. State **two** purposes of preparing a trial balance.
3. Explain what determines whether the balance of an account is entered in the debit column or the credit column of a trial balance.
4. Explain what is indicated if the totals of a trial balance agree.

In practice, a trial balance is drawn up using the actual ledger accounts. It is necessary to know the type of accounts which have a debit balance and those which have a credit balance. These are shown in the following table:

Cambridge IGCSE and O Level Accounting

Debit balances	Credit balances
Assets	Liabilities
Expenses	Incomes
Drawings	Capital
Purchases	Sales
Sales returns	Purchases returns

You can now answer Questions 1 and 2 at the end of this chapter.

Walkthrough 3.2

The following trial balance was prepared by an inexperienced book-keeper and contains errors. Prepare a corrected trial balance at 31 December 20–9.

Jasmine
Trial balance for the year ended 31 December 20–9

	Debit $	Credit $
Cash		300
Bank overdraft	3 000	
Capital		42 500
Drawings		750
Land and buildings	30 000	
Office equipment		1 050
Loan from AB Company	2 200	
Inventory	7 500	
Purchases		9 850
Sales	10 650	
Sales returns		940
Purchases returns	1 030	
Carriage inwards		400
Wages	1 500	
Rent receivable	830	
Sundry expenses	1 290	
Trade receivables		12 300
Trade payables	5 670	
	63 670	68 090

Chapter 3: The trial balance

Jasmine		
Corrected trial balance at 31 December 20–9		
	Debit $	Credit $
Cash	300	
Bank overdraft		3 000
Capital		42 500
Drawings	750	
Land and buildings	30 000	
Office equipment	1 050	
Loan from AB Company		2 200
Inventory	7 500	
Purchases	9 850	
Sales		10 650
Sales returns	940	
Purchases returns		1 030
Carriage inwards	400	
Wages	1 500	
Rent receivable		830
Sundry expenses	1 290	
Trade receivables	12 300	
Trade payables		5 670
	65 880	65 880

> **TIP**
> The opening inventory is included in a trial balance. The closing inventory does not appear on the books when a trial balance is prepared so cannot be included in a trial balance.

- The heading of the trial balance was incorrect and required amending.
- Each item had to be considered to decide whether it was in the correct column or it required amending.

You can now answer Question 3 at the end of this chapter.

TEST YOURSELF 3.2

1. State the column of a trial balance in which the balance of **each** of the following accounts would appear. Give a reason for your answer in each case.
   a Loan from WQ Loans
   b Motor expenses
   c Motor vehicles
   d Bank overdraft
   e Carriage outwards
   f Commission receivable

3.4 The trial balance and errors

If the trial balance fails to balance

When a trail balance fails to balance, it is obvious that an error has been made somewhere. This may be:

1. an error of addition within the trial balance
2. an error of addition within one of the ledger accounts
3. entering a different figure on the credit to that entered on the debit when making a double entry in the ledger
4. making a single entry for a transaction rather than a double entry
5. entering a transaction twice on the same side of the ledger

> **TIP**
> If the totals of a trial balance do not agree you know an error has been made in the ledger or in the preparation of the trial balance.

Checklist for locating errors

- Check the addition of the trial balance.
- Check the addition of the balance of each ledger account.
- Check that each ledger account balance has been entered in the correct column of the trial balance.
- Check that every ledger account balance has been entered in the trial balance.
- Look for a transaction equal to the difference in the trial balance and check that a double entry has been made for that transaction.
- Look for a transaction equal to half the difference in the trial balance and check if it has been entered twice on the same side of the ledger rather than once on each side.
- Check the double entry for every transaction entered in the books since the date of the last trial balance.

If the trial balance balances

When a trial balance balances, it simply means that the total of the debit balances is equal to the total of the credit balances. It does not imply that the double entry is error-free. The trial balance will still balance if any of the following errors are made:

Name of error	Description of error	Example
Error of commission	This occurs when a transaction is entered using the correct amount and on the correct side, but in the wrong account of the same class.	Cash received from Malini credited to Mallika's account.
Error of complete reversal	This occurs when the correct amount is entered in the correct accounts, but the entry has been made on the wrong side of each account.	Cash drawings debited to the cash account and credited to the drawings account.
Error of omission	This occurs when a transaction has been completely omitted from the accounting records. Neither a debit entry nor a credit entry has been made.	Payment of wages not entered in the books.

> **TIP**
> There are six types of error which may occur that a trial balance will not reveal.

Chapter 3: The trial balance

Name of error	Description of error	Example
Error of original entry	This occurs when an incorrect figure is used when a transaction is first entered in the accounting records. The double entry will therefore use the incorrect figure.	Goods, $100, bought on credit but recorded as $1 000.
Error of principle	This occurs when a transaction is entered using the correct amount and on the correct side, but in the wrong class of account.	Motor expenses debited to the motor vehicles account.
Compensating errors	These occur when two or more errors cancel each other out.	Purchases account under-added by $100 and sales returns account over-added by $100.

TIP

In addition to learning the names of the types of error not revealed by a trial balance, you must be able to explain and provide examples of each of these types of error.

TEST YOURSELF 3.3

1 For **each** of the following state the type of error which has been made.
  a Rent of premises debited to the premises account
  b Sales to R Singh debited to H Singh's account
  c Balance on cash account overstated by $10 and balance on sales account overstated by $10
  d Cash sales debited to the sales account and credited to the cash account

LINK

You will learn more about errors in the accounting records in Chapter 15.

You can now answer Questions 4–6 at the end of this chapter.

Revision checklist

- A trial balance is a list of the balances on the accounts in the ledger at a certain date.
- A trial balance is prepared to check the arithmetical accuracy of the double entry book-keeping.
- If a trial balance fails to balance, it indicates that an error has been made.
- There are six types of error which are not revealed by a trial balance.

Cambridge IGCSE and O Level Accounting

Exam-style questions

1. The balance of which account may appear on the debit side of a trial balance?

    A Carriage inwards
    B Purchases returns
    C Rent receivable
    D Sales

2. Jai is a trader. The following balances appeared in his books on 31 March 20–8.

	$
Sales	86 000
Purchases	51 500
Bank overdraft	1 100
Cash	50
Trade payables	4 900
Trade receivables	6 900
Furniture and equipment	26 400
Wages	21 300
Sundry expenses	3 100
Rent payable	3 200
Purchases returns	350
Inventory	9 200
Drawings	10 100
Capital	39 400

    Prepare Jai's trial balance at 31 March 20–8.

3. Sayeeda provided the following list of balances on 30 April 20–4, but was not able to provide her bank account balance.

	$
Capital	392 000
Drawings	18 000
Premises	210 000
Fixtures and fittings	66 100
Inventory	11 950
Trade receivables	13 160
Trade payables	12 280
Loan from FH	20 000
Cash	100
Sales	157 280
Purchases	143 400
Rates	6 000
General expenses	11 540
Wages	96 750
Bank	?

    Prepare Sayeeda's trial balance at 30 April 20–4, inserting the missing bank balance.

Chapter 3: The trial balance

4 The totals of a trial balance did not agree.

Which error may have caused this?

- **A** Expenses paid in cash omitted from the accounting records
- **B** Goods sold on credit to Jones debited in Jenson's account
- **C** Repairs to machinery debited to machinery account
- **D** Total of the purchases returns account overcast

5 Rent received from a tenant in cash, $450, was entered in the accounts as $460.

How will this affect the trial balance?

	Debit balances in trial balance	Credit balances in trial balance
A	cash overstated	no effect
B	cash overstated	rent receivable overstated
C	no effect	rent receivable overstated
D	rent receivable overstated	cash overstated

6 A trial balance drawn up at the end of Jim's financial year balanced. The following errors were then discovered:

1. Goods returned to K Weston had been debited to K Wilton.
2. Repairs to office equipment had been debited in the office equipment account.
3. An invoice, $1 000, for goods sold on credit to Jacob & Co had been recorded in the accounts as $100.
4. Goods purchased on credit from Brixton Ltd had been debited in Brixton's account and credited in the purchases account.

a State the type of error made in **each** of the errors 1–4.
b Name **two** further errors not revealed by a trial balance.

Chapter 4
Double entry book-keeping – Part B

Learning objectives

In this chapter you will learn to:

- recognise the division of the ledger into the sales ledger, the purchases ledger and the nominal (general) ledger   2.1
- explain the use of, and process, accounting information in the cash book   2.3
- distinguish between and account for trade discount and cash discount   2.3
- explain the dual function of the cash book as a book of prime entry and as a ledger account for bank and cash   2.3
- explain the use of, and record, payments and receipts made by bank transfers and other electronic means.   2.3

Chapter 4: Double entry book-keeping – Part B

4.1 Introduction

Chapter 2 introduced the basic principles of double entry book-keeping. It was explained how a ledger account is opened for each type of asset, expense, liability and income, and for every individual debtor and creditor. As the business grows, so does the number of ledger accounts, so it becomes necessary to divide the ledger into different sections.

4.2 Division of the ledger into specialist areas

Dividing the ledger into sections makes it more convenient to use as the same type of accounts can be kept together and the task of maintaining the ledger can be divided between several people. It also enables checking procedures (in the form of control accounts) to be introduced and may reduce the possibility of fraud.

The ledger is usually divided into the following specialised areas:

- **Sales ledger**: This is also referred to as the **debtors ledger or trade receivables ledger**. All the **personal** accounts of credit customers are kept in the sales ledger.
- **Purchases ledger**: This is also referred to as the **creditors ledger or trade payables ledger**. All the **personal** accounts of credit suppliers are kept in the purchases ledger.
- **Nominal ledger**: This is also referred to as the **general ledger**. Apart from the cash account, the bank account and the accounts of credit customers and credit suppliers, all the remaining accounts are kept in the nominal ledger. This ledger will contain accounts of assets, liabilities, expenses, incomes, sales, purchases and returns. Asset accounts are known as **real** accounts. Accounts for expenses, income and capital are known as **nominal** accounts.
- **Cash books**: These contain the main cash book (see Section 4.3) and the petty cash book.

LINK

You will learn more about control accounts in Chapter 16.

TIP

Only the personal accounts of credit customers are recorded in the sales ledger. The sales account is recorded in the nominal (general) ledger.

TIP

Only the personal accounts of credit suppliers are recorded in the purchases ledger. The purchases account is recorded in the nominal (general) ledger.

> **KEY TERMS**
>
> **Sales ledger:** the ledger in which the accounts of credit customers are maintained.
> **Purchases ledger:** ledger in which the accounts of credit suppliers are maintained.
> **Nominal (general) ledger:** the ledger where all the other accounts are maintained.

LINK

You will learn about petty cash books in Chapter 5.

> **TEST YOURSELF 4.1**
>
> 1 State **one** advantage of dividing the ledger into specialist areas.
> 2 State in which ledger **each** of the following accounts would appear.
>   a Rent account
>   b AB Finance Co loan account
>   c XY Stores account (a supplier)
>   d Capital account
>   e Sales returns account
>   f Gee Tee Traders account (a customer)

You can now answer Questions 1–3 at the end of this chapter.

4.3 The two column cash book

Chapter 2 explained how two separate accounts – a cash account and a bank account – are maintained to record the movements of money. In practice, it is common for these accounts to be moved from the ledger and shown in a separate book known as the cash book. The cash account and the bank account appear side-by-side in the cash book.

The rules of double entry book-keeping are still applied. Any money received is debited in the cash book. If the money is placed in the cash till, it will be entered in the cash column and if it is paid into the bank, it will be entered in the bank column. Any money paid out is credited in the cash book. If the money is paid in cash, it will be entered in the cash column and if it is paid out of the bank, it will be entered in the bank column.

Whilst the cash account and the bank account appear side-by-side, they still keep their own identity and must be balanced separately as described in Chapter 2.

Since the cash book is part of the double entry system, it represents ledger accounts for both cash and bank. It is, however, also a **book of prime entry** because it is one of the books in which transactions should be recorded before being entered in the ledger.

LINK

You will learn more about books of prime entry in Chapter 7.

4.4 Contra entries

Sometimes surplus cash is paid into the bank, or money may be withdrawn from the bank to place in the cash. Such transactions are known as **contra entries** because they appear on both sides of the cash book, debited to one account and credited to the other. These transactions are recorded by applying the usual rules of double entry by debiting the account receiving the money and crediting the account giving the money. The name of the account where the double entry is made is written in the details column. The entries are summarised as follows:

KEY TERM

A **Contra entry** is one which appears on both sides of the cash book.

1 To record surplus cash paid into the bank
  - Debit the bank account and write 'cash' in the details column.
  - Credit the cash account and write 'bank' in the details column.
2 To record cash withdrawn from the bank for office use
  - Debit the cash account and write 'bank' in the details column.
  - Credit the bank account and write 'cash' in the details column.

In each case, the letter 'c' is usually entered in the folio column to indicate that the double entry is on the opposite side of the same book.

In addition to making payments by cheque, businesses can pay by electronic means. These are much quicker and safer means than payments made by cheque. A person can pay another by means of a credit transfer which involves instructing their bank to transfer an amount to the bank account of the other person. Payments can also be made by standing order and direct debit. A standing order is when a person instructs the bank to pay a fixed sum at fixed intervals to another person. A direct debit is when a person notifies the bank that permission has been given for a named person to collect an amount directly from their bank account. Direct debits are used for recurring payments where the amounts and dates vary. Other popular means of payment are debit cards and credit cards. When a person uses a debit card, the money comes directly from his/her bank account. When a person uses a credit card, the credit card company pays the person to whom money is owed and the cardholder pays some or all of the money back to the card company (usually at monthly intervals).

TIP

To make a contra entry:
- In the details column on the debit side, write the name of the account where the money has come from.
- In the details column on the credit side, write the name of the account to which the money is going.

Chapter 4: Double entry book-keeping – Part B

Walkthrough 4.1

20–6

December		
1	Mamata started business with a capital of $20 000 which she transferred into a business bank account
2	Paid rent of premises, $650, by standing order
5	Purchased goods, $9 500, on credit from Lodi Road Traders
9	Withdrew $150 from the bank account for office use
14	Paid advertising expenses, $90, in cash
18	Sold goods, $4 120, on credit to Central Dealers
23	Paid Lodi Road Traders' account by cheque
26	Bought motor vehicle, $5 760, and paid by credit transfer
28	Mamata took $3 000 from the business bank account for personal use

Enter these transactions in the books of Mamata. The cash account and the bank account should be shown in a two column cash book. The ledger should be divided into sales ledger, purchases ledger and nominal ledger. Balance the cash book on 31 December.

Mamata

Sales ledger

Central Dealers account — Page 1

Date	Details	Folio	$	Date	Details	Folio	$
20–6							
Dec 18	Sales	nl 5	4 120				

Purchases ledger

Lodi Road Traders account — Page 1

Date	Details	Folio	$	Date	Details	Folio	$
20–6				20–6			
Dec 23	Bank	cb 1	9 500	Dec 5	Purchases	nl 3	9 500
			9 500				9 500

Nominal ledger

Capital account — Page 1

Date	Details	Folio	$	Date	Details	Folio	$
				20–7			
				Dec 1	Bank	cb 1	20 000

Rent payable account — Page 2

Date	Details	Folio	$	Date	Details	Folio	$
20–6							
Dec 2	Bank	cb 1	650				

Purchases account — Page 3

Date	Details	Folio	$	Date	Details	Folio	$
20–6							
Dec 5	Lodi Road Traders	pl 1	9 500				

Advertising account — Page 4

Date	Details	Folio	$	Date	Details	Folio	$
20–6							
Dec 14	Cash	cb 1	90				

Sales account — Page 5

Date	Details	Folio	$	Date	Details	Folio	$
				20–6			
				Dec 18	Central Dealers	sl 1	4 120

Motor vehicles account — Page 6

Date	Details	Folio	$	Date	Details	Folio	$
20–6							
Dec 26	Bank	cb 1	5 760				

Drawings account — Page 7

Date	Details	Folio	$	Date	Details	Folio	$
20–6							
Dec 28	Bank	cb 1	3 000				

<table>
<tr><th colspan="11">Mamata
Cash book</th></tr>
<tr><th colspan="10"></th><th>Page 1</th></tr>
<tr><th>Date</th><th>Details</th><th>Folio</th><th>Cash $</th><th>Bank $</th><th>Date</th><th>Details</th><th>Folio</th><th>Cash $</th><th>Bank $</th></tr>
<tr><td>---</td><td>---</td><td>---</td><td>---</td><td>---</td><td>---</td><td>---</td><td>---</td><td>---</td><td>---</td></tr>
<tr><td>20–6</td><td></td><td></td><td></td><td></td><td>20–6</td><td></td><td></td><td></td><td></td></tr>
<tr><td>Dec 1</td><td>Capital</td><td>nl 1</td><td></td><td>20 000</td><td>Dec 2</td><td>Rent payable</td><td>nl 2</td><td></td><td>650</td></tr>
<tr><td>9</td><td>Bank</td><td>c</td><td>150</td><td></td><td>9</td><td>Cash</td><td>c</td><td></td><td>150</td></tr>
<tr><td></td><td></td><td></td><td></td><td></td><td>14</td><td>Advertising</td><td>nl 4</td><td>90</td><td></td></tr>
<tr><td></td><td></td><td></td><td></td><td></td><td>23</td><td>Lodi Road Traders</td><td>nl 1</td><td></td><td>9 500</td></tr>
<tr><td></td><td></td><td></td><td></td><td></td><td>26</td><td>Motor vehicles</td><td>nl 6</td><td></td><td>5 760</td></tr>
<tr><td></td><td></td><td></td><td></td><td></td><td>28</td><td>Drawings</td><td>nl 7</td><td></td><td>3 000</td></tr>
<tr><td></td><td></td><td></td><td></td><td></td><td>31</td><td>Balance</td><td>c/d</td><td>60</td><td>940</td></tr>
<tr><td></td><td></td><td></td><td>150</td><td>20 000</td><td></td><td></td><td></td><td>150</td><td>20 000</td></tr>
<tr><td>20–7</td><td></td><td></td><td></td><td></td><td></td><td></td><td></td><td></td><td></td></tr>
<tr><td>Jan 1</td><td>Balance</td><td>b/d</td><td>60</td><td>940</td><td></td><td></td><td></td><td></td><td></td></tr>
</table>

TEST YOURSELF 4.2

1 Explain what is meant by a contra entry in a cash book.
2 Give **two** examples of contra entries in a cash book.

4.5 Bank overdraft

As explained earlier, the cash column and the bank column of a cash book are balanced separately as they represent two separate accounts.

The balance on the cash column will always be brought down as a debit balance at the start of the next trading period. The only exception to this is when there is no cash left in the cash account, in which case the balance will be nil. It is not possible to have a credit balance on a cash account.

It is, however, possible to have a credit balance on a bank account. The bank may allow the business to have a **bank overdraft**. This means that the bank allows the business to pay out more from the bank than is put into the bank (interest will be charged by the bank on the amount overdrawn). In the cash book, the bank account is balanced in the usual way and the balance will be brought down on the credit side. This represents the amount the business owes the bank and is a liability.

KEY TERM

A **bank overdraft** occurs when more has been paid out of the bank than was put into the bank account.

TIP

A bank loan is different to a bank overdraft because:
- it is a fixed amount which is paid into the business bank account
- it must be repaid by an agreed date
- interest at a fixed rate is payable on the total amount borrowed.

Cambridge IGCSE and O Level Accounting

Walkthrough 4.2

Mamata started business on 1 December 20–6. Her transactions for the first month of trading were the same as those shown in **Walkthrough 4.1**, except that her drawings on 28 December amounted to $5 000 rather than $3 000.

Enter Mamata's transactions for December 20–6 in her two column cash book. Balance the book on 31 December and bring down the balances on 1 January 20–7.

Mamata

Cash book — Page 1

Date	Details	Folio	Cash $	Bank $	Date	Details	Folio	Cash $	Bank $
20–6					20–6				
Dec 1	Capital	nl 1		20 000	Dec 2	Rent payable	nl 2		650
9	Bank	c	150		9	Cash	c		150
31	Balance	c/d		1 060	14	Advertising	nl 4	90	
					23	Lodi Road Traders	nl 1		9 500
					26	Motor vehicles	nl 6		5 760
					28	Drawings	nl 7		5 000
					31	Balance	c/d	60	
			150	21 060				150	21 060
20–7					20–6				
Jan 1	Balance	b/d	60		Jan 1	Balance	b/d		1 060

You can now answer Question 4 at the end of this chapter.

4.6 The three column cash book

Many businesses maintain a three column cash book rather than a two column cash book. The difference is that a three column cash book has an extra money column on each side to record **cash discount**.

KEY TERM

Cash discount is an allowance given to a customer when an account is settled within a time limit set by the supplier.

TIP

An account does not necessarily have to be paid in cash to qualify for cash discount.

Cash discount

Cash discount is an allowance given to a customer when an account is settled within a time limit set by the supplier. An account does not have to be paid in cash to qualify for cash discount. The **time** of payment is the deciding factor rather than **how** the account is paid. Cash discount is a means of encouraging customers to pay their accounts promptly. The supplier will receive an amount slightly less than the due amount. However, the money is paid earlier and so it is available for use within the business.

Discount allowed is the discount a business allows its credit customers (debtors) when they pay their accounts within a set time. This is an expense of the business as it is the cost of having debts settled promptly. **Discount received** is the discount a business receives from its credit suppliers (creditors) when it pays their accounts within a set time. This is an income of the business as it is the benefit received from settling debts promptly. It is important to realise that discount received does not involve the receipt of money: the supplier simply accepts less money in settlement of the account.

In addition to recording the cash or cheque in settlement of debt, it is also necessary to record cash discount. The entries are summarised as follows:

1 When an account is paid by a debtor and a discount is allowed

   Credit the discount in the debtor's account to show that this amount is no longer owing. Enter the amount of the discount in the discount allowed column of the cash book.

2 When an account of a creditor is paid and a discount is received

   Debit the discount in the creditor's account to show that this amount is no longer owing. Enter the amount of the discount in the discount received column of the cash book.

The discount columns in the cash book are **not** a part of the double entry system. They are used for convenience to make a note of discount at the time an account is paid or received. At the end of the trading period the totals must be transferred to the double entry system. The steps for this are as follows:

1 Total each discount column.
2 Debit the discount allowed account in the nominal ledger with the total of the discount allowed column. This now represents the double entry for all the individual credits in the accounts of debtors.
3 Credit the discount received account in the nominal ledger with the total of the discount received column. This now represents the double entry for all the individual debits in the accounts of creditors.

Trade discount must not be confused with cash discount. Trade discount is a reduction in the price of goods when goods are purchased, rather than when payment is made and is often dependent on the quantity purchased.

You can now answer Questions 5 and 6 at the end of this chapter.

TIP

Do not attempt to balance the discount columns in the cash book. They represent different types of cash discount: the column on the debit side is discount allowed and the column on the credit side is discount received.

LINK

You will learn more about trade discount in Chapter 6.

4.7 Dishonoured cheque

A **dishonoured cheque** is a cheque received which the debtor's bank refuses to pay. This may occur because the debtor does not have enough money in his/her bank account, or it may be because of an error on the cheque, e.g. no signature, no date, the amount in words and the amount in figures do not agree.

If a cheque is dishonoured, it is returned to the business that paid the cheque into the bank. The business must record the return of this cheque by crediting the bank account and debiting the debtor's account (the reverse of the entries made when the cheque was received). The business will also inform the debtor that this amount is unpaid.

KEY TERM

A **dishonoured cheque** is a cheque received which the debtor's bank refuses to pay.

TEST YOURSELF 4.3

1 Explain why it is **not** possible to have a credit balance brought down in the cash column of a cash book.
2 Explain the meaning of the term bank overdraft.
3 Explain why a business may allow its credit customers cash discount.
4 Explain the meaning of the term 'dishonoured cheque'.

Cambridge IGCSE and O Level Accounting

Walkthrough 4.3

Enter the following transactions in the books of Mamata. She maintains a three column cash book and divides the ledger into three sections – sales ledger, purchases ledger and nominal ledger.

Balance the cash book on 31 January 20–7 and transfer the totals of the discount columns to the relevant accounts in the nominal ledger. Balance the accounts in the sales and purchases ledgers where necessary.

20–7

January	1	Mamata had a cash balance of $60 and a bank overdraft of $1 060
	4	Bought goods, $5 200, on credit from Lodi Road Traders
	8	Returned goods, $200, to Lodi Road Traders
	12	Sold goods, $770, on credit to A & J Singh
	14	Cash sales $680
	17	Paid $650 cash into the business bank account
	21	Received a cheque from A & J Singh in settlement of their account
	24	Sold goods, $1 200, on credit to North East Stores
	26	A & H Singh's cheque was dishonoured and returned by the bank
	28	Paid Lodi Road Traders the amount due, by credit transfer, after deducting a discount of $2\frac{1}{2}\%$
	31	North East Stores paid the amount due by credit transfer, less a cash discount of 3%

Mamata

Sales ledger

A & J Singh account — Page 2

Date	Details	Folio	$	Date	Details	Folio	$
20–7				20–7			
Jan 12	Sales	nl 5	770	Jan 21	Bank	cb 2	770
26	Bank (dishonoured cheque)	cb 2	770	31	Balance	c/d	770
			1 540				1 540
20–7							
Feb 1	Balance	b/d	770				

North East Stores account — Page 3

Date	Details	Folio	$	Date	Details	Folio	$
20–7				20–7			
Jan 24	Sales	nl 5	1 200	Jan 31	Bank	cb 2	1 164
					Discount	cb 2	36
			1 200				1 200

Purchases ledger

Lodi Road Traders account — Page 1

Date	Details	Folio	$	Date	Details	Folio	$
20–7				20–7			
Jan 8	Purchases Returns	nl 8	200	Jan 4	Purchases	nl 3	5 200
28	Bank	cb 2	4 875				
	Discount	cb 2	125				
			5 200				5 200

Nominal ledger

Purchases account — Page 3

Date	Details	Folio	$	Date	Details	Folio	$
20–7							
Jan 4	Lodi Road Traders	pl 1	5 200				

Sales account — Page 5

Date	Details	Folio	$	Date	Details	Folio	$
				20–7			
				Jan 12	A & J Singh	sl 2	770
				14	Cash	cb 2	680
				24	North East Stores	sl 3	1 200

Purchases returns account — Page 8

Date	Details	Folio	$	Date	Details	Folio	$
				20–7			
				Jan 8	Lodi Road Traders	pl 1	200

Discount allowed account Page 9

Date	Details	Folio	$	Date	Details	Folio	$
20–7							
Jan 31	Total for month	cb 2	36				

Discount received account Page 10

Date	Details	Folio	$	Date	Details	Folio	$
				20–7			
				Jan 31	Total for month	cb 2	125

Mamata
Cash book Page 2

Date	Details	Folio	Discount allowed $	Cash $	Bank $	Date	Details	Folio	Discount received $	Cash $	Bank $
20–7						20–7					
Jan 1	Balance	b/d		60		Jan 1	Balance	b/d			1 060
14	Sales	nl 5		680		17	Bank	c		650	
17	Cash	c			650	26	A & J Singh				
21	A & J Singh	sl 2			770		(dishonoured				
31	North East						cheque)	sl 2			770
	Stores	sl 3	36		1 164	28	Lodi Road Traders	pl 1	125		4 875
	Balance	c/d			4 121	31	Balance	c/d		90	
			36	740	6 705				125	740	6 705
20–7			nl 9			20–7			nl 10		
Feb 1	Balance	b/d			90	Feb 1	Balance	b/d			4 121

Revision checklist

- The ledger is usually divided into three specialist areas – sales ledger, purchases ledger and nominal (general) ledger.
- The cash account and the bank account are usually kept side-by-side in a cash book.
- A contra entry appears on both sides of a cash book.
- Payments can be made by cheque, credit transfer, direct debit, standing order and credit and debit cards.
- A credit balance brought down in the bank column of a cash book indicates a bank overdraft.
- Cash discount is given to encourage customers to pay their accounts within a set time limit.
- The totals of the discount columns in the cash book are transferred to the discount accounts in the ledger.

Chapter 4: Double entry book-keeping – Part B

Exam-style questions

1. Which account will appear in the sales ledger?

   A Dan, a credit supplier
   B Gill, a credit customer
   C Sales
   D Sales returns

2. Mariam is a trader. On 1 March 20–2 the balances in her cash book were:

   Cash $100 debit
   Bank $494 credit

   The following transactions took place in March 20–2:

   March 4 Paid for repairs to office equipment by cheque, $293
         7 Received a cheque from Nawaz, $110
        11 Purchased motor vehicle paying by credit transfer, $5 130
        13 Took $1 500 from the bank for personal use
        19 Paid $286 to Anwar by credit transfer
        21 Paid office expenses in cash, $67
        27 Cash sales, $2 150
        28 Paid wages in cash, $953
        31 Paid all cash into bank except $150

   a Prepare Mariam's cash book for March 20–2. Balance the book and bring down the balances on 1 April 20–2.
   b Explain the significance of the credit balance on the bank column on 1 March 20–2.
   c Explain why it is not possible to have a credit balance on the cash column.
   d Explain the term 'contra'. Illustrate your answer with reference to an appropriate entry in the cash book in **a**.

3. Raminder paid a cheque, $975, to Kumar in full settlement of a debt of $1 000.
   How did Kumar record this?

	Debit	$	Credit	$
A	bank discount allowed	975 25	Raminder	1 000
B	bank discount received	975 25	Raminder	1 000
C	Raminder	1 000	bank discount allowed	975 25
D	Raminder	1 000	bank discount received	975 25

4 Where is the total of the discount column on the credit side of a cash book posted?

    A To the credit side of the discount allowed account

    B To the credit side of the discount received account

    C To the debit side of the discount allowed account

    D To the debit side of the discount received account

5 Samuel maintains a full set of accounting records including a three column cash book. He provided the following information for October 20–5.

Oct 1 Cash $110, bank $5 150 (debit)

       Trade receivables – Paul $160, Jasmine $880

       Trade payables – Adele $350

   4 Paid a cheque to Adele in settlement of her account of $350 less 2% discount

   9 Purchased a motor vehicle, $9 500, and paid by credit transfer

  12 Cash sales, $1 270, of which $1 220 was paid into the bank

  15 Received a cheque, $160, from Paul

  19 Took $1 000 from the bank for personal use

  24 Paid office expenses in cash, $35

  26 Received a cheque from Jasmine for $858 in settlement of her account of $880

  29 The cheque received from Paul on 15 October was returned dishonoured

  30 Paid all cash into the bank except $80

  a Enter the balances in the appropriate accounts on 1 October.

  b Enter the transactions in the cash book and the ledgers. Balance the cash book on 31 October and bring down the balances on 1 November 20–5.

  c Transfer the totals of the discount columns in the cash book to the ledger.

  d Total or balance the accounts of the trade receivables and trade payables as required.

6 Kalpana is a trader. On 1 February 20–8 she had the following balances on her books:

	$
Cash book – Cash	100
Bank overdraft	480
Sales ledger – Srivastava	200
Purchases ledger – Ahmed	320
Nominal ledger – Premises	60 000
Fixtures and fittings	5 500
Capital	65 000

  a Enter these balances in the appropriate accounts on 1 February 20–8.

The following transactions took place during the month of February 20–8:

February 3 Sold goods, $300, on credit to Srivastava
7 Srivastava returned faulty goods, $50
11 Purchased goods, $390, paying by cheque
Paid $10 by cheque for carriage on goods purchased
15 Cash sales, $610, of which $600 was paid into the bank
19 Srivastava paid the amount owing on 1 February by credit transfer, after deducting 3% cash discount
21 Paid general expenses, $75, in cash
23 Paid Ahmed by credit transfer the amount due, less a cash discount of $2\frac{1}{2}\%$
25 Sublet part of the premises and received $400 rent in cash
27 Paid $15 by cheque for repairs to fixtures
28 Paid all the cash into the bank except $100

b Enter these transactions in the books of Kalpana.
c Balance the cash book and the personal accounts on 28 February. Transfer the totals of the discount columns to the nominal (general) ledger on 28 February.
d Draw up a trial balance at 28 February 20–8.

Chapter 5
Petty cash books

Learning objectives

In this chapter you will learn to:

- explain the use of, and process, accounting data in the petty cash book   2.3
- explain and apply the imprest system of petty cash.   2.3

Chapter 5: Petty cash books

5.1 Introduction

A **petty cash book** is used to record low-value (petty) cash payments. These may include postages and stationery, cleaning, travelling expenses and even small cash payments to creditors.

The petty cash book serves two purposes: **a** it lists the transactions for transferring to ledger accounts; **b** it acts as a ledger account for petty cash transactions. Like the cash book, the petty cash book is a book of prime entry and since it is part of the double entry system, it is also a ledger account.

Maintaining a petty cash book means that it is not necessary to record small cash payments individually in either the cash book or the ledger. This reduces the number of entries in these books.

The task of maintaining a petty cash book is often given to a junior member of staff who is given an amount of cash to act as a **float** from which to make small cash payments. Whilst this allows the chief cashier to concentrate on more important tasks, it also provides valuable training for a junior member of staff. The chief cashier must check the work of the petty cashier at regular intervals.

When a member of staff wishes to obtain some petty cash, he/she should present the petty cashier with a completed **petty cash voucher**. This should show the purpose for which the money is required, the date and the signature of the person receiving the cash. At regular intervals the petty cashier should check these vouchers against the total cash spent.

> **LINK**
> You will learn more about books of prime entry in Chapter 7.

> **KEY TERMS**
> A **petty cash book** is used to record low-value cash payments.
> The **imprest system** of petty cash is where the amount spent each period is restored so that the petty cashier starts each period with the same amount.

TEST YOURSELF 5.1

1. State **two** advantages of maintaining a petty cash book.
2. Explain the purpose of a petty cash voucher.

5.2 The imprest system

Most petty cash books are maintained using the **imprest system**. Under this system the petty cashier starts each period (week, fortnight, month and so on) with a fixed amount of money. This is known as the **imprest amount** or the **float**. During the period, payments are made out of this cash and are recorded in the petty cash book. At the end of the period, after the petty cash book is balanced, the chief cashier will provide the petty cashier with enough cash to restore the balance to the amount of the imprest (float). The petty cashier therefore starts each period with the same amount of cash.

Under this system the chief cashier is aware of exactly how much petty cash has been spent in each period. This means that the petty cash expenditure can be controlled. The amount of the imprest can be adjusted as necessary if it is too much or not enough. The imprest system can also help to reduce fraud.

Cambridge IGCSE and O Level Accounting

> **TIP**
> The imprest is sometimes referred to as 'the float'.

> **TEST YOURSELF 5.2**
> 1. Explain the meaning of the imprest system of petty cash.
> 2. Explain what the petty cashier should do if he/she thinks that the imprest amount is inadequate.

> **KEY TERM**
> **Analysis columns** are used to divide the payments into different categories.

5.3 The layout of a petty cash book

A petty cash book resembles a ledger account with several money columns on the credit side. These are known as **analysis columns** and are used to divide the payments into different categories. A column is used for each of the main types of expenses paid out of petty cash. Instead of a folio column on the credit side there is a column for recording the number of the voucher to which the payment relates.

The number of columns and the main types of expenses will be determined by each individual business.

A layout of a petty cash book is shown as follows:

									Petty cash book				
Dr													Cr
Date	Details	Folio	Total received	Date	Details	Vo. no.*	Total paid		Analysis columns				
			$				$	$		$		$	$

*'Vo. no.' is the abbreviation for 'voucher number'.

5.4 Preparation of a petty cash book

The entries in a petty cash book are summarised as follows:

During the period

1. **Money received**
   a. Debit the total received column with any money received from the chief cashier.
      Insert the word 'cash' or 'bank' in the details column.
   b. Debit the total received column with any money received from any other source.
      Insert the name of the account to be credited in the details column, e.g. the name of a debtor (where a debtor pays an account in cash), travel expenses (where an employee reimburses the petty cash for private travel expenses), telephone expenses (where an employee reimburses the petty cash for private telephone calls) and so on.

2. **Money paid**
   Credit the total paid column with any money paid out and also enter the amount in the analysis column for that particular expense. A brief description of the reason for the payment should be entered in the details column.

Chapter 5: Petty cash books

At the end of the period

1. Add the total paid column. Insert the total.
2. Add each of the analysis columns and insert the totals. If these totals are then added horizontally they should agree with the total paid column. The analysis columns are now complete.
3. Balance the total received column and the total paid column in the same way as balancing any other ledger account. Carry down the balance from the credit side to the debit side to start the new period.
4. When the imprest is restored, enter as described earlier.
5. Complete the double entry for the totals of the analysis columns.
   a. The totals of the analysis columns for expenses should be debited to the appropriate expense account in the nominal ledger. To indicate that the double entry has been completed the folio number of the relevant account is often written below the total of the appropriate analysis column in the petty cash book.
   b. Any entries in the analysis column headed 'ledger accounts' should be debited individually to the purchases ledger account of the creditor who made the payment.

TIP
Every payment should be entered in the appropriate analysis column as well as the total paid column.

TIP
Each of the analysis columns should be totalled. Check the arithmetic by making sure that these are equal to the total amount paid.

Walkthrough 5.1

Maitreyi keeps an analysed petty cash book using the imprest system. The amount of the imprest is $150. She provided the following information:

20–1			$	Voucher number
November	1	Balance	150	
	5	Paid window cleaner	10	1
	8	Bought pens and pencils	4	2
	14	Paid H Singh, a credit supplier	20	3
	17	Paid taxi fare	9	4
	21	Bought computer paper	7	5
	25	Paid bus fares	3	6
	27	Paid A Sharma, a credit supplier	32	7
	29	Paid office cleaner	30	8

a. Write up Maitreyi's petty cash book for the month of November 20–1. The petty cash book should have four analysis columns – cleaning, stationery, travel expenses and ledger accounts.

b. Balance the petty cash book on 30 November and carry down the balance. Show the restoration of the imprest on 1 December 20–1.

c. Make the necessary entries in Maitreyi's nominal ledger and purchases ledger on 30 November 20–1.

a & b

Maitreyi
Petty cash book   Page 1

Date	Details	Fo	Total received $	Date	Details	Vo	Total paid $	Cleaning $	Stationery $	Travel expenses $	Ledger accounts $
20–1				20–1							
Nov 1	Balance	b/d	150	Nov 5	Window cleaner	1	10	10			
				8	Pens and pencils	2	4		4		
				14	H Singh	3	20				20
				17	Taxi fare	4	9			9	
				21	Computer paper	5	7		7		
				25	Bus fares	6	3			3	
				27	A Sharma	7	32				32
				29	Office cleaner	8	30	30			
							115	40	11	12	52
				30	Balance	c/d	35	nl 11	nl 17	nl 24	
			150				150				
20–1											
Dec 1	Balance	b/d	35								
	Cash		115								

c

Maitreyi
Nominal ledger
Cleaning account   Page 11

Date	Details	Folio	$	Date	Details	Folio	$
20–1							
Nov 30	Petty cash	pcb1	40				

Stationery account   Page 17

Date	Details	Folio	$	Date	Details	Folio	$
20–1							
Nov 30	Petty cash	pcb1	11				

Chapter 5: Petty cash books

Travel expenses account — Page 24

Date	Details	Folio	$	Date	Details	Folio	$
20–1							
Nov 30	Petty cash	pcb1	12				

Purchases ledger

H Singh account — Page 73

Date	Details	Folio	$	Date	Details	Folio	$
20–1							
Nov 14	Petty cash	pcb1	20				

A Sharma account — Page 69

Date	Details	Folio	$	Date	Details	Folio	$
20–1							
Nov 27	Petty cash	pcb1	32				

- Each of the accounts in the purchases ledger would have shown a credit balance representing the amount due. The payment from petty cash will cancel this amount.

TIP

At the end of the period:
- the total of each expense analysis column is transferred to the appropriate ledger account
- the individual entries in the ledger account column are transferred to the personal accounts of the credit suppliers.

TEST YOURSELF 5.3

1 Explain the use of analysis columns in a petty cash book.
2 State where the double entry will be made for **each** of the following items appearing in a petty cash book:
   a amount received to restore the imprest
   b payment from petty cash to a credit supplier.

You can now answer Questions 1–6 at the end of this chapter.

Revision checklist

- A petty cash book is used to record small cash payments (and occasionally small cash receipts).
- The imprest system of petty cash means that the petty cashier starts each period with the same amount.
- A petty cash book is a book of prime entry and also a ledger account.
- The totals of the analysis columns are posted to the appropriate nominal ledger accounts at the end of each period.
- Any payments to credit suppliers are posted individually to the purchases ledger account of the supplier to whom the payment was made.

Cambridge IGCSE and O Level Accounting

Exam-style questions

1 A trader maintains a petty cash book using the imprest system. The monthly imprest is $120. The petty cash transactions during August were:

		$
Payments	Taxi fare	12
	Stationery	31
	Postage	8
	Waheed, a credit supplier	43
Receipts	Refund for damaged stationery	11

How much was given to the petty cashier on 1 September to restore the imprest?

A $26   **B** $37   **C** $83   **D** $94

2 A trader provided the following extract from her petty cash book:

Date	Details	Total paid	Cleaning	Office expenses	Ledger accounts
		$	$	$	$
April 4	Tea and coffee	10		10	
18	Thomas	33			33
21	Copy paper	18		18	
29	Cleaning	250	250		

What entries are made in the ledger on 30 April?

A Credit cleaning account, office expenses account, ledger accounts
B Credit cleaning account, office expenses account, Thomas account
C Debit cleaning account, office expenses account, ledger accounts
D Debit cleaning account, office expenses account, Thomas account.

3 On 1 August the petty cash balance equalled the imprest amount of $100. During August the petty cashier spent $83 and received $20 from a member of staff in repayment of a loan.

What entry will be made on 31 August to restore the imprest?

	Debit	$	Credit	$
A	bank	63	petty cash book	63
B	bank	83	petty cash book	83
C	petty cash book	63	bank	63
D	petty cash book	83	bank	83

4 Robin is a sole trader. He operates a petty cash book using the imprest system with a float of $100 at the beginning of each month. The imprest was restored on 30 April so there is an opening balance of $100 on 1 May.

Details of petty cash vouchers presented during May were as follows:

		Voucher number	Total amount $
May 1	Milk, tea and sugar	9	5.20
6	Postage stamps	10	10.50
14	Cleaner's wages	11	30.00
17	Envelopes	12	7.40
21	Parcel postage	13	2.90
24	Milk and tea	14	3.10
28	Cleaner's wages	15	30.00
30	Computer paper	16	4.70

a Write up Robin's petty cash book for May. Use analysis columns for postages, cleaning, stationery and refreshments. Total and balance the book on 31 May.

b i State **one** reason why a business may operate a petty cash book.

ii State **one** advantage of operating the imprest system of petty cash.

5 Abdul maintains a petty cash book with an imprest amount of $150, which is restored on the first day of each month.

He provided the following information on 31 August:

	$
Total of sundry expenses column	13
Total of postage column	19
Total of cleaning column	45
Total of ledger accounts column	62

a Explain the imprest system of petty cash.

b State the total amount spent by the petty cashier in August.

c State the double entry which will be made for the total of the sundry expenses column on 31 August.

d State how the double entry will be made in the ledger for the items in the ledger accounts column.

e State what entry will appear for petty cash in the statement of financial position on 31 August.

f State how much the petty cashier will receive on 1 September to restore the imprest.

6 Shilpa is a sole trader. She pays all receipts into the bank at the end of each day's trading and all payments are made by cheque, except for those less than $20 which are regarded as petty cash items.

She provided the following information:

Date	Detail	Amount	
20–9		$	
Feb 21	Balance at bank	3 120	
	Petty cash imprest	50	
22	Paid South West Traders	721	to settle an account of $750
24	Received cheques:		
	Janpath Stores	410	to settle an account of $425
	AB Trading	220	
26	Paid:		
	Window cleaner	7	
	Speedy Motors	85	
	Petrol	11	
27	Paid:		
	Refreshments	5	
	Ghandi Stores	12	

a Write up the petty cash book for the week ended 28 February 20–9. Use analysis columns for refreshments, cleaning, motor expenses and ledger accounts.

Balance the book on 27 February 20–9 and restore the imprest on 28 February 20–9.

b Write up the cash book for the week ended 28 February 20–9.

Balance the book at 28 February 20–9 (after the restoration of the petty cash imprest).

Section 1: Practice questions

1. Which task is **not** performed by an accountant?
   - A monitoring the progress of the business
   - B preparing a statement of financial position
   - C reporting on the trading results
   - D writing up a three column cash book

2. What is the accounting equation?
   - A assets = capital – liabilities
   - B capital = assets + liabilities
   - C capital = assets – liabilities
   - D liabilities = assets + capital

3. The following account appeared in Anna's ledger:

Jodie account			
	$		$
Jan 5 Sales	500	Jan 7 Returns	20
		29 Bank	300
		31 Balance c/d	180
	500		500

   Which statement is correct?
   - A On 5 January Jodie sold goods, $500, to Anna.
   - B On 7 January Anna returned goods, $20, to Jodie.
   - C On 29 January Anna paid Jodie $300.
   - D On 31 January Jodie owed Anna $180.

4. What is the purpose of a trial balance?
   - A to calculate the capital of the business
   - B to prove the arithmetical accuracy of the double entry
   - C to summarise the assets and liabilities
   - D to locate and correct errors in the ledger accounts

5. Which transaction will be entered in both the purchases ledger and the nominal (general) ledger?
   - A cash paid for goods for resale
   - B purchase of office furniture by cheque
   - C returns of goods by a credit customer
   - D returns of goods to a credit supplier

6 Waseem had the following assets, liabilities and capital on 1 April 20–6:

	$
Premises	100 000
Machinery	48 000
Fixtures	8 800
Cash	590
Cash at bank	3 320
Trade receivables	4 130
Inventory	5 140
Trade payables	4 980
Capital	165 000

a Explain the meaning of each of the terms 'assets', 'liabilities' and 'capital'.

b State why the assets are always equal to the total of the liabilities and capital.

c Complete the following table to state the effect of each transaction which took place on 2 April 20–6. The first one has been completed as an example. If the transaction does not affect the assets or liabilities write 'no effect'.

Transaction	Effect on assets	$	Effect on liabilities	$
Obtained a loan, $10 000, from AB Finance	Bank	+ 10 000	Loan	+ 10 000
Bought goods for resale, $500, for cash				
Paid a credit supplier $2 100 by cheque				
Bought machinery, $4 000, and paid by cheque				
Sold out of date goods at cost price, $190, on credit				

d Prepare the statement of financial position on 2 April 20–6 after these transactions have taken place.

Section 1: Practice questions

7 The following balances appeared in the books of Fabice on 30 June 20–7:

	$
Machinery and equipment	108 000
Motor vehicles	31 000
Trade payables	7 800
Balance at bank	3 830
Trade receivables	11 500
Carriage inwards	380
Carriage outwards	440
Sales	131 000
Purchases	101 900
Rent receivable	3 600
Rent payable	8 400
Inventory	13 200
Commission receivable	1 950
Administration expenses	9 600
Capital	?

a State **two** reasons why a trial balance is prepared.

b Prepare a trial balance for Fabice on 30 June 20–7, inserting a figure for the capital account.

c Name and explain three errors which will not be revealed by a trial balance.

8 Mahendra started a business on 1 November 20–7. He provided the following information for his first month of trading:

Nov 1 Introduced $160 000 capital into the business, of which $158 500 was transferred into a business bank account and the rest was placed in the business cash box

2 Purchased premises, $95 000, paying by credit transfer

5 Bought goods for resale, $2 600, on credit from Duleep

10 Returned goods, $150, to Duleep

14 Paid general expenses in cash, $275

19 Paid rates in cash, $395

21 Sold goods on credit to Anila, $124

Paid carriage on good sold, $95, in cash

24 Paid Duleep $1 000 by cheque on account

28 Took goods costing $250 for personal use

30 Rented out part of the premises and received $260 rent by cheque

a Enter these transactions in the cash book and ledgers. Balance the cash book and Duleep's account. Bring down the balances on 1 December 20–7.
b Prepare a trial balance on 30 November 20–7.

Mahendra is considering allowing credit customers a cash discount for prompt payment.

c Explain the effect that this suggestion may have on Mahendra's cash flow.
d State how this discount would be recorded if Mahendra decided to proceed with this suggestion.

9 Rachel is as trader. Her cash book for March 20–3 is shown below.

Rachel

Cash book

20–3		Cash $	Bank $	20–3		Cash $	Bank $
Mar 1	Capital	200	49 800	Mar 4	Rent		300
21	Loan		10 000	6	Office furniture		4 100
30	Sales	17 500		10	Purchases		15 250
31	Cash		15 500	19	Office expenses		414
				31	Wages	950	
					Bank	15 500	
					Balances	1 250	55 236
		17 700	75 300			17 700	75 300

Explain each entry in the cash book. State where the double entry for each transaction would be made.

10 Habib maintains a three column cash book and also a petty cash book.

The petty cash imprest is $80. All payments under $30 are made from petty cash. The petty cash book has analysis columns for travel, stationery and ledger accounts. The balances on 1 February 20–9 were:

	$
Petty cash	44
Cash	200
Bank overdraft	2 968

The following transactions took place in February 20–9:

Feb 1   Petty cash restored from business bank account
     4   Paid for taxi fares, $18
    14   Received a cheque from Nadira in settlement of her account of $440, less $2\frac{1}{2}$% cash discount
    19   Bought copy paper, $12
    24   Paid Uzma $343 by credit transfer after deducting 2% cash discount
    26   Paid Bashir, a credit supplier, $25
    27   Cash sales, $1 962
    28   Paid all office cash into the bank except $150

Write up the petty cash book and the cash book for February 20–9. Balance the books on 28 February and bring down the balances on 1 March 20–9.

Section 2

Chapter 6
Business documents

Learning objectives

In this chapter you will learn to:

- recognise and understand the following business documents: invoice, debit note, credit note, statement of account, cheque, receipt   2.2
- complete proforma business documents   2.2
- understand the use of business documents as sources of information   2.2
- account for trade discount.   2.3

Cambridge IGCSE and O Level Accounting

LINK

You will learn more about using business documents in Chapter 7.

KEY TERMS

An **invoice** is a document issued by the supplier of goods on credit showing details, quantities and prices of goods supplied.

Trade discount is a reduction in the price of goods: the rate often increases according to quantity purchased.

LINK

You have already learned about cash discount in Chapter 4.

TIP

Trade discount is shown as a deduction on an invoice, but cash discount is not deducted on an invoice.

6.1 Introduction

As explained in Chapter 2, the entries in the accounting records of a business are made using business documents. Both documents received and issued by a business are used.

The main business documents and their uses are described in this chapter.

6.2 Invoice

When a business sells goods on credit it will issue an **invoice** to the purchaser. Each business has its own style of invoice, but they all contain the following information:

- the name and address of the supplier
- the name and address of the customer
- the date
- full details, quantities and prices of the goods supplied.

Sometimes the supplier allows the customer **trade discount**. This is a reduction in the price of the goods: the rate of this discount often increases according to the quantity purchased (so encouraging customers to buy in bulk). It is also given to businesses in the same trade. Such businesses will not be prepared to pay the full rate as they need to make a profit when they sell the goods.

It is important to distinguish between **cash discount** and **trade discount**. Cash discount was explained in Chapter 4. **Trade discount** is shown as a deduction on the invoice. Cash discount is not shown as a deduction from an invoice as it is only allowed if the invoice is paid within a set time limit.

TEST YOURSELF 6.1

1. State **two** reasons why a supplier may allow a customer trade discount.
2. Explain the difference between trade discount and cash discount.

You can now answer Question 1 at the end of this chapter.

Walkthrough 6.1

Sew and Sew is a curtain making business. On 3 April 20–9 goods were purchased on credit from The Weaving Shed and the following invoice was received:

Chapter 6: Business documents

Invoice

Invoice no I 3624

The Weaving Shed
14 Industrial Street
Hightown
Telephone 111 01357

Sew and Sew
92 The Avenue
Lowtown

3 April 20–9

Quantity	Description	Unit price $	Amount $
30 metres	Brocade fabric Design: B320 Colour: Crimson	15	450 00
10 metres	Polycotton fabric Design: P21 Colour: Lemon	6	60 00
			510 00
	Less 20% trade discount		102 00
			408 00
	Terms: $2\frac{1}{2}$% cash discount if account paid by 31 May 20–9		

> **TIP**
> From the supplier's viewpoint an invoice may be described as a sales invoice; from the customer's viewpoint it may be described as a purchases invoice.

- The customer receives the original invoice and uses it to record the purchase of goods on credit.
- The supplier keeps a copy of the invoice and uses it to record the sale of goods on credit.

TEST YOURSELF 6.2

1. List **four** items of information shown on an invoice.
2. Karnail sells goods on credit to Harbhajan and issues an invoice.
   a. Name the account to be debited and the account to be credited in Karnail's books.
   b. Name the account to be debited and the account to be credited in Harbhajan's books.

6.3 Debit note

The customer should check that goods received are in a satisfactory condition and that they are exactly what was ordered (in respect of price, quantity and quality).

The supplier must be informed of any shortages, overcharges and faults. This is done by issuing a **debit note** to the supplier. Each business has its own style of debit note, but they all contain the following information:

> **KEY TERM**
> A **debit note** is a document issued by a purchaser of goods on credit to request a reduction in the invoice received.

- the name and address of the supplier
- the name and address of the customer
- the date
- full details and quantities (and sometimes the prices) of the goods returned or overcharged.

When a price is included on a debit note, it is the price which the customer was actually charged for those goods (the price after the deduction of trade discount).

TIP
Debit notes are never entered in the accounting records.

Walkthrough 6.2

On 6 April 20–9 Sew and Sew returned goods to The Weaving Shed and issued the following debit note.

DEBIT NOTE

Debit note number 29

Sew and Sew

92 The Avenue

Lowtown

The Weaving Shed
14 Industrial Street
Hightown

6 April 20–9

The following goods have been returned:

	Unit price $	Amount $
10 metres polycotton fabric Design: P21 Colour: Lemon	6	60 00
Less 20% trade discount		12 00
		48 00
Reason for return: Wrong colour supplied		
Please issue a credit note		

- Neither the supplier nor the customer makes any entries in their accounting records in respect of a debit note.
- A debit note is merely a request to the supplier to reduce the total of the original invoice.

TEST YOURSELF 6.3

1 State **two** reasons why a customer may send a debit note to a supplier of goods on credit.

Where there has been an undercharge on an invoice most businesses will issue an additional invoice. However, some businesses may issue a debit note instead. This will be entered in the books of both the supplier and the customer in the same way as the original invoice.

6.4 Credit note

When goods are returned, reported faulty, or where there has been an overcharge on an invoice, the supplier may issue a **credit note**. As with all documents, each business has its own style of credit note, but they all contain the following information:

- the name and address of the supplier
- the name and address of the customer
- the date
- full details, quantities and prices of the goods returned or overcharged.

To distinguish them from invoices, credit notes are sometimes printed in red.

> **KEY TERM**
>
> A **credit note** is a document issued by a seller of goods on credit to notify of a reduction in an invoice previously issued.

Walkthrough 6.3

On 6 April 20–9 Sew and Sew returned goods to The Weaving Shed and issued a debit note. The Weaving Shed issued the following credit note to Sew and Sew on 9 April 20–9:

Credit note

The Weaving Shed
14 Industrial Street
Hightown
Telephone 111 01357

Credit note
C529

Sew and Sew
92 The Avenue
Lowtown

9 April 20–9

Quantity	Description	Unit price $	Amount $
10 metres	Polycotton fabric Design: P21 Colour: Lemon	6	60 00
	Less 20% trade discount		12 00
			48 00
	Reason for issue of credit note: Wrong colour supplied		

- The customer receives the original credit note and uses it to record the purchases returns.
- The supplier keeps a copy of the credit note and uses it to record the sales returns.

Cambridge IGCSE and O Level Accounting

> **TEST YOURSELF 6.4**
>
> 1. State **two** reasons why a supplier may send a credit note to a customer.
> 2. Harbhajan issues a credit note to Karnail.
>   a. Name the account to be debited and the account to be credited in Karnail's books.
>   b. Name the account to be debited and the account to be credited in Harbhajan's books.

You can now answer Questions 2 and 3 at the end of this chapter.

6.5 Statement of account

> **KEY TERM**
>
> A **statement of account** is a document issued by the seller of goods on credit to summarise the transactions for the month.

At the end of each month, a supplier will usually issue each customer with a **statement of account**. This is a summary of the transactions for the month. The style of a statement of account may vary, but they all contain the following information:

- the name and address of the supplier
- the name and address of the customer
- the date
- the balance owing at the start of the period
- invoices and credit notes issued
- payments received
- any cash discounts allowed
- the balance owing at the end of the period.

Walkthrough 6.4

The Weaving Shed issued the following statement of account to Sew and Sew on 30 April 20–9.

Statement of account

The Weaving Shed
14 Industrial Street
Hightown
Telephone 111 01357

Sew and Sew
92 The Avenue
Lowtown

30 April 20–9

Date	Reference	Debit $	Credit $	Balance $
20–9				
April 3	Invoice number I 3624	408 00		408 00
9	Credit note number C529		48 00	360 00

The last amount shown in the balance column is the amount due.

Terms: $2\frac{1}{2}$% cash discount if account is paid by 31 May 20–9.

Chapter 6: Business documents

- Neither the supplier nor the customer makes any entries in their accounting records in respect of a statement of account.
- A statement of account is a reminder to the customer of the amount outstanding. This can be checked against the customer's own records to ensure that no errors have been made by either the supplier or the customer.

TIP

A statement of account is never entered in the accounting records.

TEST YOURSELF 6.5

1. State **one** purpose of a statement of account.

You can now answer Questions 4 and 5 at the end of this chapter.

6.6 Cheque

Many accounts are paid by means of a cheque. Other methods of payment through the banking system are credit transfers and standing orders. A **cheque** is a written order to a bank to pay a stated sum of money to the person or business named on the order. A book of preprinted cheques is issued by the bank, and the customer is only required to complete the necessary details of date, amount and payee (the person or business to whom the money is to be paid).

KEY TERM

A **cheque** is a written order to a bank to pay a stated sum of money to the person or business named on the order.

Walkthrough 6.5

On 28 May 20-9 Sew and Sew sent a cheque to The Weaving Shed for the amount due on that date less cash discount. The cheque and its counterfoil are shown as follows:

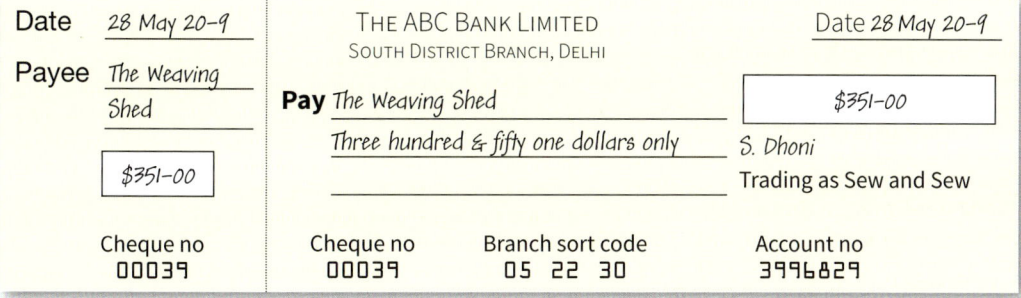

Cheque counterfoil   Actual cheque

- The supplier receives the cheque. A paying-in slip is completed when the cheque is paid into the bank. The counterfoil of this paying-in slip is used to make the entry in the cash book to show the money paid into the bank and to make a note of the discount in the discount allowed column.
- The customer keeps the cheque counterfoil and uses it to make the entry in the cash book to show the money paid out of the bank and to make a note of the discount in the discount received column.

6.7 Receipt

A **receipt** is a written acknowledgement of money received and acts as proof of payment. Since a cheque passes through the banking system it can act as a receipt, so many businesses do not issue receipts if accounts have been paid by cheque. Where goods are sold for cash, the customer is usually provided with a receipt.

> **KEY TERM**
>
> A **receipt** is a written acknowledgement of money received and acts as proof of payment.

Walkthrough 6.6

The Weaving Shed issued the following receipt to Sew and Sew on 30 May 20–9.

RECEIPT   Receipt no 44

The Weaving Shed 14 Industrial Street Hightown

Received from Sew and Sew the sum of $351 (three hundred and fifty one dollars) by cheque

30 May 20–9   *K Singh*   Chief cashier

You can now answer Question 6 at the end of this chapter.

Revision checklist

- A supplier of goods on credit issues an invoice to the customer.
- A supplier may allow a customer trade discount if the businesses are in the same trade and also for buying in bulk.
- If goods are returned or there is an overcharge, a customer may issue a debit note to the supplier asking for a reduction in the invoice.
- A supplier issues a credit note to notify the customer of any reduction in the total of an invoice.
- A supplier issues a statement of account at the end of each month to notify the customer of the amount owing and provide a summary of the account.
- Many accounts are paid by cheque, in which case it is not necessary to issue a receipt as proof of payment.

Exam-style questions

1 On 4 February Ann purchased goods, list price $5 200, on credit from Maria. The terms of trade were:

20% trade discount on orders over $5 000.

$2\frac{1}{2}$% cash discount if account paid by the end of the month.

Which amount did Ann enter in her accounts on 4 February?

  A $4 056   **B** $4 160   **C** $5 070   **D** $5 200

2 Certain items are missing from the following business document:

Credit note

AB Jones
Unit 4 Industrial Estate
Hightown

Tom Brown
123 High Street
Anytown   11 May 20–2

	Unit price $	Amount $
46 tins of paint	11.50	**i** ....
Less 20% **ii** .... discount		**iii** ....
		iv ....

---

  a Insert the missing words or figures in **i** to **iv** on the document.
  b Name the person who issued the credit note.
  c Suggest one reason why the credit note was issued.
  d Name the document which may have been issued to request this credit note.
  e State the entry AB Jones would make to record this credit note.

Account to be debited	Account to be credited

3 Kate sells goods on credit to Kylie. Kate does not allow cash discount. On 1 May Kylie owed Kate $350.

The following documents were exchanged in May:

		$
May 4	invoice	420
8	debit note	112
10	credit note	92
19	cheque	350
26	invoice	170

How much did Kylie pay on 31 May to settle her account?

A $148   B $386   C $498   D $610

4 Zodwa sold goods on credit to Elspeth.

Which document did Elspeth issue when she returned these goods?

A credit note   B debit note   C invoice   D statement

5 There are some figures missing from the following document which Dinesh received:

Trade Supplies
345 London Road
Hightown

Dinesh
110 Long Road
Northwood

31 October 20–1

Date 20–1	Details	Debit $	Credit $	Balance $
Oct 1	Balance	950		950
4	Sales	1 120		2 070
11	Sales returns		110	1 960
27	Cheque		931	?
	Discount		19	?

a Name this document.
b Suggest one reason for the issue of the document.
c State the amount owing by Dinesh on 31 October 20–1.
d Name the document sent by Trade Supplies to Dinesh on 4 October and 11 October.
e Calculate the percentage rate of discount allowed on 27 October.
f Suggest one reason why this discount was allowed.

6 Bill is a credit customer of Rick. The following documents were exchanged in June.

Complete the following table to name the person who issued each document and the entries (if any) made in the books of Bill and Rick.

Document	Person issuing document	Entries in Bill's books		Entries in Rick's books	
		Debit	Credit	Debit	Credit
Invoice					
Debit note					
Credit note					
Statement of account					

Chapter 7
Books of prime entry

Learning objectives

In this chapter you will learn to:

- understand the use of business documents as sources of information   2.2
- explain the advantages of using various books of prime entry   2.3
- explain the use of, and process, accounting data in the books of prime entry – sales journal, purchases journal, sales returns journal and purchases returns journal   2.3
- post the ledger entries from the books of prime entry   2.3
- account for trade discount.   2.3

Chapter 7: Books of prime entry

7.1 Introduction

In Chapter 4 it was explained how the ledger is divided into specialist areas and how the cash and the bank account are usually maintained in a cash book rather than in the ledger. Businesses use **books of prime entry** to record goods sold on credit, goods purchased on credit, sales returns and purchases returns. These books are basically listing devices, grouping similar types of transactions, which is useful when posting to the ledger. The use of these books means that a lot of detail is removed from the ledger. It also means that book-keeping can be divided between several people. Books of prime entry assist in the collating and summarising of accounting information and are useful when preparing control accounts.

Books of prime entry are also known as **books of original entry** or **subsidiary books**. The name of these books has arisen because all transactions should be recorded in one of these books **before** they are entered in the ledger.

The books of prime entry are:

- Cash book
- Petty cash book
- Sales journal
- Purchases journal
- Sales returns journal
- Purchases returns journal
- General journal

LINK
You have already learnt about cash books and petty cash books in Chapters 4 and 5.

LINK
You will learn about the general journal in Chapter 15.

LINK
You will learn about control accounts in Chapter 16.

TIP
Books of prime entry may be referred to as books of original entry or subsidiary books.

KEY TERMS

A **book of prime entry** is one in which transactions are recorded before being entered in the ledger.

The **sales journal** shows a list of the names of businesses to which credit sales have been made, the value of the goods sold and the date on which the sales were made.

This chapter concentrates on the sales, purchases and returns journals.

7.2 Sales journal

The **sales journal** is a list of the names of businesses to which credit sales were made, the value of the sales and the dates on which the sales were made. The sales journal is sometimes referred to as the **sales book** or the **sales day book**.

This journal is written up using copies of the invoices sent to the customers. The entries are summarised as follows:

1. **When goods are sold on credit**
   - Enter the date, customer name and the invoice total in the sales journal.
   - Debit the customer's account in the sales ledger with the invoice total.
2. **At the end of the month**
   - Credit the sales account in the nominal ledger with the sales journal total.
   - This will now form the double entry for all the individual debit entries in the sales ledger.

TIP
Only the total of the sales journal is posted to the sales account at the end of the month, not the individual transactions.

7.3 Sales returns journal

> **KEY TERM**
>
> The **sales returns journal** shows a list of the names of businesses which have returned goods previously sold on credit, the value of the goods returned and the date on which the returns were made.

The **sales returns journal** is a list of the names of businesses, the value of goods returned and the dates on which the returns were made. The sales returns journal is also known as the **sales returns book** or the **returns inwards book** (or **returns inwards journal**).

This journal is written up using copies of the credit notes sent to the customers. The entries are summarised as follows:

1 When goods are returned by a credit customer
   - Enter the date, customer name and credit note total in the sales returns journal.
   - Credit the customer's account in the sales ledger with the credit note total.

2 At the end of the month
   - Debit the sales returns account in the nominal ledger with the sales returns journal total.
   - This will now form the double entry for all the individual credit entries in the sales ledger.

> **LINK**
>
> You learnt about trade discount in Chapter 6.

> **TEST YOURSELF 7.1**
>
> 1 List **seven** books of prime entry.
> 2 When a trader sells goods on credit, he lists them in the sales journal and debits the accounts of customers. Explain where and when the double entry for these debit entries is made.

Walkthrough 7.1

20–9

April 3   The Weaving Shed issued an invoice to Sew and Sew for goods, $510, subject to a trade discount of 20%

9   The Weaving Shed issued a credit note to Sew and Sew for goods returned, list price $60

13   The Weaving Shed sold goods on credit to Fine Furnishings, $1 000, subject to a trade discount of 25%, and issued an invoice on the same day

20   The Weaving Shed sent Jaffar & Company an invoice for $220 for goods supplied on credit

28   The Weaving Shed issued a credit note to Jaffar & Company for $10 because of an overcharge

Chapter 7: Books of prime entry

Make the necessary entries in the books of The Weaving Shed for April 20–9

The Weaving Shed
Sales journal
Page 1

Date	Name	Invoice number	Folio	Amount $
20–9				
April 3	Sew and Sew	I 3624	sl 22	408
13	Fine Furnishings	I 3625	sl 14	750
20	Jaffar & Company	I 3626	sl 16	220
30	Transfer to sales account		nl 35	1 378

Sales returns journal
Page 1

Date	Name	Credit note number	Folio	Amount $
20–9				
April 9	Sew and Sew	C 529	sl 22	48
28	Jaffar & Company	C 530	sl 16	10
30	Transfer to sales returns account		nl 36	58

Sales ledger
Sew and Sew account
Page 22

Date	Details	Folio	$	Date	Details	Folio	$
20–9				20–9			
April 3	Sales	sj 1	408	April 9	Sales returns	srj 1	48

Fine Furnishings account
Page 14

Date	Details	Folio	$	Date	Details	Folio	$
20–9							
April 13	Sales	sj 1	750				

Jaffar & Company account
Page 16

Date	Details	Folio	$	Date	Details	Folio	$
20–9				20–9			
April 20	Sales	sj 1	220	April 28	Sales returns	srj 1	10

Nominal ledger

Sales account
Page 35

Date	Details	Folio	$	Date	Details	Folio	$
				20–9			
				April 30	Credit sales for month	sj 1	1 378

Sales returns account
Page 36

Date	Details	Folio	$	Date	Details	Folio	$
20–9							
April 30	Returns for month	srj 1	58				

> **TIP**
> Trade discount may be shown in the journals for information but is never entered in the double entry records. Only the net value of the goods is recorded.

- Trade discount does **not** appear in the ledger accounts. Trade discount **may** be shown in the books of prime entry for information purposes only.
- The entry in the sales account on 30 April is the double entry for the three individual debits in the customers' accounts in the sales ledger.
- The entry in the sales returns account on 30 April is the double entry for the two individual credits in the customers' accounts in the sales ledger.

7.4 Purchases journal

> **KEY TERM**
> The **purchases journal** shows a list of the names of businesses from which credit purchases have been made, the value of the goods purchased and the date on which the purchases were made.

The **purchases journal** is a list of the names of businesses from which credit purchases were made, the value of the purchases and the dates on which the purchases were made. The purchases journal is also called the **purchases book** or the **purchases day book**.

This journal is written up using the invoices received from suppliers. The entries are summarised as follows:

1. **When goods are purchased on credit**
   - Enter the date, supplier name and the invoice total in the purchases journal.
   - Credit the supplier's account in the purchases ledger with the invoice total.

2. **At the end of the month**
   - Debit the purchases account in the nominal ledger with the purchases journal total.
   - This will now form the double entry for all the individual credit entries in the purchases ledger.

> **TIP**
> Only the purchases journal total is posted to the purchases account at the end of the month, not the individual transactions.

Chapter 7: Books of prime entry

7.5 Purchases returns journal

The **purchases returns journal** is a list of the names of businesses, the value of goods returned and the dates on which the returns were made. The purchases returns journal is also known as the **purchases returns book** or the **returns outward book** (or **returns outward journal**).

This journal is written up using credit notes received from suppliers. The entries are summarised as follows:

1. **When goods are returned to a credit supplier**
   - Enter the date, supplier name and the credit note total in the purchases returns journal.
   - Debit the supplier's account in the purchases ledger with the credit note total.

2. **At the end of the month**
   - Credit the purchases returns account in the nominal ledger with the purchases returns journal total.
   - This will now form the double entry for all the individual debit entries in the purchases ledger.

KEY TERM

The **purchases returns journal** shows a list of the names of businesses to which goods, previously purchased on credit, have been returned, the value of the goods returned and the date on which the returns were made.

TIP

At the end of the month the total of the sales returns journal is posted to the sales returns account and the total of the purchases returns journal is posted to the purchases returns account.

TEST YOURSELF 7.2

1. State **two** advantages of maintaining sales, purchases and returns journals.
2. Complete the following sentence. The total of the purchases journal is .... to the .... account in the .... ledger.

Walkthrough 7.2

20–9
April 3 Sew and Sew received an invoice for goods purchased from The Weaving Shed for $510, less a trade discount of 20%

   9 Sew and Sew received a credit note from The Weaving Shed for goods returned, list price $60

   24 Sew and Sew received an invoice for goods purchased on credit from The Curtain Company for $280, less 15% trade discount

   29 Sew and Sew discovered that half of the goods purchased on 24 April were faulty and these goods were returned to The Curtain Company who issued a credit note

Make the necessary entries in the books of Sew and Sew for April 20–9.

Sew and Sew

Purchases journal — Page 1

Date	Name	Invoice number	Folio	Amount $
20–9				
April 3	The Weaving Shed	I 3624	pl 8	408
24	The Curtain Company	I 117	pl 5	238
30	Transfer to purchases account		nl 4	646

Purchases returns journal — Page 1

Date	Name	Credit note number	Folio	Amount $
20–9				
April 9	The Weaving Shed	C 529	pl 8	48
29	The Curtain Company	C 43	pl 5	119
30	Transfer to purchases returns account		nl 5	167

Purchases ledger

The Weaving Shed account — Page 8

Date	Details	Folio	$	Date	Details	Folio	$
20–9				20–9			
April 9	Purchases returns	prj 1	48	April 3	Purchases	pj 1	408

The Curtain Company account — Page 5

Date	Details	Folio	$	Date	Details	Folio	$
20–9				20–9			
April 29	Purchases returns	prj 1	119	April 24	Purchases	pj 1	238

Nominal ledger

Purchases account — Page 4

Date	Details	Folio	$	Date	Details	Folio	$
20–9							
April 30	Credit purchases for month	pj 1	646				

Purchases returns account							Page 5
Date	Details	Folio	$	Date	Details	Folio	$
				20–9			
				April 30	Returns for month	prj 1	167

TIP

If trade discount was allowed when goods were purchased (or sold), then it must be deducted when those goods are returned so that the price actual charged for those goods is recorded in the accounts.

- Trade discount does **not** appear in the ledger accounts. Trade discount **may** be shown in the books of prime entry for information purposes only.
- The entry in the purchases account on 30 April is the double entry for the two individual credits in the suppliers' accounts in the purchases ledger.
- The entry in the purchases returns account on 30 April is the double entry for the two individual debits in the suppliers' accounts in the purchases ledger.
- The Weaving Shed and Sew and Sew each record the transactions between the two businesses from their own viewpoint – The Weaving Shed is selling the goods and Sew and Sew are purchasing the goods.

You can now answer Questions 1–6 at the end of this chapter.

Revision checklist

- All transactions should be entered in a book of prime entry before they are entered in the ledger.
- The sales journal is written up from copies of invoices sent to customers and the sales returns journal is written up from copies of credit notes sent to customers.
- The purchases journal is written up from invoices received from suppliers and the purchases returns journal is written up from credit notes received from suppliers.
- At the end of each month the totals of the sales, purchases and returns journals are transferred to the sales, purchases and returns accounts, respectively.

Exam-style questions

1 Ava maintains a full set of books of prime entry.

  a State **one** advantage of maintaining purchases and sales journals.

  b Complete the following table to name the business documents which Ava will use to make entries in her books of prime entry):

Book of prime entry	Business document
sales journal	
purchases journal	
sales returns journal	
purchases returns journal	

  c State how Ava would enter the monthly totals of the following books of prime entry in her ledger. The first one has been completed as an example.

Book of prime entry	Ledger entry	
sales journal	sales account	credit
purchases journal		
sales returns journal		
purchases returns journal		

  d Name **two** other books of prime entry which Ava may use.

  e Name the ledger in which Ava will maintain the following accounts:

    i sales account

    ii purchases returns account

    iii Charles (a credit customer)

Ava provided the following information about Charles, one of her credit customers:

20–1
June 1   Charles owed $450
      5   Charles purchased goods, list price $580, less 20% trade discount
     13   Charles returned goods, list price $300, purchased on 5 June
     23   Charles purchased goods, list price $200 (no trade discount was granted)
     28   Charles paid the balance of his account on 1 June by cheque and deducted 2% cash discount

  f Write up the account of Charles in the ledger of Ava. Balance the account and bring down the balance on 1 July 20–1.

2 Dale purchased goods, list price $2 800, on credit from Jennie. Jennie offers Dale 20% trade discount and a $2\frac{1}{2}$% cash discount for prompt payment.
Which entry will Jennie make in her books of prime entry?

  A purchases journal $2 184   **B** purchases journal $2 240

  C sales journal $2 184   **D** sales journal $2 240

3 Ravi is a trader. His transactions in February 20–1 included the following.

   February 2 Sold goods on credit to Kumar, list price $7 850, less 20% trade discount
            4   Bought goods on credit from Mahela, list price $960, less 25% trade discount
            10 Returned to Mahela half of the goods purchased on 4 February
            14 Sold goods on credit to Dimuth at list price, $520
            19 Bought goods on credit from Mahela, list price $750, less 20% trade discount
            20 Dimuth returned goods purchased on 14 February, list price $110
            21 Returned goods bought from Mahela on 19 February, list price $150

   a Enter these transactions in Ravi's sales, purchases and returns journals for February 20–4.
   b Write up the following accounts in Ravi's ledger for February 20–4:
      sales, purchases, sales returns, purchases returns, Kumar, Dimuth, and Mahela.
      It is not necessary to balance or total any of the accounts.

4 In which book of prime entry will Lee record credit notes he has issued?
   A purchases journal   B purchases returns journal
   C sales journal   D sales returns journal

5 Which entries are posted from the purchases returns journal?

	Account(s) to be debited	Account(s) to be credited
A	individual credit suppliers	purchases
B	individual credit suppliers	purchases returns
C	purchases	individual credit suppliers
D	purchases returns	individual credit suppliers

6 Thembi is a trader. She maintains a full set of accounting records and posts the totals of the sales, purchases and returns journals to the ledger each month.
   On 1 March 20–1 the balances in her accounts included the following:

	$
Sales	149 200
Purchases	99 520
Sales returns	1 940
Purchases returns	2 090
Musa, a credit customer	1 110
Siwela, a credit supplier	800

The following transactions took place in March 20–1.

March 4   Sold goods on credit to Musa, list price $800, less 20% trade discount
11   Musa returned half of the goods purchased on 4 March
17   Purchased goods on credit from Siwela, list price $900, less 15% trade discount
20   Returned goods to Siwela, purchased on 17 March, list price $300
27   Paid Siwela a cheque for the amount owing on 1 March less 2% cash discount
30   Musa paid $1 000 by credit transfer on account

a Enter the balances on 1 March in the appropriate accounts.
b Enter the transactions for March in the sales journal, purchases journal, sales returns journal and purchases returns journal.
c Post the entries from the journals to the ledger accounts.
d Enter the transactions on 27 and 30 March in the accounts of Siwela and Musa respectively.
e Balance the accounts of Musa and Siwela and bring down the balances on 1 April 20–1.

Section 2: Practice questions

1. Which statement about a credit note is correct?
   - **A** It is sent to a customer when there has been an overcharge on an invoice.
   - **B** It is sent to a customer when there has been an undercharge on an invoice.
   - **C** It is sent to a supplier when there has been an overcharge on an invoice.
   - **D** It is sent to a supplier when there has been an undercharge on an invoice.

2. Which book of prime entry is part of the double entry system?
   - 1 cash book
   - 2 petty cash book
   - 3 purchases journal
   - 4 sales journal

   - **A** 1 only
   - **B** 1 and 2
   - **C** 3 and 4
   - **D** 1, 2, 3 and 4

3. Ryan buys and sells on credit terms and keeps a full set of accounting records.
   Where does he maintain the accounts of his credit customers?
   - **A** sales journal
   - **B** sales ledger
   - **C** purchases journal
   - **D** purchases ledger

4. Cheyenne sells goods on credit terms and allows her customers a trade discount of 25%.
   In June the list price of goods returned by customers totalled $2 400.
   What entry will Cheyenne make in her nominal ledger on 30 June?
   - **A** sales returns account $1 800 debit
   - **B** sales returns account $2 400 debit
   - **C** purchases returns account $1 800 credit
   - **D** purchases returns account $ 2400 credit

5. On 1 May Sally owed William $400. On 21 May she purchased goods, list price $1 440, subject to a trade discount of 25%. She returned one third of these goods on 24 May.
   How much did Sally owe William on 31 May?
   - **A** $630
   - **B** $720
   - **C** $1 030
   - **D** $1 120

6 Phayo is a trader. He maintains a full set of accounting records.

   a Complete the following table to name one source document from which Phayo will complete each book of prime entry.

Book of prime entry	Source document
Purchases journal	
Sales journal	
Purchases returns journal	
Sales returns journal	
Petty cash book	
Cash book	

   Phayo sells good on credit to Phupho. On 1 May 20–7 Phupho owed Phayo $1 350.

   They exchanged the following documents during May 20–7:

   Invoice $1 500

   Debit note $120

   Credit note $100

   Statement of account $2 750

   Cheque $1 350

   b For each document name the person who issued that document and suggest one reason for the issue of that document.

   c Prepare the account of Phupho as it would appear in the ledger of Phayo for the month of May 20–7. Balance the account and bring down the balance on 1 June 20–7.

   d Name the ledger in which Phayo would maintain the account of Phupho.

7 Aryan is a retailer. He trades with Mikhail, a wholesaler.

   The following business documents were exchanged in May:

   Cheque, credit note, debit note, invoice, receipt, statement of account.

   a List these documents in the order in which they would be issued. Name the person who issued each document.

   b Explain why each document was issued.

   c Name the book of prime entry in which each trader would record the documents. If the document would not be recorded in a book of prime entry give a reason for this.

Section 2: Practice questions

8 Nelson sells goods on credit. He maintains a full set of accounting records.

The following information was extracted form his accounting records for October 20–4.

1 October 20–4		$
Debit balances in sales ledger:	Jamil	600
	Nawaz	140

Sales journal

			$	$
Oct 4	Jamil	Goods	490	
		Trade discount	98	392
13	Nawaz	Goods		154
24	Jamil	Goods	310	
		Trade discount	62	248
31	Total for month			794

Sales returns journal

			$	$
Oct 15	Nawaz	Goods		93
26	Jamil	Goods	200	
24		Trade discount	40	160
31	Total for month			253

Extract from debit side of cash book

		$ Discount allowed	$ Cash	$ Bank
Oct 7	Jamil	18		582
21	Nawaz		90	
28	Jamil			400

a Write up the following accounts for the month of October 20–4: sales, sales returns, Jamil and Nawaz. Balance the accounts of Jamil and Nawaz and bring down the balances. There is no need to total or balance the other accounts.

b Suggest **two** differences between cash discount and trade discount.

c Calculate the rate of trade discount that Nelson allowed Jamil on 4 October.

d Calculate the rate of cash discount that Nelson allowed Jamil on 7 October.

9 Annie opened a wholesale clothing business on 1 August 20–6. She received the following documents during August 20–6:

Invoices

August 4   From Sue, for goods, list price $1 960 less 25% trade discount
       15   From Amos, for goods, list price $290
       21   From Jane, for goods, list price $2 950 less 20% trade discount

Credit notes

August 10   From Sue, for return of faulty goods, list price $120, purchased on 4 August
       26   From Jane, for return of all the goods purchased on 21 August as not what was ordered

Annie issued the following documents during August 20–6:

Invoices

August 7   To Andrew, for goods, list price $2 100
       18   To Ben, for goods, list price $3 150 less 20% trade discount
       27   To Andrew, for goods, list price $1 820

Credit note

August 29   To Andrew, for half of the goods purchased on 27 August returned as faulty

a Make the necessary entries in the purchases journal, sales journal, purchases returns journal and sales returns journal.

b Make the necessary posting to the appropriate accounts in the purchase ledger, sales ledger and nominal ledger. It is not necessary to balance or total any of the accounts.

c Suggest **two** reasons why Annie allowed Andrew a trade discount.

d Name the document which Annie may have issued before she received a credit note from Sue on 10 August.

e Explain why Annie may issue a statement of account to each credit customer at the end of every month.

On 21 September 20–6 Annie paid the amount owing to Sue on 31 August, less a cash discount of 3%.

f Calculate the amount paid to Sue on 31 August 20–6.

Section 3

Chapter 8
Financial statements – Part A

Learning objectives

In this chapter you will learn to:

- explain the advantages and disadvantages of operating as a sole trader   5.1
- explain the importance of preparing income statements   5.1
- explain the difference between a trading business and a service business   5.1
- prepare income statements for trading businesses and for service businesses   5.1
- make adjustments for goods taken by the owner for own use   5.1
- balance ledger accounts as required and make transfers to financial statements.   2.1

Chapter 8: Financial statements – Part A

8.1 Introduction

All the previous chapters have covered the book-keeping records maintained by a sole trader. Similar records will be maintained by other types of businesses.

When a person is operating a business alone as a sole trader, he/she is entitled to all the profits the business makes, but will be responsible for any losses the business makes. Business decisions may be made quickly, as consultation is not necessary, but there is no-one with whom to share the decision-making or the workload. The capital of the business will be restricted to what the trader is able to invest, whereas other forms of business have access to capital invested by other owners of the business.

When a person starts a business his/her aim is to make a profit. The profit (or loss) is calculated in the financial statements which are usually prepared at the end of each financial year. Financial statements basically consist of two parts:

1. An **income statement** which consists of two sections:
   - a **trading section** in which the **gross profit** of the business is calculated
   - a **profit and loss section** in which the **profit for the year** of the business is calculated.

   The trading section and the profit and loss section of the income statement are part of the double entry system.

2. A **statement of financial position** shows the **assets and liabilities** of the business at a certain date. The statement of financial position is not part of the double entry system.

Financial statements are usually prepared from a trial balance. **Every item in a trial balance appears *once* in a set of financial statements**. As each item is used, it is useful to place a tick (✓) against the item. This ensures that no items are overlooked.

It is common to find notes accompanying a trial balance about various adjustments which are to be made (these are explained in the following chapters). **Any notes to a trial balance are used *twice* in a set of financial statements**. To ensure that this is done, it is useful to place a tick (✓) against the notes each time they are used.

> **TIP**
> Every item in a trial balance is used once within a set of financial statements; any notes to a trial balance are used twice within a set of financial statements.

LINK

You will learn about partnerships and limited companies in Chapters 19 and 21.

KEY TERM

An **income statement** is a statement prepared for a trading period to show the gross profit and profit for the year.

LINK

You will learn more about statements of financial position in Chapter 9.

TIP

Tick off the items from a trial balance and the notes to a trial balance as you use them so that nothing is omitted.

Walkthrough 8.1

The following trial balance was extracted from the books of Samir at 31 May 20–8.

This trial balance will be used in **Walkthrough 8.2** to **Walkthrough 8.7**.

Samir
Trial balance at 31 May 20–8

	Dr $	Cr $
Revenue		95 700
Sales returns	1 000	
Purchases	65 000	
Purchases returns		500
Carriage inwards	1 500	
Inventory 1 Jun 20–8	7 100	
Discount received		400
Discount allowed	900	
Wages	11 200	
General expenses	2 800	
Property tax	600	
Loan interest	500	
Premises	80 000	
Fixtures and equipment	13 900	
Trade receivables	7 500	
Trade payables		7 800
Bank	3 300	
Cash	100	
Long-term loan		10 000
Capital		90 000
Drawings	9 000	
	204 400	204 400

- The inventory at 31 May 20–8 was valued at $7 600.
- During the year ended 31 May 20–8, Samir took goods costing $300 for his own use. No entries have been made in the accounting records.

> **TIP**
> The term 'revenue' is used instead of 'sales' in a trial balance and in an income statement.

8.2 Trading section of the income statement

The **trading section** is concerned with buying and selling, and its purpose is to calculate the profit earned on the goods sold. This is known as the **gross profit**. The formula for calculating gross profit is:

Gross profit = Selling price of goods − Cost of sales

The selling price represents the total sales less any sales returns.

The cost of sales represents the total cost of the goods actually sold. This is not necessarily the cost of goods purchased during the year: some goods may have been in stock at the start of the year, and some of the goods purchased during the year may remain unsold at the end of the year. The formula for calculating cost of sales is:

Cost of sales = Opening inventory + Purchases − Closing inventory

The purchases figure represents the total cost of purchases less any purchases returns. If carriage inwards has been paid on goods purchased this must be added to the purchases as it increases the cost of the goods. If the owner of the business has withdrawn goods for personal use the cost of these is credited to the purchases account, so reducing the cost of goods available for sale. If goods taken by the owner have not already been recorded they must be deducted from the purchases. The formula for calculating the net purchases figure is:

Net purchases = Purchases − Purchases returns + Carriage inwards − Goods for own use

The calculation of gross profit is shown in the trading section of the income statement. This must have a heading which includes the period of time covered by the statement. It is also usual to include the name under which the business trades.

> **KEY TERM**
>
> The **gross profit** is the difference between the selling price and the cost of those goods.

> **TEST YOURSELF 8.1**
>
> 1. State what is calculated in:
>   a. a trading account section of an income statement
>   b. a profit and loss account section of an income statement.
> 2. State the formula for calculating gross profit.
> 3. State the formula for calculating cost of sales.

There are two ways in which a trading section of an income statement can be prepared – **horizontal** and **vertical**.

The **horizontal format** is similar to a traditional ledger account. Using this method, the revenue is shown on the credit side and the cost of sales on the debit side. The difference (or balance) between the two sides equals the gross profit.

Walkthrough 8.2

Using the trial balance and accompanying notes shown in **Walkthrough 8.1**, prepare the trading section of the income statement of Samir for the year ended 31 May 20–8. Use the horizontal format.

Samir
Income statement (trading section) for the year ended 31 May 20–8

	$	$		$	$
Opening inventory		7 100	Revenue		95 700
Purchases	65 000		Less Sales returns		1 000 94 700
Less Purchases returns	500				
	64 500				
Less Goods for own use	300				
	64 200				
Carriage inwards	1 500	65 700			
		72 800			
Less Closing inventory		7 600			
Cost of sales		65 200			
Gross profit c/d		29 500			
		94 700			94 700

- As these items are entered in the trading section of the income statement, they should be ticked-off in the trial balance and accompanying notes.
- The gross profit is carried down to the profit and loss section (see Section 8.3).
- The first money column on each side has been used for adding and subtracting items and the final column had been used for the section total.

A trading section of an income statement can also be prepared using the **vertical format**. This is the format used by most businesses. A statement prepared using this method contains the same information as a horizontal account, but looks like an arithmetic calculation.

Walkthrough 8.3

Using the trial balance and accompanying notes shown in **Walkthrough 8.1**, prepare the trading section of the income statement of Samir for the year ended 31 May 20–8. Use the vertical format.

Samir
Income statement (Trading Section) for the year ended 31 May 20–8

	$	$	$
Revenue		95 700	
Less Sales returns		1 000	94 700
Less Cost of sales			
Opening inventory		7 100	
Purchases	65 000		
Less Purchases returns	500		
	64 500		
Less Goods for own use	300		
	64 200		
Carriage inwards	1 500	65 700	
		72 800	
Less Closing inventory		7 600	65 200
Gross profit			29 500

- The first two money columns have been used for adding and subtracting items and the final column for the final section total. For example, the first column has been used to adjust the purchases for returns, carriage and goods for own use and the final cost of purchases has been entered in the second column.

You can now answer Questions 1 and 2 at the end of this chapter.

8.3 Profit and loss section of the income statement

The **profit and loss** section of an income statement is concerned with profits and losses, gains and expenses. Its purpose is to calculate the final profit after all running expenses and other items of income. This is known as the **profit for the year**. The formula for calculating profit for the year is:

Profit for the year = Gross profit + Other income − Expenses

The profit and loss section of an income statement must have a heading which includes the period of time covered by the statement. It is also usual to include the name under which the business trades.

As with a trading section of an income statement, a profit and loss section can be prepared using either the **horizontal** or the **vertical** method. Using the horizontal format, the gross profit and any other income are shown on the credit side and the expenses are shown on the debit side. The difference (or balance) between the two sides equals the **profit for the year** (if the credit side is the largest) or the **loss for the year** (if the debit side is the largest).

KEY TERM

The **profit for the year** is the final profit after any other income has been added to the gross profit and the running expenses have been deducted.

Walkthrough 8.4

Using the trial balance and accompanying notes shown in **Walkthrough 8.1**, prepare the profit and loss section of the income statement of Samir for the year ended 31 May 20–8. Use the horizontal format.

Samir
Income statement (profit and loss section) for the year ended 31 May 20-8

	$	$			$	$
Discount allowed		900	Gross profit	b/d		29 500
Wages		11 200	Discount received			400
General expenses		2 800				
Property tax		600				
Loan interest		500				
Profit for the year		13 900				
		29 900				29 900

- As these items are entered in the profit and loss section of the income statement they should be ticked-off in the trial balance and accompanying notes.
- The gross profit is brought down from the trading section where it was calculated.

A profit and loss section of an income statement can also be prepared using the vertical format. This format is used by most businesses. A statement prepared using this method contains the same information but looks like an arithmetic calculation.

Walkthrough 8.5

Using the trial balance and accompanying notes shown in **Walkthrough 8.1**, prepare the profit and loss section of the income statement of Samir for the year ended 31 May 20-8. Use the vertical format.

Samir
Income statement (profit and loss section) for the year ended 31 May 20-8

	$	$	$
Gross profit			29 500
Add Discount received			400
			29 900
Less Discount allowed		900	
Wages		11 200	
General expenses		2 800	
Property tax		600	15 500
Profit from operations			14 400
Less Loan interest			500
Profit for the year			13 900

- Using the vertical presentation it is easy to show the profit earned from the normal trading or operating activities and then final profit for the year after the deduction of any finance costs.

Chapter 8: Financial statements – Part A

> **TEST YOURSELF 8.2**
>
> 1. Suggest **six** business expenses (excluding those shown in the walkthroughs).
> 2. State the formula for calculating profit for the year.

The two sections of the income statement are usually presented in the form of one combined statement, which is normally presented in vertical format. The profit and loss section follows on immediately after the trading section, with the words 'gross profit' being written only once. The heading of the income statement includes the period of time covered by the statement and the name under which the business trades.

As most businesses prepare their income statements using the vertical format this method will be followed in the remainder of this book.

Walkthrough 8.6

Using either the trial balance and accompanying notes shown in **Walkthrough 8.1** or the separate sections of the income statement prepared in **Walkthroughs 8.3** and **8.5**, prepare the income statement of Samir for the year ended 31 May 20–8.

Samir			
Income statement for the year ended 31 May 20–8			
	$	$	$
Revenue		95 700	
Less Sales returns		1 000	94 700
Less Cost of sales			
Opening inventory		7 100	
Purchases	65 000		
Less Purchases returns	500		
	64 500		
Less Goods for own use	300		
	64 200		
Carriage inwards	1 500	65 700	
		72 800	
Less Closing inventory		7 600	65 200
Gross profit			29 500
Add Discount received			400
			29 900
Less Discount allowed		900	
Wages		11 200	
General expenses		2 800	
Property tax		600	15 500
Profit from operations			14 400
Less Loan interest			500
Profit for the year			13 900

> **LINK**
>
> You will learn more about income statements in Chapters 11, 12 and 13.

You can now answer Questions 3 and 4 at the end of this chapter.

8.4 Transferring ledger account totals to the income statement

Anything appearing in the income statement must have a double entry in another account. Anything credited to the income statement must be debited in the appropriate ledger account. Anything debited to the income statement must be credited in the appropriate ledger account.

When something is deducted from a debit item in the income statement this is equal to a credit entry, so a debit entry is required in the ledger. In the same way, when something is deducted from a credit item in the income statement this is equal to a debit entry, so a credit entry is required in the ledger.

Walkthrough 8.7

Using the income statement prepared for Samir in Walkthrough 8.6, prepare the following ledger accounts to show how **each** is closed by transfer to the income statement:

a   purchases account
b   purchases returns account
c   discount received account
d   wages account

a

Samir
Nominal ledger
Purchases account

Date	Details	Folio	$	Date	Details	Folio	$
20–8				20–8			
May 31	Total to date		65 000	May 31	Income statement		65 000
			65 000				65 000

b

Purchases returns account

Date	Details	Folio	$	Date	Details	Folio	$
20–8				20–8			
May 31	Income statement		500	May 31	Total to date		500
			500				500

c

Discount received account

Date	Details	Folio	$	Date	Details	Folio	$
20–8				20–8			
May 31	Income statement		400	May 31	Total to date		400
			400				400

d

		Wages account					
Date	Details	Folio	$	Date	Details	Folio	$
20–8				20–8			
May 31	Total to date		11 200	May 31	Income statement		11 200
			11 200				11 200

- The entries shown as 'totals to date' represent the total of the individual entries made in the account for the year ended 31 May 20–8.
- All the other items in the income statement (excluding inventory, gross profit and profit for the year) have similar transfers from the appropriate ledger accounts.
- The gross profit technically has a double entry within the income statement as it is transferred from the trading account section to the profit and loss account section (refer to **Walkthroughs 8.2 and 8.4**).
- The entries for inventory and profit for the year are explained next.

There are two entries for inventory in the income statement – the inventory at the start of the year and the inventory at the end of the year. The inventory account will have a debit balance representing the inventory at the start of the year – this is credited to the inventory account and transferred to the debit of the income statement. The inventory at the end of the year is shown as a deduction from the debit entries in the income statement (which is equal to a credit entry), so this must be debited in the inventory account.

Walkthrough 8.8

Using the income statement prepared for Samir in **Walkthrough 8.6**, prepare the inventory account in Samir's ledger on 31 May 20–8.

		Samir					
		Nominal ledger					
		Inventory account					
Date	Details	Folio	$	Date	Details	Folio	$
20–7				20–8			
Jun 1	Balance	b/d	7 100	May 31	Income statement		7 100
			7 100				7 100
20–8							
May 31	Income statement		7 600				

> **TIP**
> The income statement consists of the trading account and the profit and loss account which are part of the double entry system.

- The entry of $7 600 on the debit side, representing the inventory at the end of the financial year on 31 May 20–8, becomes the opening inventory for the year beginning 1 June 20–8.

A profit for the year represents the return on the owner's investment. This will appear as a debit entry in the income statement and should be transferred to the credit of the capital account as it increases the amount the business owes the owner. A loss for the year will appear as a credit entry in the income statement and should be transferred to the debit of the capital account as it reduces the amount the business owes the owner.

As explained in Chapter 2, the total of the drawings account is transferred to the capital account at the end of the year.

Walkthrough 8.9

On 1 June 20–7 the credit balance on Samir's capital account was $90 000. During the year ended 31 May 20–8 he had withdrawn $9 000 in cash and $300 in goods. His profit for the year ended 31 May 20–8 was $13 900.

Prepare the capital account and the drawings account in Samir's ledger on 31 May 20–8.

Samir
Nominal ledger
Capital account

Date	Details	Folio	$	Date	Details	Folio	$
20–8				20–7			
May 31	Drawings		9 300	Jun 1	Balance	b/d	90 000
	Balance	c/d	94 600	20–8			
				May 31	Profit		13 900
			103 900				103 900
				20–8			
				Jun 1	Balance	b/d	94 600

Drawings account

Date	Details	Folio	$	Date	Details	Folio	$
20–8				20–8			
May 31	Total to date			May 31	Capital		9 300
	Cash		9 000				
	Purchases		300				
			9 300				9 300

> **TIP**
> If a business makes a profit it is credited to the capital account as it increases the owner's capital. If a business makes a loss it is debited to the capital account as it reduces the owner's capital.

TEST YOURSELF 8.3

1. Explain why it is necessary to make two transfers from the income statement to the inventory account at the end of the financial year.
2. Explain why a loss for the year is debited to the owner's capital account.

You can now answer Question 5 at the end of this chapter.

8.5 Income statement of a service business

A **service business** is one which does not buy and sell goods, such as an accountant, an insurance company, a travel agent, a hairdresser and so on. At the end of the financial year, these businesses still need to prepare financial statements. However, the trading account section of the income statement is not prepared as no goods are bought and sold. Only the profit and loss section of the income statement and a statement of financial position are prepared.

In the income statement all the items of revenue receivable such as fees from clients, commission and other income are credited and expenses are debited. The statement of financial position is exactly the same as the statement of financial position of a **trading business**.

> **KEY TERMS**
>
> A **service business** is one which provides a service.
>
> A **trading business** is one which buys and sells goods.

Walkthrough 8.10

Anita is a business consultant. She provided the following information at the end of her financial year on 30 September 20–5.

	$
Property tax	6 400
General expenses	8 950
Insurance	2 670
Printing and stationery	4 560
Loan interest	1 500
Wages	43 500
Rent receivable	7 300
Commissions received	92 150

a Prepare the income statement for Anita for the year ended 30 September 20–5. Use the horizontal format.

Anita
Income statement for the year ended 30 September 20–5

	$	$		$	$
Property tax		6 400	Commissions received		92 150
General expenses		8 950	Rent receivable		7 300
Insurance		2 670			
Printing and stationery		4 560			
Loan interest		1 500			
Wages		43 500			
Profit for the year		31 870			
		99 450			99 450

TIP
The income statement of a service business does not have a trading account section.

b Prepare the income statement for Anita for the year ended 30 September 20–5. Use the vertical format.

Anita
Income statement for the year ended 30 September 20–5

	$	$	$
Commissions received			92 150
Add Rent receivable			7 300
			99 450
Less Property tax		6 400	
General expenses		8 950	
Insurance		2 670	
Printing and stationery		4 560	
Wages		43 500	66 080
Profit from operations			33 370
Less Loan interest			1 500
Profit for the year			31 870

You can now answer Question 6 at the end of this chapter.

Revision checklist

- The difference between the selling price and the cost price is known as the gross profit. This is calculated in the trading account section of the income statement.
- The difference between the gross profit, plus other income, less expenses is known as the profit for the year. This is calculated in the profit and loss account section of the income statement.
- All the items appearing in the income statement are transferred from the ledger accounts to complete the double entry.
- A profit for the year is transferred to the credit of the capital account and a loss for the year is transferred to the debit of the capital account.
- A business which provides a service only prepares the profit and loss account section of the income statement.

Exam-style questions

1 How is the cost of sales calculated?

   A opening inventory + purchases − carriage inwards − purchases returns − closing inventory
   B opening inventory + purchases − carriage inwards + purchases returns − closing inventory
   C opening inventory + purchases + carriage inwards − purchases returns − closing inventory
   D opening inventory + purchases + carriage inwards + purchases returns + closing inventory

2 At the end of his first year of trading, Rashid provided the following information.

	$
Revenue	72 500
Purchases	49 700
Closing inventory	4 800
Carriage inwards	1 150
Carriage outwards	2 950

What was Rashid's gross profit?

   A $22 800   B $24 650   C $26 450   D $27 600

3 Mai, a fashion retailer, did not record goods costing $500 taken for personal use.
   What was the effect of this error?

	Gross profit		Profit for the year	
	Overstated	Understated	Overstated	Understated
A	✓		✓	
B		✓		✓
C	✓			✓
D		✓	✓	

4 Leo is a wholesaler. He has little knowledge of accounting. He prepared the following income statement which contains some errors.

Leo
Income statement for the year ended 30 April 20–1

		$	$
Revenue			82 300
Add	Discount received		110
	Opening inventory		4 910
			87 320
Less	Purchases	49 520	
	Returns from customers	1 190	
		50 710	
	Less Closing inventory	5 080	45 630
Profit on goods			41 690
Add	Discount allowed		220
			41 910
Less	Rent payable	8 100	
	Less Rent receivable	6 000	
		2 100	
	Wages	12 100	
	Carriage inwards	100	
	Sundry expenses	960	15 260
Final profit			26 650

Prepare a corrected income statement for Leo for the year ended 30 April 20–1.

5 Oliver has been in business as a retailer for one year. He is unsure about some of the terms used in business.

   a Explain the difference between the following terms and how they are recorded in an income statement:
      i   gross profit and profit for the year
      ii carriage inwards and carriage outwards
      iii discount allowed and discount received
      iv purchases returns and sales returns

Oliver provided the following totals for the year ended 31 December 20–5:

	$
Rates	3 140
Office expenses	1 170
Commissions received	5 830
Sales returns	1 480

b Enter these totals in the appropriate accounts. Close the accounts by making transfers to the income statement.

6 Candy provided the following information at the end of her financial year on 30 September 20–3:

	$
Capital at 1 October 20–2	198 000
Fees received from clients	82 300
Staff wages	49 600
Rent and rates	7 420
Insurance	3 830
Commissions received	4 810
Light and heat	2 180
Office expenses	1 730
Drawings	18 750

a State whether Candy's business is a trading business or a service business. Give a reason for your answer.

b Prepare Candy's income statement for the year ended 30 September 20–3.

c Prepare Candy's capital account on 30 September 20–3. Balance the account and bring down the balance on 1 October 20–3.

Chapter 9
Financial statements – Part B

Learning objectives

In this chapter you will learn to:

- explain the importance of preparing statements of financial position 5.1
- understand that statements of financial position record assets and liabilities on a specified date 5.1
- recognise and define the content of a statement of financial position: non-current assets, intangible assets, current assets, current liabilities, non-current liabilities and capital 5.1
- understand the inter-relationship of items in a statement of financial position 5.1
- prepare statements of financial position for trading businesses and service businesses. 5.1

Chapter 9: Financial statements – Part B

9.1 Introduction

As explained in Chapter 8, the financial statements are prepared at the end of each financial year. These consist of an **income statement** and a **statement of financial position**.

A **statement of the financial position** shows the assets of a business (what the business owns and what is owing to the business) and the liabilities of a business (what the business owes) on a certain date. The assets show how the resources are being used and the liabilities show where they come from.

> **KEY TERMS**
>
> A **statement of financial position** is a statement of the assets and liabilities of a business on a certain date.
>
> **Non-current assets** are assets which are obtained for use and not for resale, which help the business earn revenue.

> **TEST YOURSELF 9.1**
>
> 1 Define a statement of financial position.
> 2 Explain the meaning of **each** of the following terms:
>   a asset
>   b liability

TIP
If the totals of a trial balance are equal, the totals of the statement of financial position should balance. If they do not there is an error somewhere in the financial statements.

LINK
You learned how to prepare elementary statements of financial position in Chapter 1.

It is usual to arrange the assets and liabilities into different groups according to their type.

9.2 Assets

Assets are divided into two types. These are:

1 Non-current assets

   There are two types of **non-current assets:**

   a Tangible non-current assets

   Tangible non-current assets are long-term assets which are obtained for use rather than for resale. They help the business earn revenue. **Examples** of tangible non-current assets include land and buildings, machinery, fixtures and motors.

   In a statement of financial position, it is usual for the **non-current assets** to be **arranged in increasing order of liquidity**. This means that the most permanent assets are shown first.

   A typical order for showing tangible non-current assets in a statement of financial position is as follows:

   Land and buildings
   Machinery
   Fixtures and equipment
   Motor vehicles

   b Intangible non-current assets

   Intangible non-current assets are long-term assets which do not have material substance (they cannot be seen or touched). However, they belong to the business

TIP
An intangible asset is something owned by a business which cannot be touched.

LINK

You will learn more about goodwill in Chapter 22.

KEY TERMS

Goodwill is the amount by which the value of a business as a whole exceeds the value of the separate assets and liabilities.

Current assets are short-term assets whose amounts are constantly changing.

Non-current liabilities are amounts owed which are not due for repayment within the next 12 months.

Current liabilities are amounts owed which are due for repayment within the next 12 months.

and do have a value. **Examples** of intangible non-current assets include **goodwill**, brand names and trademarks.

In a statement of financial position the intangible non-current assets are shown before the tangible non-current assets.

2 Current assets

Current assets are short-term assets. Because they arise from the normal trading activities of the business their amounts are constantly changing. These are assets which are either in the form of cash or which can be turned into cash relatively easily.

Examples of current assets include inventory, trade receivables, bank and cash.

In a statement of financial position, it is usual for **current assets** to be **arranged in increasing order of liquidity**. This means that the assets furthest away from cash are shown first.

A typical order for showing current assets in a statement of financial position is:

    Inventory

    Trade receivables

    Bank

    Cash

9.3 Liabilities

Liabilities are divided into three types. These are:

1 Capital

Capital represents the owner's investment in the business and is the amount owed by the business to the owner.

2 Non-current liabilities

Non-current liabilities are amounts owed by the business which are not due for repayment within the next 12 months.

Examples of non-current liabilities include long-term loan and mortgage.

3 Current liabilities

Current liabilities are short-term liabilities. Since current liabilities, like current assets, arise from the normal trading activities of the business, their amounts are constantly changing. They are amounts owed by the business which are due for repayment within the next 12 months.

Examples of current liabilities include trade payables and bank overdraft.

TEST YOURSELF 9.2

1 Define the term non-current assets. Illustrate your answer by giving **two** examples.
2 State the order in which current assets are arranged in a statement of financial position.
3 Explain how to distinguish between a non-current liability and a current liability.

A statement of financial position must have a heading which includes the date to which it relates. It is also usual to include the name under which the business trades.

Chapter 9: Financial statements – Part B

There are two ways in which a statement of financial position can be prepared – **horizontal** and **vertical**. A **horizontal** statement of financial position is prepared in a two-sided format. It is usual for the assets to be listed on the left and the liabilities to be listed on the right.

Walkthrough 9.1

The following trial balance was extracted from the books of Samir at 31 May 20–8.

This trial balance was used in Chapter 8 to prepare an income statement for the year ended 31 May 20–8.

The profit for the year of $13 900 was calculated in the income statement.

Samir
Trial balance at 31 May 20–8

	Dr $	Cr $
✓ Revenue (sales)		95 700
✓ Sales returns	1 000	
✓ Purchases	65 000	
✓ Purchases returns		500
✓ Carriage inwards	1 500	
✓ Inventory 1 Jun 20–8	7 100	
✓ Discount received		400
✓ Discount allowed	900	
✓ Wages	11 200	
✓ General expenses	2 800	
✓ Property tax	600	
✓ Loan interest	500	
Premises	80 000	
Fixtures and equipment	13 900	
Trade receivables	7 500	
Trade payables		7 800
Bank	3 300	
Cash	100	
Long-term loan		10 000
Capital		90 000
Drawings	9 000	
	204 400	204 400

- The inventory at 31 May 20–8 was valued at $7 600.
- During the year ended 31 May 20–8 Samir took goods costing $300 for his own use.
- No entries have been made in the accounting records.

As explained in Chapter 8, every item within a trial balance is used once in the preparation of a set of financial statements, and any notes to a trial balance are used twice. The items already used in the preparation of the income statement in Chapter 8 have been ticked.

Walkthrough 9.2

Using the trial balance and accompanying notes shown in **Walkthrough 9.1**, prepare a balance statement of financial position for Samir at 31 May 20–9. Use the horizontal format.

Samir
Statement of financial position at 31 May 20–9

	$	$		$	$
Non-current assets			**Capital**		
Premises		80 000	Opening balance		90 000
Fixtures and equipment		13 900	Plus Profit for the year		13 900
		93 900			103 900
Current assets			Less Drawings		
			(9 000 + 300)		9 300
Inventory	7 600				94 600
Trade receivables	7 500		**Non-current liabilities**		
Bank	3 300		Loan		10 000
Cash	100	18 500	**Current liabilities**		
			Trade payables		7 800
		112 400			112 400

- As these items are entered in the statement of financial position they should be ticked-off in the trial balance and accompanying notes.
- Once the statement of financial position is completed all the items in the trial balance should have a tick and the notes to the trial balance should have two ticks.
- The assets and liabilities have been arranged in their different categories.
- The balance on the capital account has increased because the business made a profit (which the business owes to the owner of the business), but has decreased because the owner made drawings (money and goods).

If a statement of financial position is prepared using the **vertical** format, the assets are listed (showing how the resources are used) and underneath them the liabilities are listed (showing where the resources have come from).

> **TIP**
> There are several acceptable formats for presenting statements of financial position. Whichever format is selected it is important to classify the assets and liabilities into the different types.

Walkthrough 9.3

Using the trial balance and accompanying notes shown in **Walkthrough 9.1**, prepare a statement of financial position for Samir at 31 May 20–9. Use the vertical format.

Samir
Statement of financial position at 31 May 20–9

	$	$	$
Assets			
Non-current assets			
Premises			80 000
Fixtures and equipment			13 900
			93 900
Current assets			
Inventory			7 600
Trade receivables			7 500
Bank			3 300
Cash			100
			18 500
Total assets			112 400
Capital and liabilities			
Capital			
Opening balance			90 000
Plus Profit for the year			13 900
			103 900
Less Drawings (9 000 + 300)			9 300
			94 600
Non-current liabilities			
Loan			10 000
Current liabilities			
Trade payables			7 800
Total capital and liabilities			112 400

> **TIP**
> When the statement of financial position is completed, every item in the trial balance should have a tick against it and each note to the trial balance should have two ticks against it.

- The first section of the statement shows how the resources are being used and the second section shows where those resources have come from.

As most businesses prepare their statement of financial position using the vertical format, this method will be followed in the remainder of this book.

You can now answer Questions 1–6 at the end of this chapter.

Revision checklist

- A statement of financial position shows the assets and liabilities of a business on a certain date.
- Non-current assets are long-term assets. In a statement of financial position the most permanent are shown first.
- Current assets are short-term assets and their values are constantly changing. In a statement of financial position the furthest away from cash are shown first.
- Non-current liabilities are amounts which are not due for repayment within the next 12 months.
- Current liabilities are amounts which are due for repayment within the next 12 months.

Chapter 9: Financial statements – Part B

Exam-style questions

1. Lydia is a wholesaler. She has very little knowledge about accounting, but attempted to prepare a statement of financial position. The statement she prepared contains errors.

Lydia			
Statement of financial position at 31 July 20–5			
Assets	$	Liabilities	$
Premises	82 500	Trade receivables	2 140
Capital	100 000	Drawings	16 120
Cash	250	Loan (repayable in 5 years)	20 000
Profit for the year	14 350	Cash at bank	4 360
Fixtures and fittings	11 980		
Inventory	2 480		
Motor vehicle	16 500		
Trade payables	1 980		
	230 040		52 620

Prepare a corrected statement of financial positon at 31 July 20–5. Use the vertical format.

2. Dwayne's assets and liabilities on 29 September 20–1 were as follows:

	$
Fixtures and fittings	49 500
Inventory	9 050
Trade payables	7 450
Trade receivables	8 150
Cash at bank	750

Dwayne invested $10 000 additional capital on 30 September 20–1.
What was Dwayne's capital after this transaction?

A $62 500   **B** $67 450   **C** $70 000   **D** $77 450

3. A trader took cash from the business for personal use.
What effect would this have on the financial statements?

	Current assets	Profit for the year
A	decrease	increase
B	decrease	no effect
C	increase	decrease
D	increase	increase

4 A trader repaid a long-term loan of $10 000. She used all the money in the business bank account, $7 000, and paid the balance from her personal bank account.

How did this affect the statement of financial position?

	Assets	Liabilities	Capital
A	no effect	decrease $3 000	increase $3 000
B	decrease $7 000	decrease $10 000	increase $3 000
C	decrease $10 000	decrease $7 000	decrease $3 000
D	decrease $10 000	decrease $10 000	no effect

5 Ayesha is a business adviser. Her financial year ends on 30 September. She provided the following trial balance at 30 September 20–3:

	$	$
Capital		125 000
Drawings	15 200	
Premises	95 000	
Office equipment	21 600	
Fees from clients		65 950
Insurance	3 110	
Printing and stationery	2 480	
Wages	59 650	
Office expenses	3 120	
Rent receivable		6 000
Trade receivables	6 150	
Bank overdraft		9 510
Cash	150	
	206 460	206 460

Prepare Ayesha's income statement for the year ended 30 September 20–3 and a statement of financial position at 30 September 20–3.

6 Abhinav is a trader.

Using the following information taken from Abhinav's books on 30 June 20–8:

a prepare a trial balance at 30 June 20–8
b prepare an income statement for the year ended 30 June 20–8
c prepare a statement of financial position at 30 June 20–8.

	$
Capital	54 400
Drawings	1 300
Premises	30 000
Fixtures	4 000
Revenue	82 000
Purchases	70 100
Inventory 1 July 20–7	18 600
Carriage inwards	400
Carriage outwards	1 500
Trade receivables	14 000
Trade payables	8 000
Discount received	210
Insurance	390
Sundry expenses	340
Wages	10 300
Rates	1 200
Loan interest	500
Long-term loan from ABC Loans	10 000
Cash at bank	1 980

Inventory at 30 June 20–8 was valued at $20 100.

Chapter 10
Accounting rules

Learning objectives

In this chapter you will learn to:

- explain and recognise the application of the following accounting principles: business entity, consistency, duality, going concern, historic cost, matching, materiality, money measurement, prudence, realisation   7.1
- recognise the influence of international accounting standards and understand the following objectives in selecting accounting policies: comparability, relevance, reliability and understandability   7.2
- distinguish between and account for capital expenditure and revenue expenditure   4.1
- distinguish between and account for capital receipts and revenue receipts   4.1
- calculate and comment on the effect on profit of incorrect treatment   4.1
- calculate and comment on the effect on asset valuations of incorrect treatment   4.1
- understand the basis of the valuation of inventory at the lower of cost and net realisable value   4.5
- prepare simple inventory valuation statements   4.5
- recognise the importance of valuation of inventory and the effect of an incorrect valuation of inventory on gross profit, profit for the year, equity and asset valuation.   4.5

Chapter 10: Accounting rules

10.1 Introduction

Accounting has developed a number of rules which must be applied by everyone who is involved with the recording of financial information. If every accountant or book-keeper followed their own rules it would be impossible for others to fully understand the financial position of a business. In the same way, it would be impossible to make a comparison between the financial results of two or more businesses if they had each applied their own rules in the preparation of their accounting statements. The accounting principles which must be applied by every business are explained in this chapter.

It also describes how capital and revenue expenditure and capital and revenue receipts should be recorded. It is important that all businesses follow the same procedures for these items. Similarly, all businesses should apply the same principles of inventory valuation. This is also explained in Section 10.5.

> **TEST YOURSELF 10.1**
>
> 1 State **one** reason why accounting rules are necessary.

10.2 Accounting principles

Accounting principles are sometimes referred to as **concepts** and **conventions**. A **concept** is a rule which sets down how the financial activities of a business are recorded. A **convention** is an acceptable method by which the rule is applied to a given situation. Some of the main accounting principles have already been applied to the practical accounting examples in the previous chapters.

The main accounting principles are explained next.

TIP

In addition to learning the names of the principles, you must be able to explain and provide examples of each principle.

Business entity

The **business entity principle** is also known as the **accounting entity** principle. This means that the **business is treated as being completely separate from the owner of the business**. The personal assets of the owner, the personal spending of the owner, etc. do not appear in the accounting records of the business. The accounting records relate only to the business and record the assets of the business, the liabilities of the business, the money spent by the business and so on. Everything is recorded from the viewpoint of the business.

If there is a transaction concerning both the business and its owner then it is recorded in the accounting records of the business. When the owner introduces capital into the business, it is credited to the capital account (to show the funds coming from the owner). The capital account shows a credit balance representing the amount owed by the business to the owner. When the owner makes drawings from the business a debit entry will be made in the drawings account (to show the value going to the owner) which reduces the amount owed by the business to the owner.

KEY TERM

The **business entity principle** means that the business is treated as being completely separate from the owner of the business.

LINK

The practical application of the principle of business entity has already been explained in Chapters 2, 4 and 9.

Consistency

There are some areas of accounting where a choice of method is available. For example, there are several different ways to calculate the depreciation of a non-current asset.

LINK

You will learn about depreciation in Chapter 12.

> **KEY TERMS**
>
> The **consistency principle** means that accounting methods must be used consistently from one accounting period to the next.
>
> The **principle of duality** means that every transaction is recorded twice – once on the debit side and once on the credit side.
>
> The **going concern principle** means that the accounting records are maintained on the basis that the business will continue to operate for an indefinite period of time.
>
> The **historic cost principle** means that all assets and expenses are initially recorded at their actual cost.

Where a choice of method is available, the one with the most realistic outcome should be selected. Once a method has been selected, **the method must be used consistently from one accounting period to the next.** This is known as the **consistency principle**. If this is not done, a comparison of the financial results from year to year is impossible, and the profit of a particular year can be distorted.

There may be a good reason why it is necessary to change a method or valuation. In such a situation, the change may be made, but the effects of this should be noted in the financial statements.

> **TEST YOURSELF 10.2**
>
> 1. Explain the meaning of the term business entity.
> 2. State why a business should apply the principle of consistency.

Duality

The **principle of duality** is also referred to as the **dual aspect** principle. It has been explained in Chapter 2 how **every transaction has two aspects – a giving and a receiving**. The term **double entry** is used to describe how these two aspects of a transaction are recorded in the accounting records.

Going concern

The accounting records of a business are always maintained on the basis of assumed continuity. This means that **it is assumed that the business will continue to operate for an indefinite period of time and that there is no intention to close down the business or reduce the size of the business by any significant amount**. This is the **going concern principle**.

This continuity means that the non-current assets shown in a statement of financial position will appear at their book value, which is the original cost less depreciation (see Chapter 12), and inventory will appear at the lower of cost or net realisable value (see Section 10.5).

If it is expected that the business will cease to operate in the near future, the asset values in the statement of financial position will be adjusted. Assets will be shown at their expected sale values which are more meaningful than their book value in this situation.

Historic cost

The **historic cost principle** requires that **all assets and expenses are initially recorded in the ledger accounts at their actual cost**. It is closely linked to the money measurement principle. Cost is a known fact and can be verified.

Applying this principle makes it difficult to make comparisons about transactions occurring at different times because of the effect of inflation.

Sometimes it is necessary to adopt a more prudent approach to ensure that the non-current assets are shown at a more realistic value, so the cost price is reduced by depreciation (see Chapter 12).

Matching

The **matching principle** is also referred to as the **accruals principle**. This is an extension of the realisation principle to include other income and expenses. **The revenue of the accounting period is matched against the costs of the same period** (the timing of the actual receipts and payments is ignored).

The figures shown in an income statement must relate to the period of time covered by that statement, whether or not any money has changed hands. This means that a more meaningful comparison can be made of the profits, sales, expenses, and so on from year to year.

You will learn how the matching principle is applied to capital and revenue expenditure later in this section.

 LINK

In Chapter 11 you will learn why it is sometimes necessary to adjust the items of income and expense in an income statement for amounts prepaid or accrued.

Materiality

The **materiality principle** applies to items of very low value (items which are not 'material') which are not worth recording as separate items. Other principles can be ignored if the time and cost involved in recording such low value items far outweigh any benefits to be gained from the strict application of these principles. For example, a pocket calculator purchased for office use is strictly a non-current asset, part of its value being 'lost' each year through normal usage. The cost of calculating and recording this each year would amount to more than the cost of the asset. Instead of the calculator being recorded as a non-current asset, it would be regarded as an office expense in the year of purchase. What is material for one business may not be so for another business. A laptop computer may be regarded as immaterial for a large multi-national business, but would be material for a small sole trader. A large business may decide that non-current assets costing less than $1 000 will be regarded as immaterial and be charged as expenses. A small business may have a much lower figure.

This principle is also applied by entering small expenses in one account known as 'general expenses' or 'sundry expenses' rather than having individual ledger accounts for office expenses like light bulbs, flower displays and so on. Materiality is also applied in relation to inventories of office supplies like envelopes when the total cost of envelopes purchased during the year is treated as an expense even though there are some left at the end of the year.

 **KEY TERMS**

The **matching principle** means that the revenue of the accounting period is matched against the costs of the same period.

The **materiality principle** means that individual items which will not significantly affect either the profit or the assets of a business do not need to be recorded separately.

TEST YOURSELF 10.3

1. Explain how the principle of duality is carried out in recording the day-to-day transactions of a business.
2. State **one** situation when the principle of going concern is **not** applied.
3. Explain what is meant by the principle of matching.
4. Explain why the principle of materiality may be applied to the purchase of an office stapler.

Money measurement

The **money measurement principle** means that **only information which can be expressed in terms of money can be recorded in the accounting records**. Money is a recognised unit of measure and is a traditional way of valuing transactions. It does not rely on personal opinions and it is factual.

There are many aspects of a business which cannot be measured in terms of money and, therefore, do not appear in the accounting records. The morale of the workforce, the effectiveness of a good manager, the benefits of a staff training course all play an important part in the success of the business, but they will not appear in the accounting records as their value cannot be expressed in monetary terms. In a similar way, the launch of a rival product or increased competition cannot be recorded in the accounting records as their effects cannot be measured in monetary terms.

Prudence

The **prudence principle** is also known as the principle of **conservatism**. This principle ensures that the accounting records present a realistic picture of the position of the business. However, the exercise of prudence does not allow the deliberate understatement of assets or income, or the deliberate overstatement of liabilities or expenses. In short, prudence does not permit bias. **Accountants should ensure that profits and assets are not overstated and that liabilities are not understated.** The phrase 'never anticipate a profit, but provide for all possible losses' is often used to describe the principle of **prudence**. Profit should only be recognised when it is reasonably certain that such a profit has been realised and all possible losses should be provided for.

Prudence is a very important principle. If a situation arises where applying another accounting principle would be contrary to the principle of prudence, then the principle of prudence is applied. For example, under the realisation principle, profit is earned when goods actually change hands; but if the customer fails to pay after a reasonable time, the principle of prudence may be applied and the debt is written off.

Realisation

The **realisation principle** emphasises the importance of not recording a profit until it has actually been earned. This means that **revenue is only regarded as being earned when the legal title to goods or services passes from the seller to the buyer**, who has then an obligation (liability) to pay for those goods.

When an order is placed by a customer no goods change hands, and no profit is earned. Profit is regarded as being realised when the goods actually change hands. This is the same even if the goods are sold on credit and the customer does not pay for them immediately.

> **KEY TERMS**
>
> The **money measurement principle** means that only information which can be expressed in terms of money can be recorded in the accounting records.
>
> The **prudence principle** means that profits and assets should not be overstated and losses and liabilities should not be understated.
>
> The **realisation principle** means that revenue is only regarded as being earned when the legal title to goods passes from the seller to the buyer.

> **LINKS**
>
> You will learn about providing for the loss in value of non-current assets in Chapter 12.
>
> You will learn about providing for the loss when customers do not pay their accounts in Chapter 13.

> **TEST YOURSELF 10.4**
>
> 1. No entry is made in the accounting records of Park Street Stores when a competitor reduces his prices by 15%. Explain why.
> 2. 'If in doubt, understate profits and overstate losses'. State which accounting principle is being described.
> 3. A customer orders goods on 2 February. The goods are delivered to the customer on 16 February. A cheque in full settlement is received from the customer on 28 February. State the date on which the revenue is regarded as realised. Give a reason for your answer.

You can now answer Questions 1 and 2 at the end of this chapter.

10.3 International accounting standards

International accounting standards ensure that financial statements are prepared using the same rules and guidelines internationally. Knowledge of the individual accounting standards is outside the scope of the syllabus.

The objectives of the standards are to ensure that users of financial statements are protected and not misled. The quality of information contained in financial statements determines the usefulness of these statements. This quality of information can be measured in terms of four factors – comparability, relevance, reliability and understandability.

Comparability

The information contained in financial statements can be useful if it can be compared with similar information about the same business for another accounting period or at another point in time. It is also useful to be able to compare the information with similar information about other business.

In order to make comparisons, it is necessary to be aware of any different policies used in the preparation of the financial statements, any changes in these policies and the effects of such changes. It is important to be able to identify similarities and differences between the information in the financial statement and the information relating to other accounting periods or other businesses.

Relevance

Financial statements provide information about a business's financial performance and position. These can be used as the basis for financial decisions. It is important that the information is provided in time for these decisions to be made: information not available when required is of little use.

It is also important that the information is relevant to users of the financial statements. This means that it can be used to confirm, or correct, prior expectations about past events and also to help forming, revising or confirming expectations about the future.

Reliability

The information provided in financial statements can be reliable if it is:

- capable of being depended upon by users as being a true representation of the underlying transactions and events which it is representing
- capable of being independently verified
- free from bias
- free from significant errors
- prepared with suitable caution being applied to any judgements and estimates which are necessary.

Understandability

It is important that financial statements can be understood by the users of those statements. This depends partly on the clarity of the information provided.

TIP
You need to be able to explain these four accounting objectives.

It also depends on the abilities of the users of the financial statements. It is normally assumed that users of financial statements have a reasonable knowledge of business and economic activities and accounting and that they will be reasonably diligent when studying the financial statements. However, information should not be omitted from financial statements because it is decided that it is too difficult for users to understand.

TEST YOURSELF 10.5

1. State **two** ways in which information can be regarded as being relevant.
2. State **three** ways in which information can be regarded as being reliable.
3. Explain why it is necessary to know any changes in accounting policy when comparing financial statements with those of a previous year.
4. Explain the meaning of the term 'understandability'.

10.4 Capital and revenue expenditure and receipts

Capital expenditure

Capital expenditure is money spent by a business on purchasing non-current assets and improving or extending non-current assets. This includes all the legal costs incurred in the purchase of non-current assets, costs of carriage for the delivery of non-current assets and costs of installing non-current assets.

These costs will appear as non-current assets in the statement of financial position of a business. They should **not** be charged as expenses in the year of purchase as they benefit the business for several years. The value of non-current assets often decreases because of depreciation (see Chapter 12). This cost will be **matched** against the annual revenue which the non-current asset has helped the business to earn.

KEY TERMS

Capital expenditure is money spent on purchasing, improving or extending non-current assets.

Revenue expenditure is money spent on running a business on a day-to-day basis.

A **capital receipt** is money received by a business from a source other than the normal trading activities.

Revenue expenditure

Revenue expenditure is money spent on running a business on a day-to-day basis. This includes the administration expenses, the selling expenses, the financial expenses and the cost of maintaining and running non-current assets. It also includes the cost of goods purchased for the purpose of resale.

These costs will appear in the income statement. They are **matched** against the revenue of the period.

If these two types of expenditure are treated incorrectly the profit for the year will be inaccurate and the statement of financial position (whilst still balancing) will also be incorrect. For example, if repairs to a machine were treated as an improvement to that machine the expenses in the income statement would be understated, so the profit for the year would be overstated. In the statement of financial position, the non-current assets would be overstated and the capital would also be overstated because of the incorrect profit for the year.

Capital receipt

A **capital receipt** occurs when money is received other than from normal trading activities. This includes the receipt of capital from the owner, the receipt of loans and the proceeds of sale of a non-current asset.

A capital receipt should **not** be entered in the income statement. If, however, a profit or loss is made on the sale of a non-current asset then this will be included in the income statement for the year in which the asset was sold.

> **LINK**
> You will learn about the disposal of non-current assets in Chapter 12.

Revenue receipt

A **revenue receipt** is money received by a business from normal trading activities.

These include revenue from the sale of goods, fees from clients and other income such as rent received, commission received, discount received and so on.

Because these arise from the normal trading activities they are entered in the income statement.

> **KEY TERM**
> A **revenue receipt** is money received by a business from normal trading activities.

> **TEST YOURSELF 10.6**
>
> 1 Explain why it is important to distinguish between capital expenditure and revenue expenditure.
> 2 Give **one** example of **each** of the following: **a** capital receipt, **b** revenue receipt.

You can now answer Questions 3 and 4 at the end of this chapter.

10.5 Inventory valuation

It is necessary for a business to value its inventory at the end of each financial year.

Inventory is always valued at the **lower of cost or net realisable value**. This is an application of the principle of **prudence** as overvaluing the inventory causes both the profit and the assets to be overvalued.

> **TIP**
> Inventory must always be valued at the lower of cost and net realisable value.

The cost of the inventory is the actual purchase price plus any additional costs (such as carriage inwards) incurred in bringing the inventory to its present position and condition. The net realisable value is the estimated receipts from the sale of the inventory, less any costs of completing the goods or costs of selling the goods.

Usually the cost of the inventory will be lower than the net realisable value. It may happen that the goods are damaged or there is no demand for such type of goods because of change in taste or fashion. In this situation, the net realisable value will be lower than cost.

> **TEST YOURSELF 10.7**
>
> 1 State the basis on which inventory should be valued.
> 2 Explain the meaning of the term 'net realisable value'.

Walkthrough 10.1

Dhaval sells two different types of goods (Type A and B). He provided the following information at 31 December 20–6:

Type	Units	Cost price per unit	Net realisable value per unit
A	94	$20	$18
B	38	$15	$19

The cost price per unit of Type A does not include carriage inwards of $1 per unit.

It will cost $0.50 per unit to bring Type A goods into a saleable condition

12 units of Type B were damaged and would only be able to be sold for $10 per unit.

Prepare a statement to show the value of the closing inventory at 31 December 20–6.

Dhaval
Valuation of inventory at 31 December 20–6

	$	$
Type A – 94 units at $17.50		1 645
Type B – 12 units at $10	120	
26 units at $15	390	510
		2 155

Calculations

Type A   Cost $20 + Carriage $1 = $21
Net realisable value $18 – costs to complete $0.50 = $17.50
Valued at net realisable value as it is lower than cost

Type B   12 units Cost $15
Net realisable value $10
Valued at net realisable value as it is lower than cost
26 units Cost $15
Net realisable value $19
Valued at cost as it is lower than net realisable value

You can now answer Question 5 at the end of this chapter.

> **LINK**
>
> You will learn about correcting errors in Chapter 15.

As explained earlier, the inventory at the end of one year becomes the inventory at the start of the next year. If an incorrect value is placed on the inventory it will affect the gross profit and the profit for the year for both the current financial year and the following financial year. Incorrect values will also be shown for both current assets and capital in the statement of financial position.

Walkthrough 10.2

After the preparation of his financial statements for the year ended 31 December 20–7 Dhaval discovered that he had over-valued his closing inventory by $50

Complete the following table by placing a tick in the correct columns to show the effect of this.

	Overstated	Understated	No effect
gross profit for the year ended 31 December 20–7	✓		
gross profit for the year ending 31 December 20–8		✓	

	Overstated	Understated	No effect
profit for the year ended 31 December 20–7	✓		
profit for the year ending 31 December 20–8		✓	
Dhaval's capital at 31 December 20–7	✓		
Dhaval's capital at 31 December 20–8			✓
current assets at 31 December 20–7	✓		
current assets at 31 December 20–8			✓

Over-valuing the inventory at 31 December 20–7 will affect the financial statements for that year because

- the cost of sales is under-stated so both the gross profit and the profit for the year will be overstated
- over-stating the profit for the year means that the balance of the capital account on 31 December 20–7 will also be over-stated
- the total of the current assets at 31 December 20–7 will be over-stated if the inventory at that date is over-valued.

Over-valuing the inventory at 31 December 20–7 will affect the financial statements for the year ending 31 December 20–8 because

- the cost of sales is over-stated so both the gross profit and the profit for the year will be under-stated
- under-stating the profit for the year means that the balance of the capital account on 31 December 20–7 will have been corrected at 31 December 20–8
- the total of the current assets at 31 December 20–8 will not be affected.

You can now answer Question 6 at the end of this chapter.

Revision checklist

- Accounting has developed a set of principles which are applied in the preparation of accounting statements.
- The main accounting principles are – business entity, consistency, duality, going concern, historic cost, matching, materiality, money measurement, prudence and realisation.
- The quality of information contained in financial statements can be measured in terms of four factors – comparability, relevance, reliability and understandability.
- It is important to distinguish between capital and revenue expenditure and also between capital and revenue receipts. If these items are treated incorrectly the financial statements will also be inaccurate.
- At the end of every financial year inventory must be valued. It is always valued at the lower of cost or net realisable value.

Exam-style questions

1. The cost of insuring the owner's personal motor vehicle was not included in the income statement of the business. Which accounting principle was applied?

   A business entity
   B going concern
   C money measurement
   D prudence

2. Name the accounting principle applied in each of the following:

	Principle
Rent for business premises relating to 20–9 was not included in the income statement for 20–8.	
Credit sales were recorded when the goods were dispatched (sent), not When the customer placed the order.	
The value of the assets of a business was not reduced when the manager of the business retired.	
Cash purchases were debited to the purchases account and credited to the cash account.	

3. Repairs to office machinery were entered as capital expenditure in the accounting records. How did this affect the financial statements?

	Profit for the year		Non-current assets	
	Overstated	Understated	Overstated	Understated
A	✓		✓	
B		✓		✓
C	✓			✓
D		✓	✓	

4. **a** Explain the difference between each of the following pairs of terms. Give an example of each

   i capital expenditure and capital receipts

   ii revenue expenditure and revenue receipts

   b Explain why it is important that capital receipts are not recorded as revenue receipts.

5 Abeba provided the following information about her closing inventory:

	Number of units	Cost price per unit	Net realisable value per unit
Product X	500	$1.00	$1.80
Product Y	2 000	$2.00	$1.90

200 units of Product Y were damaged and unsaleable.

What was the value of Abeba's inventory?

A $3 920   B $4 100   C $4 320   D $4 700

6 a Explain the meaning of the terms 'cost' and 'net realisable value'.
   b State how a trader should value the inventory at the end of the financial year.
   c At the end of the financial year on 30 June 20–6, a trader discovered that he had undervalued his closing inventory by $1 000.

   Complete the following table by placing a tick in the correct columns to show the effect of this:

	Overstated	Understated	No effect
Profit for the year ended 30 June 20–6			
Gross profit for the year ended 30 June 20–7			
Current assets on 30 June 20–7			

Chapter 11
Other payables and other receivables

Learning objectives

In this chapter you will learn to:

- recognise the importance of matching costs and revenues   4.3
- prepare ledger accounts to record accrued and prepaid expenses   4.3
- prepare ledger accounts to record accrued and prepaid incomes   4.3
- make adjustments for accrued and prepaid expenses and accrued and prepaid incomes.   5.1

Chapter 11: Other payables and other receivables

11.1 Introduction

It is often necessary to make adjustments to the accounting records in order to present a more accurate view of the profit or loss of the business and the financial position of the business. Such adjustments are referred to as **year-end adjustments**.

The examples used in previous chapters assumed that all the expenses in the profit and loss section of the income statement were paid until the end of the financial year, with nothing paid beyond that date and nothing unpaid. A similar approach was used in relation to revenue items within the profit and loss section of the income statement when it was assumed that all the items were received up to the end of the financial year with nothing relating to a period beyond that date and nothing outstanding. In practice, this is rarely the case: it is common to find expenses or income unpaid, or to find expenses or income paid in one financial year but which relate to other financial years.

Only items relating to that particular time period should be included in the statement: the timing of the actual receipts and payments is not relevant.

An income statement is prepared for a definite period of time (the period of time covered by the statement being included as part of the statement heading).

This is a practical application of the **matching principle**.

It is necessary to adjust the items within an income statement for amounts **prepaid** or **accrued**. This means that the profit or loss will be shown at a more accurate figure, and it allows for more meaningful comparisons of the financial statements from year to year.

The use of a simple diagram is often helpful when calculating the expense or income relating to a particular financial year. This is illustrated in the examples used in this chapter.

LINK

You will learn more about year-end adjustments in Chapters 12 and 13.

LINK

You learned about income statements in Chapter 8.

LINK

You learned about the matching principle in Chapter 10.

TIP

Only those expenses and incomes which relate to the current financial year are included in the income statement.

11.2 Accrued and prepaid expenses

Accrued expenses

An **accrual** is an amount due in an accounting period which remains unpaid at the end of that accounting period. Where an expense is accrued it means that some benefit or service has been received during the accounting period but this benefit or service has not been paid for by the end of the period.

To apply the **matching principle**, the amount transferred to the income statement should represent the expense for the accounting period covered by that account. This means that **any amount due but unpaid at the end of the financial year must be added to the amount paid** and the total expense relating to the accounting period transferred to the income statement.

The expense account will now show a balance equal to the amount unpaid. To complete the double entry, this **balance is brought down on the credit side of the ledger account**. As the balance represents an amount owing, due for payment in the near future, it will be included as a **current liability** in the **statement of financial position**.

KEY TERM

An **accrued expense** is an expense relating to a particular accounting period which is unpaid at the end of that period.

LINK

You learned in Chapter 8 how the totals of the expense accounts and income accounts are transferred to the income statement at the end of the financial year.

The entries are summarised as follows:

During the year – debit the expense account and credit the cash book with the amount paid.

At the year-end – debit the expense account with any amount due but unpaid and carry down as a credit balance

credit the expense account and debit the income statement with the difference on the expense account (this represents the expense for the year)

include the balance on the expense account as a current liability in the statement of financial position.

> **TEST YOURSELF 11.1**
>
> 1 State what is meant by an accrued expense.
> 2 State where an accrued expense is shown in a statement of financial position.
> 3 Explain why accrued expenses should be included when calculating the profit.

Walkthrough 11.1

Salman started a business on 1 April 20–7.

He receives an invoice for telephone expenses quarterly in arrears. During the year ended 31 March 20–8 his payments for expenses included the following:

20–7	30 June	Telephone expenses paid in cash, $44
	4 October	Telephone expenses paid by credit transfer, $56
20–8	3 January	Telephone expenses paid by credit transfer, $62

An invoice for telephone expenses for $59 was received on 31 March 20–8. This was for telephone expenses up to the end of March, but was not paid until 5 April 20–8.

a Write up the telephone expenses account in Salman's nominal ledger for the year ended 31 March 20–8.
b Prepare a relevant extract from Salman's income statement for the year ended 31 March 20–8.
c Prepare a relevant extract from Salman's statement of financial position at 31 March 20–8.

Before attempting to answer the question it may be helpful to consider the problem by the use of a diagram.

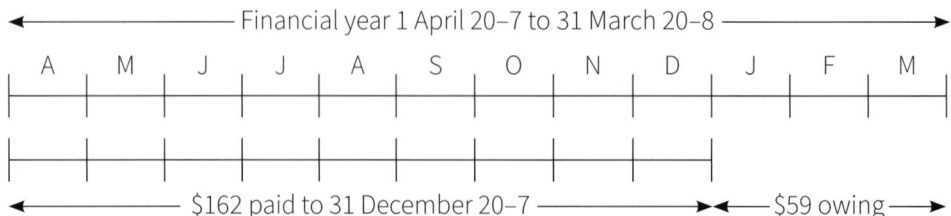

The diagram shows that the expenses paid do not match the period covered by the financial year, so it is necessary to add the amount owing at the end of the year.

a

Salman
Nominal ledger
Telephone expenses account

Date	Details	Folio	$	Date	Details	Folio	$
20–7				20–8			
Jun 30	Cash		44	Mar 31	Income statement		221
Oct 4	Bank		56				
20–8							
Jan 3	Bank		62				
Mar 31	Balance	c/d	59				
			221				221
				20–8			
				Apr 1	Balance	b/d	59

b

Salman
Extract from income statement for the year ended 31 March 20–8

	$
Expenses – Telephone expenses	221

c

Salman
Extract from statement of financial position at 31 March 20–8

	$
Current liabilities	
Other payables	59

- The telephone expenses relating to the financial year ended on 31 March 20–8 amount to $221, which is the total paid plus the amount unpaid.
- The telephone expenses would be listed with the other expenses in the income statement and deducted from the gross profit.
- Where there are several accrued expenses it is usual to show one combined figure in the statement of financial position under 'other payables' rather than showing the amount of each separate accrual.

Cambridge IGCSE and O Level Accounting

> **KEY TERM**
>
> A **prepaid expense** is an expense paid during the financial year which relates to a future accounting period.

Prepaid expenses

A **prepayment** is an amount that is paid in advance. Where an expense is prepaid it means that a payment has been made during the financial year for some benefit or service to be received in a future accounting period.

As with accrued expenses, the **matching principle** must be applied so that the amount transferred to the income statement represents the expense for the accounting period covered by that statement. Any amount paid during the financial year relating to a future accounting period must be deducted from the amount paid so that only the expense relating to the accounting period is transferred to the income statement.

The expense account will now show a balance equal to the amount paid in advance. To complete the double entry, this **balance is brought down on the debit side of the ledger account**. As the balance represents a short term benefit, which the business has paid for but which is not used up, it will be included as a **current asset** in the **statement of financial position**.

The entries are summarised as follows:

During the year – debit the expense account and credit the cash book with the amount paid.

At the year-end – credit the expense account with any amount paid in advance and carry down as a debit balance

credit the expense account and debit the income statement with the difference on the expense account (this represents the expense for the year)

include the balance on the expense account as a current asset in the statement of financial position.

> **TEST YOURSELF 11.2**
>
> 1 State what is meant by a prepaid expense.
> 2 State where a prepaid expense is shown in a statement of financial position.
> 3 Explain how the matching principle is applied to expenses shown in the income statement.

Walkthrough 11.2

Salman started a business on 1 April 20–7.

Salman rented premises until 1 July 20–7 when he purchased premises. He paid a cheque for $600 for one year's insurance on his premises on 1 July 20–7.

a Write up the insurance account in Salman's nominal ledger for the year ended 31 March 20–8.

b Prepare a relevant extract from Salman's income statement for the year ended 31 March 20–8.

c Prepare a relevant extract from Salman's statement of financial position at 31 March 20–8.

Before attempting to answer the question it may be helpful to consider the problem by the use of a diagram.

Chapter 11: Other payables and other receivables

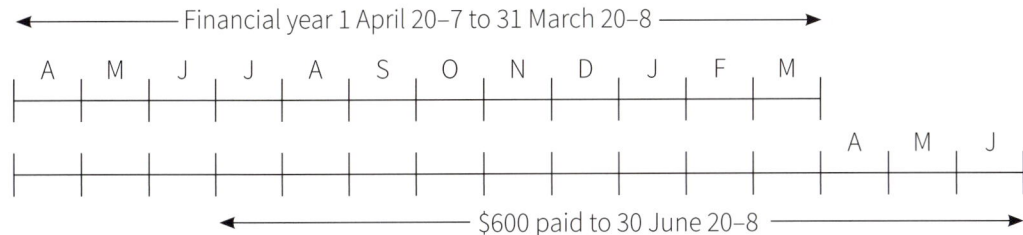

The diagram shows that the expenses paid do not match the period covered by the financial year, so it is necessary to deduct that portion of the $600 which falls outside the financial year (3 months/12 months or $\frac{1}{4}$ of $600 relates to the following financial year).

a

Salman
Nominal ledger
Insurance account

Date	Details	Folio	$	Date	Details	Folio	$
20–7				20–8			
Jul 1	Bank		600	Mar 31	Income statement		450
					Balance	c/d	150
			600				600
20–8							
Apr 1	Balance	b/d	150				

b

Salman
Extract from income statement for the year ended 31 March 20–8

	$
Expenses – Insurance	450

c

Salman
Extract from statement of financial position at 31 March 20–8

	$
Current assets	
Other receivables	150

- The insurance relating to the financial year ended on 31 March 20–8 amounts to $450, which is the insurance from 1 July 20–7 to 31 March 20–8.
- The insurance expense would be listed with the other expenses in the income statement and deducted from the gross profit.
- Where there are several prepaid expenses it is usual to show one combined figure in the statement of financial position under 'other receivables' rather than showing the amount of each separate prepayment.

If a business has an inventory of stationery, postage stamps, wrapping paper and so on at the end of a financial year, this can be regarded as a prepaid expense. Money has been spent, but the benefit will not be received until the following accounting period, when these are actually used. The entries are similar to those for a prepaid expense.

Walkthrough 11.3

Salman started a business on 1 April 20–7.

During the year ended 31 March 20–8 he purchased stationery costing $113.

On 31 March 20–8 the inventory of stationery was valued at $36.

Write up the stationery account in Salman's nominal ledger for the year ended 31 March 20–8.

Salman

Nominal ledger

Stationery account

Date	Details	Folio	$	Date	Details	Folio	$
20–8				20–8			
Mar 31	Bank/cash		113	Mar 31	Income statement		77
					Balance	c/d	36
			113				113
20–8							
Apr 1	Balance	b/d	36				

- The date of 31 March 20–8 has been used for the total paid as no individual dates and amounts were shown in the question.
- The expense of $77 would be listed with the other expenses in the income statement and deducted from the gross profit.
- The balance representing the inventory at 31 March 20–8 would appear as a current asset in the statement of financial position.
- The inventory of stationery must not be included in the inventory of goods for resale.

You can now answer Questions 1–3 at the end of this chapter.

11.3 Opening balances on expense accounts

The trader mentioned in **Walkthrough 11.1** to **11.3** was in his first year of business, so none of the expense accounts prepared in these examples had an opening balance. There was, however, a closing balance on each account which became the opening balance for the second year of trading. This must be considered when calculating the expense relating to the next financial year.

Walkthrough 11.4

Salman's financial year ends on 31 March.

He receives an invoice for telephone expenses quarterly in arrears.

On 1 April 20–8 the telephone expenses account in Salman's nominal ledger showed a credit balance of $59.

During the year ended 31 March 20–9 his payments for expenses included the following:

20–8	5 April	Telephone expenses paid in cash, $59
20–8	30 June	Telephone expenses paid by cheque, $60
	2 October	Telephone expenses paid by credit transfer, $48
	31 December	Telephone expenses paid by credit transfer, $56

An invoice for telephone expenses for $63 was received on 31 March 20–9. This was for telephone expenses up to the end of March, but was not paid until 2 April 20–9.

Write up the telephone expenses account in Salman's nominal ledger for the year ended 31 March 20–9.

Before attempting to answer the question it may be helpful to consider the problem by the use of a diagram.

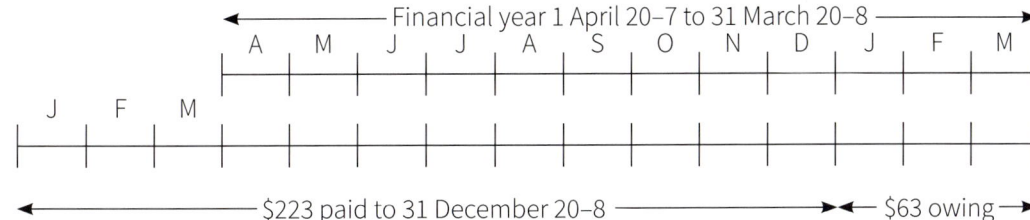

The diagram shows that the expenses paid do not match the period covered by the financial year, so it is necessary to:

- deduct that portion of the $223 which falls outside the financial year ($59 was paid during this financial year but related to the previous accounting period)
- add the $63 owing at the end of present financial year.

Salman
Nominal ledger
Telephone expenses account

Date	Details	Folio	$	Date	Details	Folio	$
20–8				20–8			
Apr 5	Cash		59	Apr 1	Balance	b/d	59
Jun 30	Bank		60	20–9			
Oct 2	Bank		48	Mar 31	Income statement		227
Dec 31	Bank		56				
20–9							
Mar 31	Balance	c/d	63				
			286				286
				20–9			
				Apr 1	Balance	b/d	63

Walkthrough 11.5

Salman's financial year ends on 31 March.

On 1 April 20–8 the insurance account in Salman's nominal ledger showed a debit balance of $150.

He paid $636 for one year's insurance on his premises by direct debit on 1 July 20–8.

Write up the insurance account in Salman's nominal ledger for the year ended 31 March 20–9.

Before attempting to answer the question it may be helpful to consider the problem by the use of a diagram.

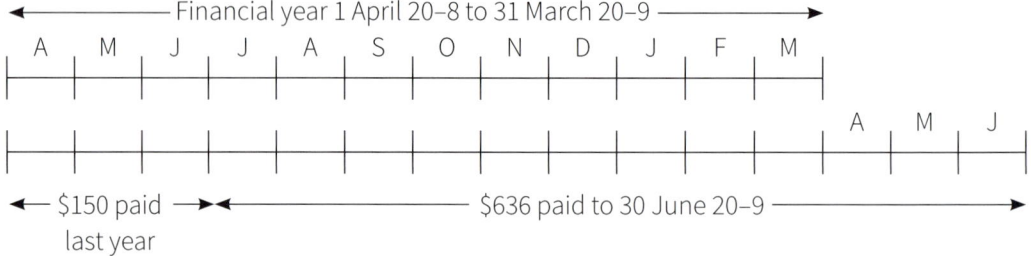

The diagram shows that the expenses paid do not match the period covered by the financial year, so it is necessary to:

- deduct that portion of the $636 which falls outside the financial year (3 months/12 months or $\frac{1}{4}$ of $636 relates to the following financial year)

- add the $150 paid in the previous financial year as it falls within the present financial year.

Salman

Nominal ledger

Insurance account

Date	Details	Folio	$	Date	Details	Folio	$
20–8				20–9			
Apr 1	Balance	b/d	150	Mar 31	Income statement		627
Jul 1	Bank		636		Balance	c/d	159
			786				786
20–9							
Apr 1	Balance	b/d	159				

Chapter 11: Other payables and other receivables

TEST YOURSELF 11.3

1. Anisha started business on 1 April 20–1. Property tax amounted to $800 for the year ended 31 March 20–2 and $880 for the year ended 31 March 20–3. Property tax of $600 was paid during the year ended 31 March 20–2 and $860 was paid during the year ended 31 March 20–3.

   For **each** of the years ended 31 March 20–2 and 31 March 20–3 state:

   a the amount charged for property tax in the income statement

   b the amount shown for property tax in the statement of financial position, indicating whether it is a current asset or a current liability.

> **TIP**
> Where an item of expense or income requires adjustment it is recommended that the calculation is shown. This can be done in brackets after the wording and the final figure shown in the money column.

11.4 Combined expense accounts

Sometimes a business may use one ledger account for two different, but related, expenses. The same principles are applied as those used for an account containing a single expense. The only difference is that there may be two opening and closing balances.

Walkthrough 11.6

Mary's financial year ends on 31 March. She maintains a combined account for rent and rates. On 1 April 20–8 Mary had prepaid one month's rates, $300, and owed two months' rent, $1 000. During the year ended 31 March 20–9 Mary made the following payments by cheque:

20–8		$
1 May	Rent for 8 months to 30 September 20–8	4 000
1 June	Rates for 13 months to 31 May 20–9	3 900
1 December	Rent for 5 months to 28 February 20–9	2 500

Write the rent and rates account in Mary's nominal ledger for the year ended 31 March 20–9.

Before attempting to answer the question it may be helpful to consider the problem by the use of a diagram.

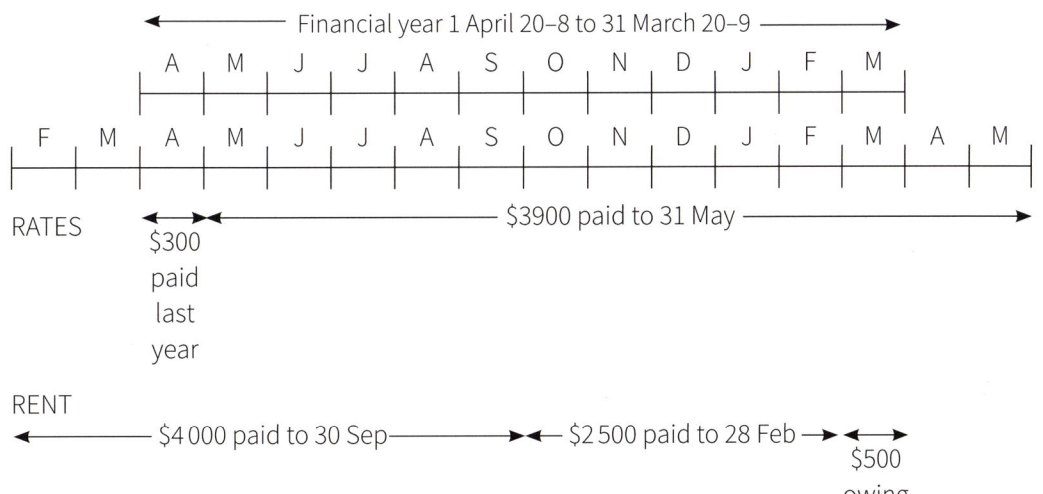

Apply the same principles as used in **Walkthrough 11.4** and **11.5** by deducting anything which falls outside the financial year and adding anything which falls within the present financial year.

Mary
Nominal ledger
Rent and rates account

Date	Details	Folio	$	Date	Details	Folio	$
20–8				20–8			
Apr 1	Balance (rates)	b/d	300	Apr 1	Balance (rent)	b/d	1 000
May 1	Bank (rent)		4 000	20–9			
Jun 1	Bank (rates)		3 900	Mar 31	Income statement		
Dec 1	Bank (rent)		2 500		Rent 6 000		
20–9					Rates 3 600		9 600
Mar 31	Balance (rent)	c/d	500		Balance (rates)	c/d	600
			11 200				11 200
20–9				20–9			
Apr 1	Balance (rates)	b/d	600	Apr 1	Balance (rent)	b/d	500

11.5 Accrued and prepaid income

Accrued income

Where **an item of income is accrued** it means that another person receiving a benefit or service from the business during the accounting period has not paid for that benefit or service by the end of the period.

The totals of income accounts in the nominal ledger are transferred to the income statement at the end of the financial year. The **matching principle** is applied to income in the same way as it is to expenses so that the amount transferred to the income statement represents the income for the accounting period covered by that statement. This means that **any amount due but not received at the end of the financial year must be added to the amount received** and the total income relating to the accounting period transferred to the income statement.

The income account will now show a balance equal to the amount not yet received. To complete the double entry, this **balance is brought down on the debit side of the ledger account**. As the balance represents an amount owing to the business, due to be received in the near future, it will be included as a **current asset** in the **statement of financial position**.

The entries are summarised as follows:

During the year – credit the income account and debit the cash book with the amount received

At the year-end – credit the income account with any amount due but not received and carry down as a debit balance

> **KEY TERM**
>
> **Accrued income** is income relating to a particular accounting period which has not been received at the end of that period.

Chapter 11: Other payables and other receivables

debit the income account and credit the income statement with the difference on the income account (this represents the income for the year)

include the balance on the income account as a current asset in the statement of financial position.

Walkthrough 11.7

Salman started a business on 1 April 20–7.

On that date he also agreed to act as an agent for Kohli & Company. Salman was to be paid a commission six monthly in arrears on all goods sold for Kohli & Company.

Commission of $120 was received by direct debit on 1 October 20–7 and $135 was received by direct debit on 2 April 20–8.

a Write up the commission receivable account in Salman's nominal ledger for the year ended 31 March 20–8.

b Prepare a relevant extract from Salman's income statement for the year ended 31 March 20–8.

c Prepare a relevant extract from Salman's statement of financial position at 31 March 20–8.

Before attempting to answer the question it may be helpful to consider the problem by the use of a diagram.

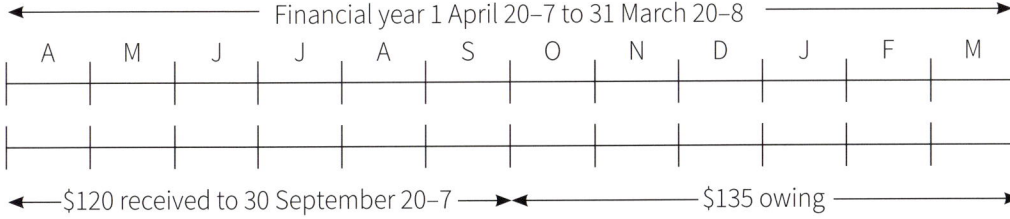

The diagram shows that the income received does not match the period covered by the financial year, so it is necessary to add the amount not yet received at the end of the year.

a

Salman
Nominal ledger
Commission receivable account

Date	Details	Folio	$	Date	Details	Folio	$
20–8				20–7			
Mar 31	Income statement		255	Oct 1	Bank		120
				20–8			
				Mar 31	Balance	c/d	135
			255				255
20–8							
Apr 1	Balance	b/d	135				

b

Salman
Extract from income statement for the year ended 31 March 20-8

	$
Gross profit	xxx
Add Commission receivable	255

c

Salman
Extract from statement of financial position at 31 March 20-8

	$
Current assets	
Income accrued	135

- The commission receivable relating to the financial year ended on 31 March 20-8 amounts to $255, which is the total received plus the amount due but not yet received.
- The commission received would be listed with the other items of income in the income statement and added to the gross profit.
- The commission due but not yet received would appear in the statement of financial position as a current asset under the description of income accrued. Alternatively, it could be included in the other receivables (in this case a note to the statement of financial position would show the breakdown of this figure).

> **KEY TERM**
>
> **Prepaid income** is income received during the financial year which relates to a future accounting period.

Prepaid income

Where **an item of income is prepaid**, it means that a person had paid for a benefit or service from the business, but this has not been provided by the business at the end of the financial year.

Once again, the **matching principle** must be applied so that the amount transferred to the income statement represents the income for the accounting period covered by that statement. Any amount received during the financial year relating to a future accounting period must be deducted from the amount received so that only the income relating to the accounting period is transferred to the income statement.

The income account will now show a balance equal to the amount received in advance. To complete the double entry, this **balance is brought down on the credit side of the ledger account**. This balance will be included as a **current liability** in the **statement of financial position** as the business has a liability to provide some service or benefit for which the business has already been paid.

Chapter 11: Other payables and other receivables

The entries are summarised as follows:

During the year – credit the income account and debit the cash book with the amount received.

At the year-end – debit the income account with any amount received in advance and carry down as a credit balance

debit the income account and credit the income statement with the difference on the income account (this represents the income for the year)

include the balance on the income account as a current liability in the statement of financial position.

Walkthrough 11.8

Salman started a business on 1 April 20–7.

Salman rented premises until 1 July 20–7 when he purchased premises. On that date he rented out part of his premises to another trader at an annual rent of $1 000, payable quarterly in advance.

The tenant paid rent of $250 by direct debit on 1 July 20–7, 1 October 20–7, 31 December 20–7 and 30 March 20–8.

a Write up the rent receivable account in Salman's nominal ledger for the year ended 31 March 20–8.

b Prepare a relevant extract from Salman's income statement for the year ended 31 March 20–8.

c Prepare a relevant extract from Salman's statement of financial position at 31 March 20–8.

Before attempting to answer the question it may be helpful to consider the problem by the use of a diagram.

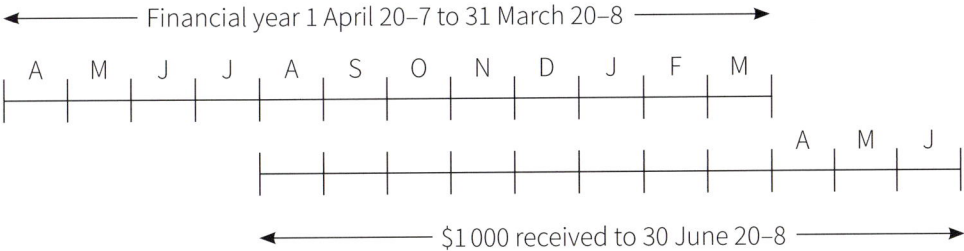

The diagram shows that the income received does not match the period covered by the financial year, so it is necessary to deduct that portion of the $1 000 which falls outside the financial year ($250 relates to the following financial year).

TIP

In a statement of financial position, the individual items of other receivables and other payables can be shown in brackets after the wording and the total figure entered in the money column.

a

Salman
Nominal ledger
Rent receivable account

Date	Details	Folio	$	Date	Details	Folio	$
20–8				20–7			
Mar 31	Income statement		750	Jul 1	Bank		250
	Balance	c/d	250	Oct 1	Bank		250
				Dec 31	Bank		250
				20–8			
				Mar 30	Bank		250
			1 000				1 000
				20–8			
				Apr 1	Balance	b/d	250

b

Salman
Extract from income statement for the year ended 31 March 20–8

	$
Gross profit	xxx
Add Rent receivable	750

c

Salman
Extract from statement of financial position at 31 March 20–8

	$
Current liabilities	
Income prepaid	250

- The rent receivable relating to the financial year ended on 31 March 20–8 amounts to $750, which is the rent received for the period 1 July 20–7 to 31 March 20–8.

- The rent received would be listed with the other items of income in the income statement and added to the gross profit.

- The rent received in advance would appear in the statement of financial position as a current liability under the description of income prepaid. Alternatively, it could be included in the other payables (in this case a note to the statement of financial position would show the breakdown of this figure).

Chapter 11: Other payables and other receivables

> **TEST YOURSELF 11.4**
>
> 1. Explain why income received in advance is shown as a current liability in a statement of financial position.
> 2. Explain why accrued income is shown as a current asset in a statement of financial position.

11.6 Opening balances on income accounts

In the second and subsequent years of trading, a business may have opening balances on income accounts as well as opening balances on expense accounts. These must be considered when calculating the income relating to the particular financial year for which the accounts are prepared.

Walkthrough 11.9

Salman's financial year ends on 31 March.

He acts as an agent for Kohli & Company and is paid a commission six monthly in arrears on all goods sold for Kohli & Company.

On 1 April 20–8 the commission receivable account in Salman's nominal ledger showed a debit balance of $135.

During the year ended 31 March 20–9 he received direct debits for commission as follows:

| 20–8 | 2 April | $135 |
| | 1 October | $145 |

At 31 March 20–9 commission due but not yet received amounted to $156.

Write up the commission receivable account in Salman's nominal ledger for the year ended 31 March 20–9.

Before attempting to answer the question it may be helpful to consider the problem by the use of a diagram.

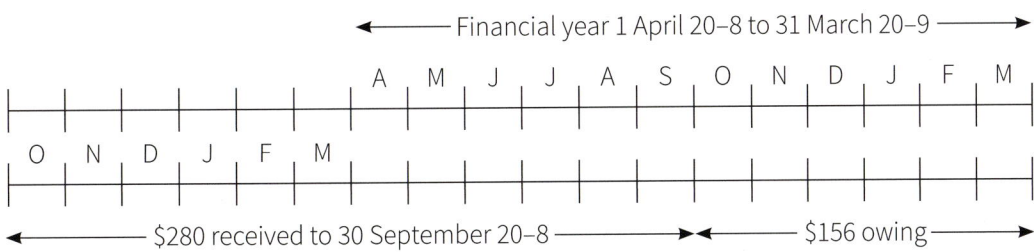

The diagram shows that the income received does not match the period covered by the financial year, so it is necessary to:

- deduct that portion of the $280 which falls outside the financial year ($135 was received during this financial year but related to the previous accounting period)
- add the $156 owing at the end of present financial year.

Salman
Nominal ledger
Commission receivable account

Date	Details	Folio	$	Date	Details	Folio	$
20–8				20–8			
Apr 1	Balance	b/d	135	Apr 2	Bank		135
20–9				Oct 1	Bank		145
Mar 31	Income statement		301	20–9			
				Mar 31	Balance	c/d	156
			436				436
20–9							
Apr 1	Balance	b/d	156				

Walkthrough 11.10

Salman's financial year ends on 31 March.

He rents part of his premises to another trader at an annual rent of $1 000, payable quarterly in advance.

On 1 April 20–8 the rent receivable account in Salman's nominal ledger showed a credit balance of $250.

The tenant paid rent of $250 by direct debit on 1 July 20–8 and 2 October 20–8. The rent due on 1 January 20–9 was not received until 2 April 20–9.

Write up the rent receivable account in Salman's nominal ledger for the year ended 31 March 20–9.

Before attempting to answer the question it may be helpful to consider the problem by the use of a diagram.

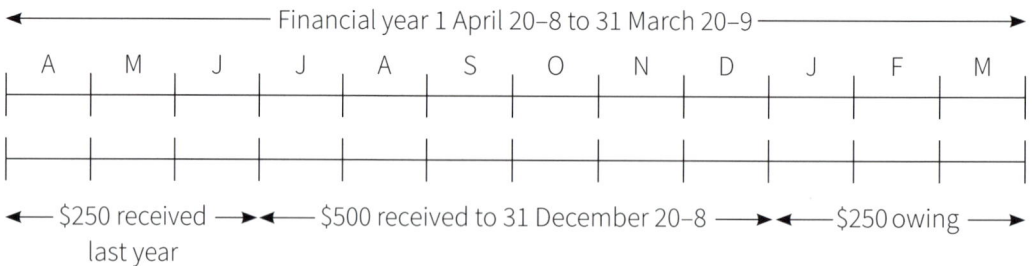

The diagram shows that the income received does not match the period covered by the financial year, so it is necessary to:

- add the $250 due but not received at the end of the financial year
- add the $250 received in the previous financial year as it falls within the present financial year.

Chapter 11: Other payables and other receivables

Salman
Nominal ledger
Rent receivable account

Date	Details	Folio	$	Date	Details	Folio	$
20–8				20–8			
Mar 31	Income statement		1 000	Apr 1	Balance	b/d	250
				Jul 1	Bank		250
				Oct 2	Bank		250
				20–9			
				Mar 31	Balance	c/d	250
			1 000				1 000
20–9							
Apr 1	Balance	b/d	250				

TEST YOURSELF 11.5

1 Whabi & Company's financial year ends on 31 December. They act as agent for another business and receive a commission on goods sold.

   The following information is provided:

   20–6 Jan 1   Commission, $94, was owing to Whabi & Company
         Dec 31 Commission, $1 350, was received
                 Commission, $76, was owing to Whabi & Company
   20–7 Dec 31 Commission, $1 480, was received

   For **each** of the years ended 31 December 20–6 and 31 December 20–7 state:

   a the amount shown for commission receivable in the income statement

   b the amount (if any) shown for commission receivable in the statement of financial position, indicating whether it is a current asset or a current liability.

You can now answer Questions 4–6 at the end of this chapter.

Revision checklist

- The expenses for an accounting period must be matched against the income of that particular period.
- An accrual is an amount due in an accounting period which remains unpaid at the end of that period. A prepayment is an amount that has been paid or received in one accounting period which relates to a future period.
- In the income statement an accrued expense is added to the total paid. The accrued amount is a current liability in the statement of financial position.
- In the income statement a prepaid expense is deducted from the total paid. The prepaid amount is a current asset in the statement of financial position.
- In the income statement accrued income is added to the total received. The accrued amount is a current asset in the statement of financial position.
- In the income statement income received in advance is deducted from the total received. The amount received in advance is a current liability in the statement of financial position.

Exam-style questions

1. Zaid's financial year ends on 31 October. On 1 November 20–6 he owed advertising costs of $40. During the year ended 31 October 20–7 he paid advertising costs of $530. This included $270 for an advertising campaign for six months to 29 February 20–8.

   How much did Zaid charge to the income statement for the year ended 31 October 20–7 for advertising costs?

   A $220   B $260   C $310   D $350

2. Aryani started a fashion boutique on 1 March 20–6. On that date she purchased stationery, $395. During the year she took stationery, $15, for her own use. On 28 February 20–7 the stationery was valued at $174. Which amount was charged to the income statement for the year ended 28 February 20–7 for stationery?

   A $206   B $221   C $236   D $380

3. Nasir's financial year ends of 31 December. On 1 April 20–9 she paid $1800 for one year's insurance on new premises.

   What entry would be made for insurance in the statement of financial positon on 31 December 20–9?

   A $450 asset   B $450 liability   C $1 350 asset   D $1 350 liability

4. William is a trader. His financial year ends on 31 December. He rents business premises. The monthly rent of $1 350, payable in advance on the first day of each month, was increased to $1 380 from 1 July 20–1. William paid six months' rent in advance by direct debit on the following dates in 20–1: 1 January, 1 July and 31 December.

   a i Prepare the rent payable account in William's ledger for the year ended 31 December 20–1.

      Balance the account and bring down the balance on 1 January 20–2.

      ii Prepare a relevant extract from William's statement of financial positon at 31 December 20–1.

   William sublets part of his business premises to a tenant. The monthly rent is $450. The rent receivable account in William's ledger for the year ended 31 December 20–1 was as follows:

William							
Rent receivable account							
Date	Details	Folio	$	Date	Details	Folio	$
20–1				20–1			
Jan 1	Balance	b/d	900	Jan 10	Bank		3 600
Dec 31	Income statement		5 400	Jun 1	Bank		4 050
	Balance	c/d	1 350				
			7 650				7 650
				20–2			
				Jan 1	Balance	b/d	1 350

b **i** Name the ledger in which this account would appear.

  ii Explain each entry in the account.

  iii State where the balance on the account on 31 December 20–1 would appear in the statement of financial positon.

On 1 January 20–1 William had stationery valued at $80. During the year ended 31 December 20–1 the following transactions took place:

February 1 Purchased stationery, $64, and paid in cash.

August 31 Purchased stationery, $18, using petty cash.

William's inventory of stationery on 31 December 20–1 was valued at $75.

c Write up the stationery account in William's ledger for the year ended 31 December 20–1. Balance the account and bring down the balance on 1 January 20–2.

5 Miriam is a business consultant. She provided the following information at the end of her first year on 30 September 20–4.

	$
Office expenses	7 250
Wages	27 500
Insurance	1 800
Rates	800
Motor vehicle expenses	1 840
Fees received from clients	40 900
Commission receivable	5 600

The following information is also available:

1 The office expenses include stationery. On 30 September 20–4 the inventory of stationery was valued at $250.

2 It is estimated that half of the motor vehicle expenses relate to Miriam's personal use.

3 On 30 September 20–4:

   Rates due amounted to $160

   Office expenses due amounted to $45

   Commission receivable outstanding amounted to $250.

4 The insurance covers a period of 15 months to 31 December 20–4.

5 Wages paid in cash, $115, have not been entered in the accounting records.

Prepare Miriam's income statement for the year ended 30 September 20–4.

6 Luc owns a wholesale furniture store. His financial year ends on 30 June. He provided the following trial balance on 30 June 20–1:

	$	$
Revenue		112 650
Purchases	86 270	
Purchases returns		410
Inventory 1 Jul 20–0	7 010	
Premises	80 000	
Fixtures and fittings	19 700	
Trade payables		7 136
Trade receivables	9 175	
Bank	867	
Rent receivable		840
Discount received		170
Insurance	728	
Rates	600	
Wages	25 600	
Office expenses	256	
Capital		101 000
Drawings	2 000	
3% 10 year loan from AB Finance		10 000
	232 206	232 206

Additional information:

1 At 30 June 20–1:

   Inventory was valued at $6 840

   Rent receivable prepaid amounted to $60

   Insurance prepaid amounted to $104

   Rates accrued amounted to $120

   A whole year's interest on the loan is outstanding.

2 During the year ended 30 June 20–1 Luc took goods, $930, for his own use. This was not entered in the accounting records.

Prepare an income statement for the year ended 30 June 20–1 and a statement of financial position on 30 June 20–1.

Chapter 12
Accounting for depreciation and disposal of non-current assets

Learning objectives

In this chapter you will learn to:

- define depreciation   4.2
- explain the reasons for accounting for deprecation   4.2
- name and describe the straight line, reducing balance and revaluation methods of depreciation   4.2
- prepare ledger accounts for the provision of depreciation   4.2
- prepare ledger accounts to record the sale of non-current assets, including the use of disposal accounts   4.2
- make adjustments for provision for depreciation using the straight line, reducing balance and revaluation methods.   5.1

Cambridge IGCSE and O Level Accounting

LINK

You learned about the year-end adjustments for accruals and prepayments in Chapter 11 and will learn about other year-end adjustments in Chapter 13.

KEY TERM

Depreciation is an estimate of the loss in value of a non-current asset over its expected working life.

LINK

You learned about capital expenditure in Chapter 10.

LINK

You learned about the accounting principles of matching, prudence and historic cost in Chapter 10.

TIP

Depreciation is a non-monetary expense as it does not involve an outflow of money, nor does it provide a cash fund to use for the replacement of a non-current asset.

12.1 Introduction

As explained in Chapter 11, it is often necessary to include year-end adjustments in a set of financial statements. This ensures that the accounts provide a more accurate view of the profit or loss of the business and the financial position of the business. This chapter focuses on the year-end adjustments made for depreciation of non-current assets.

Depreciation is an estimate of the loss in value of a non-current asset over its expected working life. Most of the non-current assets of a business lose value over a period of time that they are used by the business. If the accounting records continue to show these assets at their cost prices then the accounts will provide misleading information. It is, therefore, necessary to record an estimate of the loss in value. The records can only show an **estimate** of the loss in value of a non-current asset because of depreciation. The **exact** amount will only be known when the asset is disposed of or sold. Buildings depreciate over time but land does not usually lose value (unless it is something like a well or mine when value is removed from the land).

The purchase of a non-current asset is **capital expenditure.**

The cost of a non-current asset is not charged as an expense in the year of purchase as it benefits the business for several years. **Matching** the capital expenditure against the sales it has helped the business to earn is done by an annual charge for depreciation. **This means that the cost of the non-current asset is spread over the years which benefit from the use of that asset.** The depreciation for the year is included in the expenses in the income statement, so the profit for the year is not overstated. This is an application of the **principle of prudence.** If the profit is overstated, the owner of a business may be tempted to withdraw more cash than the business can actually afford.

The principle of prudence is also applied in the statement of financial position as the non-current assets are recorded at a figure less than the cost price (this is known as the **net book value** or the **written down value**). This overrides the **historic cost principle** as it ensures that the non-current assets are shown at more realistic values.

12.2 Causes of depreciation

The four main causes of depreciation are physical deterioration, economic reasons, passage of time and depletion.

Physical deterioration

This is the result of 'wear and tear' due to the normal usage of the non-current asset. It can also be because the asset falls into a poor physical state due to rust, rot, decay and so on.

Economic reasons

The non-current asset may become inadequate as it can no longer meet the needs of the business. It can also be because the non-current asset has become obsolete as newer and more efficient assets are now available.

Passage of time

This arises where a non-current asset, for example a lease, has a fixed life of a set number of years.

Chapter 12: Accounting for depreciation and disposal of non-current assets

Depletion
This arises in connection with non-current assets such as wells and mines. The worth of the asset reduces as value is taken from the asset.

> **TEST YOURSELF 12.1**
>
> 1 Explain the meaning of depreciation.
> 2 Explain how depreciation is an application of the matching principle.
> 3 List **four** causes of depreciation of non-current assets.

12.3 Methods of calculating depreciation

There are several methods used to calculate the estimated loss in value of a non-current asset. Different types of non-current assets are often depreciated using different methods. The method selected should be the one which spreads the cost of the asset as fairly as possible over the periods which benefit from its use. Once a method has been selected for a particular non-current asset, it should be applied each year. This is an application of the **principle of consistency**.

LINK
You learned about the principle of consistency in Chapter 10.

In practice, many factors are considered before a depreciation method is selected. These are:
- How long is the asset expected to last?
- How much will the asset be sold for when it is put out of use?
- How can the benefits from the use of the asset be measured?

There are three main methods of depreciation:
- Straight line method
- Reducing balance method
- Revaluation method

These are explained below. There are several other methods, but they are outside the scope of the syllabus.

Straight line method of depreciation
This is also known as the **fixed instalment method**.

The formula used for calculating the annual depreciation using this method is:

$$\frac{\text{Cost of asset}}{\text{Number of expected years of use}}$$

This expresses the annual depreciation as an amount of money. The answer to this formula is expressed as a percentage of the total cost.

This method applies the **same amount of depreciation (or the same percentage rate of the cost price) each year**. The value of the asset can fall to nil if there is no residual value (see below).

This method is used where each year is expected to benefit equally from the use of the asset.

KEY TERM

The **straight line method of depreciation** is where the same amount of depreciation is charged each year.

Walkthrough 12.1

Kavita's financial year ends on 30 June.

On 1 July 20–3 she purchased fixtures costing $25 000 and paid by cheque. She estimated that she would be able to use the fixtures for four years.

Calculate the annual depreciation charge:

a as an amount of money

b as a percentage.

a $\dfrac{\$25\,000}{4 \text{ years}} = \$6\,250$

b $\dfrac{\$6\,250}{\$25\,000} = 25\%$

> **KEY TERM**
>
> The **residual value** is the value of a non-current asset at the end of its useful life.

Where it is estimated that the asset will have some value at the end of its working life, this must be included in the calculation. Such a value is known as a **residual value**. The formula then becomes:

$$\dfrac{\text{Cost of asset} - \text{Residual value}}{\text{Number of expected years of use}}$$

Walkthrough 12.2

Kavita's financial year ends on 30 June.

On 1 July 20–3 she purchased fixtures costing $25 000 and paid by cheque. She estimated that she would be able to use the fixtures for four years and then be able to sell them for $3 000.

Calculate the annual depreciation charge:

a as an amount of money

b as a percentage (based on the original cost).

a $\dfrac{\$25\,000 - \$3\,000}{4 \text{ years}} = \$5\,500$

b $\dfrac{\$5\,500}{\$25\,000} \times \dfrac{100}{1} = 22\%$

> **TIP**
>
> Advantages of the straight line method of deprecation.
> 1 It is relatively easy to calculate.
> 2 It is useful when a non-current asset provides equal benefit for each year of its useful life.
>
> Disadvantages of the straight line method of depreciation.
> 1 It is necessary to estimate the useful life and the residual value of the non-current asset.
> 2 It ignores the actual rate at which the non-current asset will lose value.

Chapter 12: Accounting for depreciation and disposal of non-current assets

Reducing balance method of depreciation

As the name implies, the amount of depreciation reduces each year. **The same percentage rate is applied, but it is calculated on a different value each year.** At the end of the first year the depreciation for that year is calculated on the cost of the asset. The depreciation for the following year is calculated (using the same percentage) on the cost of the asset less the depreciation previously written off. The figure of cost less depreciation is known as the **net book value** (or **written down value**) of the asset.

The value of the asset can never fall to nil as the depreciation is always calculated as a percentage of the net book value.

This method is used where the greater benefits from the use of the asset will be gained in the early years of its life. Assets depreciated by this method often have lower maintenance costs in the early years. This method is often used for those assets which quickly become out of data because of advancing technological progress.

Any residual value is taken into consideration when the percentage rate is selected.

> **KEY TERMS**
>
> The **reducing balance method of depreciation** is where the depreciation charged each year decreases as it is calculated on the net book value rather than the cost.
>
> The **net book value** of a non-current asset is the cost price minus the total depreciation to date.

Walkthrough 12.3

Kavita's financial year ends on 30 June.

On 1 July 20–3 she purchased fixtures costing $25 000 and paid by cheque. She estimated that she would be able to use the fixtures for four years and then be able to sell them for $3 000.

Calculate the depreciation for **each** of the four years of the fixtures' working life using the reducing balance method at the rate of 40% per annum.

	$
Cost	25 000
Depreciation for year ended 30 June 20–4 at 40%	10 000
Book value at 1 July 20–4	15 000
Depreciation for year ended 30 June 20–5 at 40%	6 000
Book value at 1 July 20–5	9 000
Depreciation for year ended 30 June 20–6 at 40%	3 600
Book value at 1 July 20–6	5 400
Deprecation for year ended 30 June 20–7 at 40%	2 160
Book value at 1 July 20–7	3 240

TIP

Depreciation is always expressed in units of whole dollars so it may be necessary to adjust a figure to eliminate any cents.

TIP

Advantages of the reducing balance method of deprecation.
1. It matches costs with revenue.
2. It is useful for those non-current assets where greater benefits are gained in the early years of usage.

Disadvantages of the reducing balance method of deprecation.
1. The depreciation has to be recalculated each year.
2. The depreciation charge against profit is greater in the early years of the non-current asset's life.

You can now answer Questions 1 and 2 at the end of this chapter.

KEY TERM

The **revaluation method of depreciation** is where the opening and closing value of a non-current asset are compared (after adjusting for any additions during the year) to determine the depreciation for the year.

Revaluation method of depreciation

This method is used where it is not practical, or it is difficult, to keep detailed records of certain types of non-current assets. If detailed records are not available then the straight line and the reducing balance methods of depreciation cannot be calculated. Small items of equipment used in offices and laboratories, packing cases, loose tools, etc. are usually depreciated using the revaluation method as no detailed records are kept for these assets.

The assets are valued at the end of each financial year. This value is compared with the value at the end of the previous financial year (or with the cost if it is the first year of ownership). **The amount by which the value of the asset has fallen is the depreciation for the year.**

Walkthrough 12.4

Kavita's financial year ends on 30 June.

On 1 July 20–3 she purchased fixtures costing $25 000 and paid by cheque. She decided to revalue the fixtures at the end of each year.

On 30 June 20–4 the fixtures were valued at $20 500.

Calculate the depreciation for the year ended 30 June 20–4.

	$
Cost of fixtures on 1 July 20–3	25 000
Value of fixtures on 30 June 20–4	20 500
Depreciation for the year ended 30 June 20–4	4 500

TIP

Advantages of the revaluation method of deprecation.
1 It is not necessary to estimate the useful life and the residual value of the non-current asset.
2 No complex calculations are required.

Disadvantages of the revaluation method of depreciation.
1 The non-current asset has to be revalued at the end of each year.
2 The valuation may be based on personal opinion.

TEST YOURSELF 12.2

1 Explain the straight line method of depreciation.
2 Explain how, using the reducing balance method, the **amount** of depreciation decreases each year even though the same **percentage rate** is applied.
3 State when the revaluation method is used to depreciate non-current assets.

You can now answer Question 3 at the end of this chapter.

12.4 Recording depreciation in the ledger

Recording depreciation using the straight line method and the reducing balance method

The procedure for entering depreciation calculated using the straight line method and the reducing balance method is exactly the same.

Each type of non-current asset has two ledger accounts:

- an account for recording the cost of the asset (the asset account)
- an account for recording the depreciation (the provision for depreciation of asset account).

The asset account always has a debit balance and the provision for depreciation always has a credit balance. These two accounts must always be considered together. The difference between the balances of these accounts represents the net book value of the asset.

The entries are summarised as follows:

During the year – when the asset is purchased

debit the asset account and credit either the cash book or the supplier's account with the cost price.

At the year-end – debit the income statement and credit the provision for depreciation account with the depreciation for the year

balance the provision for depreciation account and carry down as a credit balance

balance the asset account if there have been any transactions during the year and carry down as a debit balance.

Walkthrough 12.5

Kavita's financial year ends on 30 June.

On 1 July 20–3 she purchased fixtures costing $25 000 and paid by cheque. She estimated that she would be able to use the fixtures for four years and then be able to sell them for $3 000.

Kavita decided to use the reducing balance method of depreciation at 40% per annum.

Make the entries in Kavita's nominal ledger accounts for **each** of the years ended 30 June 20–4, 20–5, 20–6 and 20–7.

Kavita

Nominal ledger

Fixtures account

Date	Details	Folio	$	Date	Details	Folio	$
20–3							
Jul 1	Bank		25 000				

Provision for depreciation of fixtures account

Date	Details	Folio	$	Date	Details	Folio	$
20–4				20–4			
Jun 30	Balance	c/d	10 000	Jun 30	Income statement		10 000
			10 000				10 000
20–5				20–4			
Jun 30	Balance	c/d	16 000	Jul 1	Balance	b/d	10 000
				20–5			
				Jun 30	Income statement		6 000
			16 000				16 000
20–6				20–5			
Jun 30	Balance	c/d	19 600	Jul 1	Balance	b/d	16 000
				20–6			
				June 30	Income statement		3 600
			19 600				19 600
20–7				20–6			
Jun 30	Balance	c/d	21 760	Jul 1	Balance	b/d	19 600
				20–7			
				June 30	Income statement		2 160
			21 760				21 760
				20–7			
				Jul 1	Balance	b/d	21 760

- The asset account was not balanced at the end of each year as there is only one entry in the account.
- Before the transfer to the income statement can be made each year it is necessary to calculate the depreciation for the year. The calculations have been shown in **Walkthrough 12.3**.
- The difference between the balance on the asset account and the balance on the provision for depreciation account on the same date represents the net book value of the fixtures on that date.
- If the straight line method of depreciation had been selected the entry in the fixtures account would be exactly the same.
- If the straight line method of depreciation had been selected the entries in the provision for depreciation of fixtures account would be very similar. The transfer to the income statement would be $5 500 each year, so the totals and balances on the account would differ to those shown earlier.

Chapter 12: Accounting for depreciation and disposal of non-current assets

> **TEST YOURSELF 12.3**
>
> 1 Referring to **Walkthrough 12.5**:
>   a state the total amount of depreciation up to 30 June 20–6
>   b state the net book value of the fixtures on 30 June 20–7.
> 2 Explain why the asset account and the provision for depreciation account of that asset should both be referred to when the asset is being considered.

Where a non-current asset is purchased **during** the financial year, a business may decide to charge depreciation from the date of purchase. This means that in the first year of ownership only a proportion of the annual depreciation will be charged to the income statement.

Walkthrough 12.6

Kavita's financial year ends on 30 June.

On 1 July 20–4 she purchased a motor vehicle costing $9 000 and paid by credit transfer. On 1 April 20–5 an additional motor vehicle costing $8 000 was purchased and paid for by credit transfer.

She decided to use the straight line method of deprecation at 20% per annum, depreciation to be calculated from the date of purchase.

Make the entries in Kavita's nominal ledger accounts for the year ended 30 June 20–5.

Kavita
Nominal ledger
Motor vehicles account

Date	Details	Folio	$	Date	Details	Folio	$
20–4				20–5			
Jul 1	Bank (A)		9 000	Jun 30	Balance	c/d	17 000
20–5							
Apr 1	Bank (B)		8 000				
			17 000				17 000
20–5							
Jul 1	Balance	b/d	17 000				

Provision for depreciation of motor vehicles account

Date	Details	Folio	$	Date	Details	Folio	$
20–5				20–5			
Jun 30	Balance	c/d	2 200	Jun 30	Income statement		
					(A) 1 800		
					(B) 400		2 200
			2 200				2 200
				20–5			
				Jul 1	Balance	b/d	2 200

Sometimes a business may decide to ignore the date of purchase when calculating depreciation. This means that a whole year's depreciation will be charged on all the assets held at the end of the financial year.

Recording depreciation using the revaluation method

The cost of the asset and the depreciation are recorded in the same account.

The entries are summarised as follows:

During the year – when the asset is purchased

debit the asset account and credit either the cash book or the supplier's account with the cost price.

At the year-end – credit the asset account with the value of the asset at that date and carry down as a debit balance

transfer the difference on the account to the income statement as this is the depreciation for the year.

Walkthrough 12.7

Kavita's financial year ends on 30 June.

On 1 July 20–3 she purchased fixtures costing $25 000 and paid by cheque. She decided to revalue the fixtures at the end of each year.

On 30 June 20–4 the fixtures were valued at $20 500.

Make the entries in the fixtures account in the nominal ledger for the year ended 30 June 20–4.

Kavita

Nominal ledger

Fixtures account

Date	Details	Folio	$	Date	Details	Folio	$
20–3				20–4			
Jul 1	Bank		25 000	Jun 30	Balance	c/d	20 500
					Income statement		4 500
			25 000				25 000
20–4							
Jul 1	Balance	b/d	20 500				

12.5 Recording depreciation in the financial statements

Recording depreciation in the income statement

The depreciation for the year for each type of asset is credited to the provision for depreciation account in the nominal ledger and is debited to the income statement. This reduces the business's profit for the year. As depreciation is a non-monetary expense, it is usually shown after the monetary expenses in the income statement.

If the business is a manufacturing business, depreciation of assets used in the manufacturing process will be debited to the manufacturing account rather than the income statement. This increases the cost of manufacturing which, in turn, reduces the profit for the year.

> **LINK**
>
> You will learn about preparing manufacturing accounts in Chapter 20.

Recording depreciation in the statement of financial position

It is usual to show the total cost of each type of non-current asset less the total depreciation written off up to the date of the statement of financial position (referred to as **accumulated depreciation** or **depreciation to date**). The difference between these figures is the net book value.

Walkthrough 12.8

Kavita's financial year ends on 30 June.

On 1 July 20–3 she purchased fixtures costing $25 000 and paid by cheque. She estimated that she would be able to use the fixtures for four years and then be able to sell them for $3 000.

Kavita decided to use the reducing balance method of depreciation at 40% per annum.

a Prepare a relevant extract from Kavita's income statement for **each** of the years ended 30 June 20–4 and 30 June 20–5.

b Prepare a relevant extract from Kavita's statement of financial position at 30 June 20–4 and at 30 June 20–5.

a

Kavita
Extract from income statement for the year ended 30 June 20–4

	$
Expenses – Depreciation of fixtures	10 000

Kavita
Extract from income statement for the year ended 30 June 20–5

	$
Expenses – Depreciation of fixtures	6 000

b

Kavita
Extract from statement of financial position at 30 June 20–4

Non-current assets	$ Cost	$ Accumulated depreciation	$ Net book value
Fixtures	25 000	10 000	15 000

Kavita
Extract from statement of financial position at 30 June 20–5

Non-current assets	$ Cost	$ Accumulated depreciation	$ Net book value
Fixtures	25 000	16 000	9 000

The financial statements are prepared from a trial balance and its accompanying notes. In the trial balance, the balances on the asset accounts are shown in the debit column and the balances on the provision for depreciation accounts are shown in the credit column. One of the notes will indicate the depreciation to be charged for the current financial year.

The depreciation for the year will appear twice in the financial statements: It is an expense in the income statement, and it is included in the statement of financial position as part of the provision for depreciation (the depreciation for the year is added to the balance shown in the trial balance).

> **LINK**
> You learned how to prepare financial statements in Chapters 8 and 9.

Walkthrough 12.9

Kavita's financial year ends on 30 June.

She depreciates her fixtures using the reducing balance method of depreciation at 40% per annum.

Her trial balance drawn up on 30 June 20–6 included the following:

	Dr $	Cr $
Fixtures	25 000	
Provision for depreciation of fixtures		16 000

a Prepare a relevant extract from Kavita's income statement for the year ended 30 June 20–6.

b Prepare a relevant extract from Kavita's statement of financial position at 30 June 20–6.

a

Kavita
Extract from income statement for the year ended 30 June 20–6

	$
Expenses – Depreciation of fixtures	3 600

b

Kavita
Extract from statement of financial position at 30 June 20–6

Non-current assets	$ Cost	$ Accumulated depreciation	$ Net book value
Fixtures	25 000	19 600	5 400

> **TIP**
> An income statement includes the depreciation of non-current assets for that particular year. A statement of financial position includes the cost and the accumulated depreciation to date of non-current assets.

- The deprecation relating to the current financial year is included as an expense in the income statement.
- In the statement of financial position the total depreciation up to that date ($16 000 shown in the trial balance plus the depreciation for the year of $3 600) are deducted from the cost price of the asset.

> **TEST YOURSELF 12.4**
>
> 1. Explain why depreciation is a non-monetary expense.
> 2. Referring to **Walkthrough 12.9**, explain why the figure of $16 000 provision for depreciation does not actually appear in the financial statements.

You can now answer Question 4 at the end of this chapter.

12.6 Disposal of non-current assets

Because the purchase of a non-current asset is **capital expenditure** it is recorded in an account for the non-current asset rather than in the purchases account. When a non-current asset is sold it is a **capital receipt** and is recorded in a special account known as a **disposal of non-current asset account** rather than in the sales account.

When a non-current asset is sold or disposed of, it must be removed from the ledger records. The cost of the asset and the depreciation on the asset are removed from the asset account and the provision for depreciation account and transferred to a disposal account. The proceeds of sale are also entered in this account. It is quite likely that this account will not balance. This is because the depreciation was only an estimate of the loss in value. Only when the asset is sold can the actual loss in value be calculated. The difference on the disposal account represents either a loss on disposal (when the actual depreciation proved to be more than the estimate) or a profit on disposal (when the actual depreciation proved to be less than the estimate).

The entries are summarised as follows.

On the date of sale – credit the asset account and debit the disposal of non-current asset account with the original cost price (of the asset being sold)

debit the provision for depreciation account and credit the disposal of non-current asset account with the total depreciation charged (on the asset being sold)

credit the disposal of non-current asset account and debit either the cash book or the debtor's account with the proceeds of sale.

At the year-end – transfer any difference on the disposal of non-current asset account to the income statement.

Walkthrough 12.10

Kavita's financial year ends on 30 June.

On 1 July 20–3 she purchased fixtures costing $25 000 and paid by cheque. She decided to depreciate the fixtures using the reducing balance method.

On 1 July 20–7 the provision for depreciation of fixtures account showed a credit balance of $21 760.

Kavita sold all the fixtures on credit to Traders Ltd for $3 100 on 1 July 20–7.

Make the entries in Kavita's nominal ledger accounts for the year ended 30 June 20–8.

Kavita
Nominal ledger
Fixtures account

Date	Details	Folio	$	Date	Details	Folio	$
20–3				20–7			
Jul 1	Bank		25 000	Jul 1	Disposal		25 000
			25 000				25 000

Provision for depreciation of fixtures account

Date	Details	Folio	$	Date	Details	Folio	$
20–7				20–7			
Jul 1	Disposal		21 760	Jul 1	Balance	b/d	21 760
			21 760				21 760

Disposal of fixtures account

Date	Details	Folio	$	Date	Details	Folio	$
20–7				20–7			
Jul 1	Fixtures		25 000	Jul 1	Provision for depreciation		21 760
					Traders Ltd		3 100
				20–8			
				Jun 30	Income statement		140
			25 000				25 000

- The difference on the disposal account remains in that account until the end of the financial year when it is transferred to the income statement.
- In this case the depreciation had been under-provided so there was a small loss of $140 to transfer to the income statement.
- If the total of the credit side of the account had exceeded the debit side, there would have been an over-provision of depreciation. The transfer to the income statement would have been shown on the debit of this account and on the credit of the income statement.

Chapter 12: Accounting for depreciation and disposal of non-current assets

If only some of the assets of a particular type are being sold, it is important that only the entries relating to the assets being sold are removed from the ledger records.

Businesses may operate different policies in relation to depreciation where an asset is sold or disposed of part-way through the year. Some ignore depreciation in the year of sale; others charge depreciation up to the date of disposal of the asset. Once a method has been selected it should be employed **consistently**.

You can now answer Questions 5 and 6 at the end of this chapter.

Revision checklist

- Depreciation is an estimate of the loss in value of a non-current asset over its expected working life.
- The main causes of depreciation are physical deterioration, economic reasons, passage of time and depletion.
- The three main methods of calculating depreciation are straight line, reducing balance and revaluation.
- Depreciation is shown as an expense in the income statement.
- In the statement of financial position the total depreciation to date is deducted from the cost of the asset.
- When a non-current asset is sold it is removed from the ledger records by transfer to a disposal of non-current asset account.

Exam-style questions

1 Halima's financial year ends on 31 October. She depreciates her motor vehicles using the reducing balance method at 20% per annum. On 1 November 20–6 she bought a motor vehicle for $14 200. What was the charge for depreciation for the year ended 31 October 20–8?

   A $2 272   **B** $2 840   **C** $5 110   **D** $5 680

2 Salim purchased machinery for $15 000 on 1 January 20–1. He decided to depreciate it using the straight line method at 10% per annum. On 31 December 20–2 he incorrectly charged depreciation using the reducing balance method at 10% per annum.

What was the effect on the profit for the year ended 31 December 20–2?

   A overstated by $150   **B** understated by $150
   C overstated by $1 350   **D** understated by $1 350

3 Zareb started a business on 1 April 20–4. He decided to use the revaluation method to calculate the depreciation on his fixtures and fittings.

Fixtures and fittings, $9 800 were purchased on 1 April 20–4 which Zareb expected to have a useful life of four years. Additional fixtures and fittings, $1 200, were purchased during the year. On 31 March 20–5 Zareb valued his fixtures and fittings at $8 700.

What was the depreciation charge for the year ended 31 March 20–5?

   A $1 100   **B** $2 300   **C** $2 450   **D** $2 750

4 Elsa's financial year ends on 31 March. She depreciates her office equipment at 20% per annum on cost. Depreciation is calculated from the date of purchase.

On 1 April the balances in Elsa's books included the following:

	$
Office equipment	2 500
Provision for depreciation of office equipment	750

She purchased additional office equipment by cheque on the following dates:

	$
31 August 20–4	1 200
1 December 20–4	900

   a Write up the office equipment account and the provision for depreciation of office equipment account for the year ended 31 March 20–5. Balance the accounts and bring down the balances on 1 April 20–5.

   b Prepare a relevant extract from Elsa's income statement for the year ended 31 March 20–5.

   c Prepare a relevant extract from Elsa's statement of financial position at 31 March 20–5.

5 Beketele started a business on 1 July 20–6. On that date she made the following payments.

	$
Premises	215 000
Legal costs relating to purchase of premises	2 150
Motor vehicle	9 800
Delivery costs of motor vehicle	200
Fuel for motor vehicle	50
Insurance of motor vehicle	495

a State whether each of these payments is capital expenditure or revenue expenditure.

Beketele decided to depreciate the motor vehicle by 20% per annum using the straight line method.

b Calculate the accumulated depreciation on the motor vehicle on 1 July 20–8.

On 1 July 20–8 Beketele decided that the motor vehicle was no longer suitable and sold it for $5 600 which was received in cash.

d Complete the following table to show the debit and credit entries Beketele would make to record the disposal of the motor vehicle.

		Account debited $	Account credited $
i	transfer of original cost from motor vehicle account		
ii	transfer of accumulated depreciation from provision for depreciation account		
iii	receipt of the proceeds from the sale of motor vehicle		

6 Tebogo owns an advertising agency. His financial year ends on 31 May. He provided the following information for the year ended 31 May 20–1:

	$
Fees received from clients	37 130
Office expenses	9 435
Rates	2 125
Wages of assistant	19 500
Rent received from tenant	2 300
Cash drawings	9 000

The following additional information is also available:
1 On 31 May 20–1 fees due from clients amounted to $1 030.
2 The rent received includes $200 which was accrued on 1 June 20–0 and $300 which was prepaid for the year ending 31 May 20–2.
3 The wages paid included $180 which was accrued on 1 June 20–0. On 31 May 20–1 wages accrued amounted to $210.

4 Office equipment was sold on 1 September 20–0 for $2 200. This had cost $3 650 and had been deprecated by $1 560 at the date of sale.

5 New office equipment, $4 200, was purchased on 1 September 20–0. This is to be depreciated at the rate of 20% per annum from the date of purchase.

6 On 1 June 20–0 Tebogo's capital was $82 000.

a Prepare Tebogo's income statement for the year ended 31 May 20–1.

b Prepare Tebogo's capital account for the year ended 31 May 20–1. Balance the account and bring down the balance on 1 June 20–1.

Chapter 13
Irrecoverable debts and provisions for doubtful debts

Learning objectives

In this chapter you will learn to:

- understand the meaning of irrecoverable debts and recovery of debts written off   4.4
- prepare ledger accounts to record irrecoverable debts   4.4
- prepare ledger accounts to record recovery of debts written off   4.4
- explain the reasons for maintaining a provision for doubtful debts   4.4
- prepare ledger accounts to record the creation of, and adjustments to, a provision for doubtful debts   4.4
- make adjustments for irrecoverable debts and provisions for doubtful debts.   5.1

> **KEY TERMS**
>
> An **irrecoverable debt** is an amount owing to a business which will not be paid by the credit customer.
>
> A **debt written off** may be recovered if a credit customer pays some, or all, the amount owed, after the amount was written off.

>  **LINK**
>
> You learned about the principle of prudence in Chapter 10.

13.1 Introduction

When goods are sold on credit the customer is allowed to pay for the goods at a later date. There is always a risk that the customer may not pay for those goods. **An irrecoverable debt is an amount owing to a business which will not be paid by the credit customer.** This may be because the customer has disappeared, has gone out of business or because he is unable to pay.

If all reasonable steps to obtain payment have failed the debt is **written off**.

The account of the customer is closed by transferring the amount written off to the irrecoverable debts account. At the end of the year, the total of the irrecoverable debts account is transferred to the income statement where it is regarded as an expense for the year.

The entries are summarised as follows:

When the debt is written off – credit the customer's account and debit the irrecoverable debts account.

At the year-end – credit the irrecoverable debts account and debit the income statement.

Writing off irrecoverable debts is an example of the application of the principle of **prudence**. If a debt cannot be regarded as an asset it is written off so that the assets are not overstated. The amount of the irrecoverable debt is regarded as a loss for the year so must be included in the income statement otherwise the profit for the year will be overstated.

You can now answer Question 1 at the end of this chapter.

13.2 Recovery of debts written off

A debt written off may be recovered if a credit customer pays some, or all, of the amount owed, after the amount was written off.

As the account of the customer has been closed, the amount received is debited in the cash book and credited to a debts recovered account. An alternative method is to reinstate the debt by crediting the debts recovered account and debiting the customer with the amount previously written off. The amount received would then be entered by debiting the cash book and crediting the customer. The advantage of this method is that all the transactions relating to that customer appear in their account.

The entries are summarised as follows:

When the amount is received – debit the cash book and credit the debts recovered account

or debit the cash book and credit the customer, debit the customer and credit debts recovered account

At the year-end – debit the debts recovered account and credit the income statement

or credit the irrecoverable debts account.

> **TIP**
>
> At the end of the year the total of the debts recovered account can either be transferred to the income statement (as income for the year) or transferred to the credit of the irrecoverable debts account (where it reduces the debts written off during the year).

Chapter 13: Irrecoverable debts and provisions for doubtful debts

Walkthrough 13.1

Sachin is a trader who sells goods on credit. He offers customers a cash discount of 2% if accounts are paid within 30 days.

Sachin's financial year ends on 31 December.

Sachin sold goods, $400, on credit to Bhuvan's Stores on 1 February 20–2. The account was settled by cheque on 28 February 20–2. On this date Bhuvan's Stores purchased further goods, $150, on credit. After many attempts to recover the amount due, Sachin wrote off Bhuvan's Stores account as an irrecoverable debt on 30 December 20–2.

Sachin received a cheque from Bhuvan's Stores for $150 on 31 October 20–3.

During the year ended 31 December 20–3 Sachin wrote off irrecoverable debts totalling $820.

Write up the following accounts in Sachin's ledgers for **each** of the years ended 31 December 20–2 and 20–3 – Bhuvan's Stores account, irrecoverable debts account and debts recovered account.

Sachin
Sales ledger
Bhuvan's Stores account

Date	Details	Folio	$	Date	Details	Folio	$
20–2				20–2			
Feb 1	Sales		400	Feb 28	Bank		392
28	Sales		150		Discount		8
				Dec 30	Irrecoverable debts		150
			550				550

Nominal ledger
Irrecoverable debts account

Date	Details	Folio	$	Date	Details	Folio	$
20–2				20–2			
Dec 30	Bhuvan's Stores		150	Dec 31	Income statement		150
			150				150
20–3				20–3			
Dec 31	Debtors written off		820	Dec 31	Income statement		820
			820				820

Debts recovered account							
Date	Details	Folio	$	Date	Details	Folio	$
20–3				20–3			
Dec 31	Income statement		150	Oct 31	Bank (Bhuvan's Stores)		150
			150				150

- The words 'debtors written off' have been used as no individual names, dates and amounts details have been provided.
- Alternatively, the debt could have been reinstated by debiting Bhuvan's Stores account and crediting debts recovered. The cheque would then be debited to the bank and credited to Bhuvan's Stores account.
- Alternatively, the debts recovered account could have been transferred to the credit of the irrecoverable debts account. This would result in $670 being transferred from irrecoverable debts to the income statement on 31 December 20–3.

13.3 Reducing the possibility of irrecoverable debts

The only certain way of avoiding irrecoverable debts is not to sell goods on credit. In practice, this is not always an option. All possible steps must be taken to avoid irrecoverable debts. Before allowing credit to a new customer, credit references should be obtained – one from the customer's bank and one from a present or previous supplier. A credit limit is usually fixed for each customer, which places an upper limit on the amount the customer can owe at any one time (this credit limit can be reviewed periodically). The establishing of a credit limit and the later monitoring of the customer's account is known as **credit control**.

Invoices and month-end statements of account should be issued promptly. The sales ledger accounts should be carefully monitored. Any overdue accounts should be investigated and the customers contacted by letters, emails and telephone calls if necessary. No further goods should be supplied until the amount due is paid. A more extreme measure involves taking legal action against the customer, but sometimes the amount of the debt is too small to justify costly legal proceedings.

Some businesses may make use of factoring and invoice discounting, but these are outside the scope of the syllabus.

> **TEST YOURSELF 13.1**
>
> 1 Explain how writing off irrecoverable debts is an application of the principle of prudence.
> 2 List **three** ways in which the possibility of irrecoverable debts may be reduced.

13.4 Provision for doubtful debts

A provision for doubtful debts is an estimate of the amount which a business will lose in a financial year because of irrecoverable debts.

Chapter 13: Irrecoverable debts and provisions for doubtful debts

At the end of their financial year, many businesses try to anticipate the amount which will be lost because of irrecoverable debts. This ensures that the profit for the year is not overstated and the amount of trade receivables in the statement of financial position is shown at a realistic level. This is an application of the principle of **prudence**. By maintaining a **provision for doubtful debts**, a business also observes the principle of **matching**. The amount of sales for which the business is unlikely to be paid is regarded as an expense of the year in which those sales are made (rather than an expense of the year in which the debt is actually written off).

In order to make a provision for doubtful debts, it is necessary to estimate the amount of irrecoverable debts. The amount of the provision may be established by:

- looking at each individual credit customer's account and estimating which ones will not be paid
- estimating, on the basis of past experience, the percentage of the total amount owing by credit customers that will not be paid
- considering the length of time debts have been outstanding by means of an ageing schedule. A provision of a higher percentage may be made on older debts (the longer a debt is outstanding the greater the risk it may become irrecoverable).

> **KEY TERM**
>
> A **provision for doubtful debts** is an estimate of the amount which a business will lose in a financial year because of irrecoverable debts.

> **LINK**
>
> You learned about the principles of prudence and matching in Chapter 10.

> **TEST YOURSELF 13.2**
>
> 1 Explain the meaning of a provision for doubtful debts.
> 2 Explain how maintaining a provision for doubtful debts is an application of both the principle of matching and the principle of prudence.

You can now answer Questions 2 and 3 at the end of this chapter.

13.5 Creating a provision for doubtful debts

Once it is decided to create a provision for doubtful debts and the amount or percentage has been decided, this can be recorded in the books. These entries are made at the end of the financial year.

The entries are summarised as follows:

- Debit the income statement and credit the provision for doubtful debts account.
- In the statement of financial position deduct the balance on the provision for doubtful debts account from the trade receivables.

> **Walkthrough 13.2**
>
> Sachin's financial year ends on 31 December.
>
> During the year ended 31 December 20–4 he wrote off irrecoverable debts totalling $950.
>
> On 31 December his trade receivables amounted to $25 000. He decided to create a provision for doubtful debts of 4% of the trade receivables.
>
> a Write up the irrecoverable debts account and the provision for doubtful debts account in Sachin's nominal ledger for the year ended 31 December 20–4.
> b Prepare a relevant extract from Sachin's income statement for the year ended 31 December 20–4.

c Prepare a relevant extract from Sachin's statement of financial position at 31 December 20–4.

a

Sachin

Nominal ledger

Irrecoverable debts account

Date	Details	Folio	$	Date	Details	Folio	$
20–4				20–4			
Dec 31	Debtors written off		950	Dec 31	Income statement		950
			950				950

Provision for doubtful debts account

Date	Details	Folio	$	Date	Details	Folio	$
				20–4			
				Dec 31	Income statement		1 000

- The words 'debtors written off' have been used in the irrecoverable debts account as no individual names, dates and amounts have been provided.
- The provision has been calculated at 4% of $25 000.

b

Sachin

Extract from income statement for the year ended 31 December 20–4

	$
Expenses – Irrecoverable debts	950
Provision for doubtful debts	1 000

c

Sachin

Extract from statement of financial position at 31 December 20–4

	$	$
Current assets		
Trade receivables	25 000	
Less Provision for doubtful debts	1 000	24 000

- Only the amount which is actually expected to be received from the trade receivables is added to the other current assets in the statement of financial position.

13.6 Adjusting a provision for doubtful debts

In future years it may be decided to maintain the provision for doubtful debts using the same percentage of the trade receivables. If the amount owing has increased, the provision needs to be increased and vice versa. If the original provision for doubtful debts was based on an amount of money rather than a percentage, it may be decided that this amount needs to be changed. This adjustment to the provision for doubtful debts is made at the end of the financial year.

The entries are summarised as follows:

- Debit the provision for doubtful debts account with the **new** provision and carry down as a credit balance.
- Transfer the difference on the provision for doubtful debts account to the income statement.
- In the statement of financial position deduct the balance on the provision for doubtful debts account (the **new** provision) from the trade receivables.

Walkthrough 13.3

Increasing a provision for doubtful debts

Sachin's financial year ends on 31 December.

On 31 December 20–4 Sachin created a provision for doubtful debts of $1 000.

During the year ended 31 December 20–5 Sachin wrote off debts totalling $990.

On 31 December 20–5 his trade receivables amounted to $28 000. He decided to maintain the provision for doubtful debts at the rate of 4% of the trade receivables.

a Write up the irrecoverable debts account and the provision for doubtful debts account in Sachin's nominal ledger for the year ended 31 December 20–5.

b Prepare a relevant extract from Sachin's income statement for the year ended 31 December 20–5.

c Prepare a relevant extract from Sachin's statement of financial position at 31 December 20–5.

a

Sachin
Nominal ledger
Irrecoverable debts account

Date	Details	Folio	$	Date	Details	Folio	$
20–5				20–5			
Dec 31	Debtors written off		990	Dec 31	Income statement		990
			990				990

Provision for doubtful debts account								
Date	Details	Folio	$	Date	Details	Folio	$
20–5				20–4			
Dec 31	Balance statement	c/d	1 120	Dec 31	Income statement		1 000*
				20–5			
				Dec 31	Income statement		120
			1 120				1 120
				20–6			
				Jan 1	Balance	b/d	1 120

- The words 'debtors written off' have been used in the irrecoverable debts account as no individual names, dates and amounts have been provided.
- The item indicated with * was entered in the account on 31 December 20–4 at the end of the previous financial year.
- The new provision has been calculated at 4% of $28 000.

b

Sachin
Extract from income statement for the year ended 31 December 20–5

	$
Expenses – Irrecoverable debts	990
Provision for doubtful debts	120

- Only the amount by which the provision needs to be increased is included in the expenses in the income statement.

c

Sachin
Extract from statement of financial position at 31 December 20–5

	$	$
Current assets		
Trade receivables	28 000	
Less Provision for doubtful debts	1 120	26 880

- The amount of the provision for doubtful debts at 31 December 20–5 (the balance on the provision account) is deducted from the trade receivables to show the amount expected to be received.

> **TIP**
> When a provision for doubtful debts is created, the total amount is entered in the income statement. In later years, only the amount by which the provision increases or decreases is entered in the income statement.

Chapter 13: Irrecoverable debts and provisions for doubtful debts

Walkthrough 13.4
Reducing a provision for doubtful debts

Sachin's financial year ends on 31 December.

On 31 December 20–5 Sachin's provision for doubtful debts amounted to $1 120.

On 31 December 20–6 his trade receivables amounted to $24 000. He decided to maintain the provision for doubtful debts at the rate of 4% of the trade receivables.

a Write up the provision for doubtful debts account in Sachin's nominal ledger for the year ended 31 December 20–6.

b Prepare a relevant extract from Sachin's income statement for the year ended 31 December 20–6.

c Prepare a relevant extract from Sachin's statement of financial position at 31 December 20–6.

a

Sachin
Nominal ledger
Provision for doubtful debts account

Date	Details	Folio	$	Date	Details	Folio	$
20–6				20–6			
Dec 31	Income statement		160	Jan 1	Balance	b/d	1 120
	Balance	c/d	960				
			1 120				1 120
				20–7			
				Jan 1	Balance	b/d	960

- The new provision has been calculated at 4% of $24 000.

b

Sachin
Extract from income statement for the year ended 31 December 20–6

	$
Gross profit	XXX
Add Reduction in provision for doubtful debts	160

- The surplus provision is added to the gross profit in the income statement.
- Any irrecoverable debts would be included in the expenses in the income statement in the usual way.

TIP
In the statement of financial position the total amount of the provision for doubtful debts at that date is deducted from the trade receivables.

c

Sachin
Extract from statement of financial position at 31 December 20–6

	$	$
Current assets		
Trade receivables	24 000	
Less Provision for doubtful debts	960	23 040

- The amount of the provision for doubtful debts at 31 December 20–6 (the balance on the provision account) is deducted from the trade receivables to show the amount expected to be received.

You can now answer Questions 4–6 at the end of this chapter.

Revision checklist

- An irrecoverable debt is an amount owing to a business which will not be paid by a credit customer. Irrecoverable debts are shown as an expense in the income statement.
- A debt written off may later be recovered when a credit customer pays some, or all, of the debt. Debts recovered are added to the gross profit in the income statement.
- A provision for doubtful debts is an estimate of the amount which a business will lose in a financial year because of irrecoverable debts.
- The amount required to create or increase a provision for doubtful debts is shown as an expense in the income statement. Any surplus provision is added to the gross profit in the income statement.
- The provision for doubtful debts is deducted from the trade receivables in the statement of financial position.

Exam-style questions

1. At the end of his financial year Kahili wrote off a debt owed by a credit customer.
   What was the effect of this?

	Trade Receivables	Profit for the year	Capital	Balance at bank
A	decreased	decreased	decreased	no effect
B	decreased	no effect	no effect	no effect
C	no effect	no effect	decreased	decreased
D	no effect	decreased	no effect	decreased

2. Wendy maintains a provision for doubtful debts. Which statements are correct?
   1. It is an application of the matching principle.
   2. It is an application of the prudence principle.
   3. It is an estimate of what may be lost because of irrecoverable debts.
   4. It is money set aside to cover losses because of irrecoverable debts.

   A 1, 2 and 3   B 1 and 4   C 2 and 3   D 2, 3 and 4

3. Abi maintains a provision for doubtful debts at 2% of trade receivables. On 1 January 20–5 the provision for doubtful debts was $426. The trade receivables on 31 December 20–4 amounted to $20 550.
   What entries did Abi make on 31 December 20–4 to adjust the provision for doubtful debts?

	Debit	$	Credit	$
A	income statement	15	provision for doubtful debts	15
B	income statement	411	provision for doubtful debts	411
C	provision for doubtful debts	15	income statement	15
D	provision for doubtful debts	411	income statement	411

4 K Dhoni is a business consultant.

The following trial balance is provided at 30 September 20–1:

	$	$
Capital		94 000
Drawings	12 250	
Premises at cost	82 000	
Office equipment at cost	19 000	
Provision for depreciation of office equipment		1 900
Trade receivables	5 000	
Loan (repayable 20–9)		10 000
Irrecoverable debts	100	
Provision for doubtful debts		150
Fees from clients		75 300
Insurance	2 400	
Printing and stationery	3 150	
Wages	47 000	
Office expenses	2 950	
Rent receivable		5 400
Cash	200	
Bank	12 700	
	186 750	186 750

The following additional information is supplied:

1. At 30 September 20–1 – rent received in advance amounted to $1 800
   insurance prepaid amounted to $600
   printing expenses owing amounted to $150
   loan interest owing amounted to $500.
2. The office equipment is being depreciated at the rate of 10% per annum using the straight line method.
3. The provision for doubtful debts is maintained at 4% of the trade receivables.

a Prepare the income statement of K Dhoni for the year ended 30 September 20–1.

b Prepare the statement of financial position of K Dhoni at 30 September 20–1.

Chapter 13: Irrecoverable debts and provisions for doubtful debts

5   Harry is a trader selling goods on credit. His financial year ends on 31 December. The balances on his books on 1 January 20–3 included the following:

	$
Provision for doubtful debts	300
Jane, a credit customer	900 debit

Harry's transactions for the year ended 31 December 20–3 included the following:

January 4	Received a cheque from Jane in full settlement of her account less a cash discount of 2%
March 5	Sold goods on credit to Jane, list price $200, less trade discount of 20%
May 18	Received $100 cash from Sarah whose account had been written off two years ago
December 30	Jane was declared bankrupt. She left the country and could not be traced. Her account was written off
December 31	Harry decided to increase his provision for doubtful debts by $50

Write up the accounts for Jane, irrecoverable debts, debts recovered and provision for doubtful debts for the year ended 31 December 20–3. Balance or total the accounts or make an appropriate year-end transfer as necessary.

6   Lakshmi runs a secretarial agency. The following trial balance was prepared on 31 January 20–1:

	$	$
Capital 1 February 20–0		98 000
Drawings	5 000	
10 year loan from AB Loans		15 000
Premises at cost	90 000	
Office equipment at cost	10 500	
Motor vehicles at cost	16 900	
Provision for depreciation of office equipment		4 200
Provision for depreciation of motor vehicles		6 480
Trade receivables	7 800	
Provision for doubtful debts		172
Bank		2 888
Fees		21 820
Commission receivable		490
Wages	10 200	
Insurance	2 250	
Rates	3 200	
Office expenses	2 450	
Loan interest	750	
	149 050	149 050

Additional information:

1 At 31 January 20–1:
   - commission receivable outstanding amounted to $30
   - wages accrued amounted to $320.

2 The insurance is for 15 months from 1 February 20–0.

3 Lakshmi occupies a flat above the business premises and one quarter of the rates relate to this flat.

4 Office equipment is being depreciated at 20% per annum on cost.

5 Motor vehicles are being depreciated at 20% per annum using the reducing balance method.

6 The provision for doubtful debts is to be maintained at 2% of the trade receivables.

a Prepare the income statement for the year ended 31 January 20–1.

b Prepare the statement of financial position at 31 January 20–1.

Section 3: Practice questions

1 'Profit is regarded as being earned when the legal title of the goods or services passes from the seller to the buyer.' Which accounting principle does this statement describe?
   - A going concern
   - B matching
   - C money measurement
   - D realisation

2 Which accounting objective requires that the information in financial statements is free from bias and free from significant errors?
   - A comparability
   - B relevance
   - C reliability
   - D understandability

3 A trader paid operating expenses during his financial year. There was the amount accrued at the start of the year and a prepayment at the end of the year.

   What is the formula for calculating the operating expenses for the year?
   - A amount paid + opening accrual + closing prepayment
   - B amount paid + opening accrual − closing prepayment
   - C amount paid − opening accrual + closing prepayment
   - D amount paid − opening accrual − closing prepayment

4 Why should non-current assets be depreciated?
   - A to apply the money measurement principle
   - B to charge the cost of using them against income
   - C to ensure money will be available to replace them
   - D to ensure the profit for the year is not understated

5 Dogma's credit customer, Sophie, paid her account on 20 May by cheque. On 28 May Dogma was notified that the bank had dishonoured this cheque.

   What entries would Dogma make on 28 May?

	Account to be debited	Account to be credited
A	bank	Sophie
B	irrecoverable debts	bank
C	irrecoverable debts	Sophie
D	Sophie	bank

6 Anais owns a general store. She makes payments of both capital and revenue items and has both capital and revenue receipts.

a Complete the following table by placing a tick (✓) to indicate how each item could be classified.

	Capital expenditure	Revenue expenditure	Capital receipt	Revenue receipt
Loan from AB Limited				
Purchase of additional premises				
Legal fees for purchase of additional premises				
Insurance of additional premises				
Cash sales				
Purchase of inventory				
Proceeds of sale of old motor vehicle at book value				
Discount received				

When calculating her profit for the year ended 29 February 20–4, Anais discovered some errors had been made in the accounting records.

Error 1 Redecorating of the original premises had been debited to the premises account.
Error 2 Payment of loan interest had been debited to the loan account.
Error 3 Commission received had been credited to the sales account.
Error 4 Proceeds of sale of office fixtures at book value had been credited to the sales account.

b Complete the following table by placing a tick (✓) to indicate the effect of each error on the profit for the year.

	Effect on the profit for the year		
Error	Overstated	Understated	No effect
error 1			
error 2			
error 3			
error 4			

Section 3: Practice questions

7 Nazeer is a trader. He provided the following information about his inventory at 30 November 20–8:

Inventory code number	Number of units in inventory	Cost per unit $	Selling price per unit $
BD20	300	1.50	2.30
BD23	119	0.95	0.80
BD29	410	1.78	1.85

Nazeer had to pay carriage inwards on inventory code number BD20 at the rate of $5 per 100 units (not included in the cost per unit shown in the table).

- **a** Explain the meaning of the following terms used in connection with inventory valuation:
    - **i** cost
    - **ii** net realisable value
- **b** Name one accounting principle Nazeer should apply when valuing his inventory.
- **c** Calculate the total value of Nazeer's inventory on 30 November 20–8.

After the preparation of the financial statements for the year ended 30 November 20–8 Nazeer discovered that the inventory had been understated by $15.

- **d** Complete the following table by placing a tick (✓) to show the effect of this error.

	Overstated	Understated	No effect
current assets at 30 November 20–8			
profit for the year ended 30 November 20–8			
gross profit for the year ended 30 November 20–9			

8 Karima's financial year ends on 31 December.

She maintains one combined account for rates and insurance.

On 1 January 20–4 she owed $560 for 4 months' rates and had paid 6 months' insurance, $580, in advance.

During the year ended 31 December 20–4 Karima made the following payments:

			$
February	28	Rates for 8 months by cheque	1 120
April	30	Rates for 5 months by cheque	700
July	1	Insurance for 12 months by credit transfer	1 200

- **a** Prepare the rates and insurance account for the year ended 31 December 20–4. Balance the account and bring down the balances on 1 January 20–5.
- **b** Prepare relevant extracts from the statement of financial position on 31 December 20–4.
- **c** Explain why it is important to make adjustments for accrued and prepaid expenses at the end of the financial year.

9 Tanvir is a trader. His financial year ends on 31 December.

Tanvir purchases all of his office stationery from Tabitha. He provided the following information for the year ended 31 December 20–8:

			$
January	1	Inventory of stationery	44
April	1	Purchased stationery on credit from Tabitha	313
	18	Returned damaged stationery to Tabitha	22
June	1	Paid amount owing to Tabitha by cheque	
December	31	Inventory of stationery	65

a Prepare the following ledger accounts for the year ended 31 December 20–8:
   i Tabitha account
   ii Stationery account

The accounts should be balanced, totalled or transferred to the income statement as appropriate.

Tanvir is supplied with electricity by EE Limited. He pays by bank transfer after receipt of invoices which are issued every six months by EE Limited.

Tanvir provided the following information relating to the year ended 31 December 20–8:

			$
January	1	Balance owing to EE Limited for electricity supplied	239
	30	Paid balance owing to EE Limited by bank transfer	
July	1	Received an invoice from EE Limited for electricity supplied	445
August	2	Paid balance owing to EE Limited by bank transfer	
December	31	Estimate of amount of electricity used since July	388

b Prepare the following ledger accounts for the year ended 31 December 20–8.
   i EE Limited account
   ii Electricity expense account

The accounts should be balanced, totalled or transferred to the income statement as appropriate.

10 Chibuzo's financial year ends on 31 December. He depreciates his motor vehicles at 20% per annum on the cost of motor vehicles held at the end of each financial year.

Chibuzo provided the following information:

1 January 20–7 Purchased motor vehicle A for $15 000 and motor vehicle B for $18 000

1 July 20–9   Motor vehicle A was sold for $8 600. On the same date motor vehicle C was purchased for $21 000

a Calculate the profit or loss on disposal of motor vehicle A.
b Calculate the depreciation charge for motor vehicles for the year ended 31 December 20–9.

Chibuzo provided the following additional information for the year ended 31 December 20–9:

	$
Revenue	108 200
Wages	10 300
Rent and rates	2 100
Purchases	81 140
Inventory 1 January 20–9	5 410
Administration and selling expenses	2 230
Commission receivable	2 050
Provision for doubtful debts 1 January 20–9	540

Additional information:

1 On 31 December 20–9

	$
Inventory	5 550
Wages accrued	120
Rates prepaid	300
Commission receivable outstanding	420
Provision for doubtful debts to be reduced to	450

2 Office equipment was valued at $4 320 on 1 January 20–9. Office equipment, $1 200, was purchased during the year. No office equipment was disposed of during the year. On 31 December 20–9 the office equipment was valued at $5 250.

c Prepare the income statement for the year ended 31 December 20–9.

11 Nadia's financial year ends on 31 August. She depreciates her office fixtures by 25% per annum on cost. Depreciation is calculated from the date of purchase. No depreciation is charged in the year of disposal.

a Name and explain two accounting principles Nadia is observing by depreciating her office fixtures.

On 1 September 20–3 the following balances appeared in Nadia's ledger:

	$
Office fixtures at cost	4 500
Provision for depreciation of office fixtures	2 100

On 1 December 20–3 Nadia purchased additional office fixtures, $2 400, on credit from AB Limited.

On 1 March 20–4 Nadia sold office fixtures for $120 which was received in cash. The office fixtures had been purchased on 1 September 20–0 for $1 000.

b Write up the office fixtures account, the provision for depreciation of office fixtures account and the disposal of office fixtures account for the year ended 31 August 20–4. Balance the accounts where necessary and bring down the balances on 1 September 20–4.

c Prepare a relevant extract from Nadia's statement of financial position on 31 August 20–4.

12 Charlotte maintains a provision for doubtful debts at $2\frac{1}{2}$% of her trade receivables at the end of each financial year.

    a Explain the meaning of each of the following terms:

        i irrecoverable debt

        ii provision for doubtful debts

    b Explain how Charlotte is observing the accounting principle of prudence by maintaining a provision for doubtful debts.

    c Name one other accounting principle Charlotte is observing by maintaining a provision for doubtful debts.

    d Suggest two ways in which Charlotte may reduce the possibility of irrecoverable debts.

At the end of her financial year on 31 July 20–3 Charlotte provided the following information:

		$
On 1 August 20–2	Trade receivables	8 400
During the year ended 31 July 20–3	Debts written off as irrecoverable	167
On 31 July 20–3	Trade receivables	7 546
	It was decided to write off a debt as irrecoverable	66

The provision for doubtful debts should be maintained at $2\frac{1}{2}$% of the trade receivables.

    e Prepare the provision for doubtful debts account for the year ended 31 July 20–3. Balance the account and bring down the balance on 1 August 20–3.

    f Prepare relevant extracts from the income statement for the year ended 31 July 20–3.

    g Prepare a relevant extract from the statement of financial position at 31 July 20–3.

13 Sharif is a trader. He maintains a full set of accountings records. His financial year ends on 30 April.

The balances on his ledger accounts on 30 April 20–7 included the following:

	$
Sales	49 750
Rent receivable	2 000
Irrecoverable debts	960
Provision for doubtful debts	1 400
Stationery and office expenses	3 210
Inventory (1 May 20–6)	4 520
Office fixtures at cost	14 500
Provision for depreciation of office fixtures	5 800
Disposal of office fixtures account	–

a Open an account for each of the items and enter the balance on 30 April 20–6.

Sharif provided the following additional information on 30 April 20–7.
1 Inventory was valued at $4 970.
2 Inventory of stationery was valued at $45.
3 Rent receivable outstanding amounted to $400.
4 $116 owed by Halijah should be written off as irrecoverable.
5 The provision for doubtful debts should be increased by $100.
6 Office fixtures were sold on 28 April. The proceeds of sale, $780, had been debited in the cash book, but no other entries had been made. The fixtures originally cost $2 000 and had been depreciated by $800.
7 The remaining office fixtures should be depreciated by 10% per annum on cost.

b Record this information in the accounts opened in a. Close the accounts by balancing or by making a transfer to the income statement.

14 Priti is a trader. Her financial year ends on 31 March. Her trial balance on 31 March 20–4 was as follows:

	$	$
Capital		390 000
Drawings	54 000	
Trade receivables	49 270	
Trade payables		43 500
Bank	21 335	
Premises at cost	300 000	
Fixtures and fittings at cost	35 000	
Motor vehicles at cost	24 000	
Provision for depreciation of fixtures and fittings		14 000
Provision for depreciation of motor vehicles		10 500
Provision for doubtful debts		2 360
Revenue		644 000
Inventory 1 April 20–3	36 000	
Purchases	528 850	
Sales returns	1 050	
Carriage inwards	750	
Commission receivable		1 030
Rates and insurance	10 400	
Wages	39 400	
Administration expenses	5 335	
	1 105 390	1 105 390

Additional information:

1. At 31 March 20–4:

   Inventory was valued at $41 050.

   Commission receivable outstanding amounted to $110.

   Insurance prepaid amounted to $180.

   Rates accrued amounted to $260.

   Wages accrued amounted to $1 600.

2. A debt of $150 should be written off as irrecoverable and the provision for doubtful debts should be maintained at 5% of the remaining trade receivables.

3. Fixtures and fittings are being depreciated at 20% per annum using the straight line method.

4. Motor vehicles are being depreciated at 25% per annum using the reducing balance method.

a. Prepare the income statement for the year ended 31 March 20–4.

b. Prepare the statement of financial position at 31 March 20–4.

Section 4

Chapter 14
Bank reconciliation statements

Learning objectives

In this chapter you will learn to:

- understand the use and purpose of a bank statement   3.3
- update the cash book for bank charges, bank interest paid and received, correction of errors, credit transfers, direct debits, dividends and standing orders   3.3
- understand the purpose of, and prepare, a bank reconciliation statement to include bank errors, uncredited deposits and unpresented cheques.   3.3

Chapter 14: Bank reconciliation statements

14.1 Introduction

A bank will send a statement at regular intervals to its customers detailing the transactions that have taken place during the period covered by the statement and showing the bank balance at the end of the period. This is similar to the **statement of account** issued by its suppliers to the customers who have purchased goods on credit.

A **bank statement** is a copy of the customer's account in the books of the bank. This is a record of transactions as they affect the bank. When money is paid into the bank the customer's account will be credited, as this is the amount owed by the bank to the customer and when money is taken out of the bank, the customer's account will be debited, as this reduces the amount owed by the bank to the customer. A positive bank balance will appear as a credit balance and an overdrawn balance as a debit balance.

When the entries on a bank statement are compared to those in the bank account, in the cash book it will be found that they are recorded on opposite sides of the account. The bank account is a record of transactions as they affect the business. Money paid into the bank is debited (the bank is a debtor for this amount) and money withdrawn from the bank is credited (the bank is a creditor for this amount).

It is important to compare the bank statement and the bank account in the cash book. If the two balances disagree, it is necessary to **reconcile** them to explain why the differences have arisen.

KEY TERM

A **bank statement** is a copy of a customer's account in the books of the bank which is sent to the customer at regular intervals.

TIP

The entries in the bank column of the cash book will appear on the opposite side to that on which they are recorded on the bank statement.

LINK

You learned about cash books in Chapter 4.

TEST YOURSELF 14.1

1. State why bank reconciliation should be carried out.
2. Explain why money paid into the bank appears on the debit of the bank account but on the credit of the bank statement.

14.2 Reasons why the bank account and the bank statement may differ

Differences between the two records usually occur because of:

- the different times at which the same items are recorded
- the business not recording certain items in the cash book.

Timing differences

These are usually due to:

1. **Cheques not yet presented**

   These are cheques that have been paid by the business and entered on the credit of the cash book, but which do not appear on the bank statement. This may be because the payee has not paid the cheque into his bank or because the cheque is still in the banking system and has not yet been deducted from the business's account.

2. **Amounts not yet credited**

   These are cash and cheques that have been paid into the bank and entered on the debit side of the cash book, but which do not appear on the bank statement. It usually takes a few days before the money paid into the bank is recorded in the customer's account.

Items not recorded in the cash book

It often happens that the business does not record certain items until the bank statement is received. These include:

1 **Bank charges and bank interest**

   The bank may deduct an amount from the customer's account to cover the cost of running the account and for any interest charged on overdrafts and loans.

LINK
You learned about dishonoured cheques in Chapter 4.

2 **Dishonoured cheques**

   A cheque paid into the bank may be returned because the drawer did not have sufficient funds in the account.

3 **Amounts paid directly into the bank**

   These are **credit transfers, standing orders** and **direct debits** where a person has instructed their bank to pay an amount of money directly into the bank account of the business.

4 **Amounts paid directly by the bank to others**

   These include credit transfers, standing orders and direct debits which the business has instructed the bank to pay directly from the account of the business.

Any other differences between the two records must be investigated. **Errors made by the business** should be corrected and **errors made by the bank** should be notified to the bank.

The differences between the bank account in the cash book and the bank statement are summarised as follows:

Items in cash book not in bank statement	Items in bank statement but not in cash book
Cheques not yet presented	Bank charges and bank interest
Amounts not yet credited	Dishonoured cheques
Errors in cash book	Standing orders
	Credit transfers
	Direct debits
	Errors on bank statement
	Dividends

TEST YOURSELF 14.2

1 Explain the term 'cheque not yet presented'.
2 Explain the term 'dishonoured cheque'.
3 Give an example of an expense which may be paid by standing order.

14.3 Stages of bank reconciliation

1. **Compare the bank account in the cash book with the bank statement**

   The debit side of the bank account should be compared with the credit side of the bank statement and the credit side of the bank account compared with the debit side of the bank statement. Put a tick (✓) against those items which appear in both records.

2. **Update the cash book**

   Enter in the cash book any items which appear on the bank statement but which have not yet been entered in the cash book.

   a   Items debited on the bank statement (e.g. bank charges, credit transfers paid by the bank, etc.) should be credited to the bank account in the cash book.

   b   Items credited on the bank statement (e.g. credit transfers and direct debits paid into the bank) should be debited to the bank account in the cash book.

3. **Correct any errors in the cash book**

4. **Balance the cash book and carry down the balance**

   This balance is the correct bank balance. If it is the end of the financial year, this is the balance which should appear in the statement of financial position.

5. **Prepare a bank reconciliation statement**

   This should show why the balance on the updated cash book does not agree with the balance shown on the bank statement.

   a   Start with the balance shown on the bank statement.

   b   Add any items which appear on the debit side of the cash book but which do not appear on the bank statement (e.g. amounts not yet credited).

   c   Deduct any items which appear on the credit side of the cash book but which do not appear on the bank statement (e.g. cheques not yet presented).

   d   Make any adjustments for bank errors by adding amounts debited in error by the bank and deducting amounts credited in error by the bank.

   e   The total of this calculation should equal the updated bank balance in the cash book.

It is possible to start the bank reconciliation statement with the updated bank account balance. In this case, it is necessary to reverse items **b**, **c** and **d**.

A **bank reconciliation statement does not form part of the double entry records of the business**. It is a statement which shows that, on a certain date, the bank account and the bank statement balances were reconciled.

> **KEY TERM**
>
> A **bank reconciliation statement** is a document prepared by a business to explain why the updated bank balance in the cash book does not agree with the balance on the bank statement.

> **TIP**
>
> The updated bank balance in the cash book appears in the statement of financial position.

Walkthrough 14.1

The bank columns of Fatima's cash book for the month of April 20–8 are:

Cash book (bank columns only)

Date	Details	Folio	$	Date	Details	Folio	$
20–8				20–8			
Apr 1	Balance		2970	Apr 10	Purchases		234
14	J Dhatwani		420	19	B Malukani		110
26	ABC Stores		217	29	TeeDee Co		1372
28	Sales		1460	30	Dobhal Ltd		517
					Balance	c/d	2834
			5067				5067
20–8							
May 1	Balance	b/d	2834				

Fatima's bank statement for the month of April 20–8 is:

REGIONAL BANK LTD
West District

Account: Fatima Goyal
Account no: 987654
Date: 30 April 20–8

Date	Details	Debit $	Credit $	Balance $
20–8				
April 1	Balance			2970 Cr
13	Cheque no 2388	243		2727 Cr
19	Credit no 6983		420	3147 Cr
20	Credit transfer (dividend)		150	3297 Cr
24	Cheque no 2389	110		3187 Cr
30	Bank charges	95		3092 Cr

It is discovered that Fatima has made an error on 10 April and recorded purchases as $234, when the correct figure was $243.

a Make any additional entries that are required in Fatima's cash book. Balance the bank account and bring down the balance on 1 May 20–8.

b Prepare a bank reconciliation statement at 30 April 20–8.

The first thing to do is to compare the entries in the cash book with those on the bank statement. Place a tick (✓) against the items appearing in both the records.

Chapter 14: Bank reconciliation statements

The cash book and the bank statement should now look like this:

Cash book (bank columns only)

Date	Details	Folio	$	Date	Details	Folio	$
20–8				20–8			
Apr 1	Balance	✓	2 970	Apr 10	Purchases		234
14	J Dhatwani	✓	420	19	B Malukani	✓	110
26	ABC Stores		217	29	TeeDee Co		1 372
28	Sales		1 460	30	Dobhal Ltd		517
					Balance	c/d	2 834
			5 067				5 067
20–8							
May 1	Balance	b/d	2 834				

REGIONAL BANK LTD
West District

Account: Fatima Goyal   **Account no**: 987654

Date: 30 April 20–8

Date	Details	Debit $	Credit $	Balance $
20–8				
April 1	Balance			2 970 Cr ✓
13	Cheque no 2388	243		2 727 Cr
19	Credit no 6983		420 ✓	3 147 Cr
20	Credit transfer (dividend)		150	3 297 Cr
24	Cheque no 2389	110 ✓		3 187 Cr
30	Bank charges	95		3 092 Cr

It is now possible to update the bank account in the cash book. Firstly, the error on 10 April must be corrected. Items appearing in the debit column of the bank statement which have not been ticked off (excluding 13 April which has now been corrected in the bank account) must be credited in the bank account. Items appearing in the credit column of the bank statement which have not been ticked off must be debited in the bank account.

a

Cash book (bank columns only)							
Date	Details	Folio	$	Date	Details	Folio	$
20–8				20–8			
May 1	Balance	b/d	2 834	May 1	Correction of error		9
	Dividend		150		Bank charges		95
					Balance	c/d	2 880
			2 984				2 984
20–8							
May 1	Balance	b/d	2 880				

The bank reconciliation statement can now be prepared.

b

Fatima
Bank reconciliation statement at 30 April 20–8

	$	$
Balance shown on bank statement		3 092
Add Amounts not yet credited – ABC Stores	217	
Sales	1 460	1 677
		4 769
Less Cheques not yet presented – TeeDee Co	1 372	
Dobhal Ltd	517	1 889
Balance shown in cash book		2 880

It is important to remember that the bank columns are actually part of the main three column cash book – not a separate ledger account.

> **TEST YOURSELF 14.3**
>
> **1** On 31 May a trader's bank account showed a he had $250 in the bank. On the same day his bank statement showed a credit balance of $198. The cash book was updated and the new balance showed there was $141 in the bank.
>
> In the trader's statement of financial position on 31 May:
>
> **a** Under what heading will bank be shown?
> **b** What amount will be entered for bank?

14.4 Bank reconciliation when there is a bank overdraft

Walkthrough 14.1 showed how to update the cash book and prepare a bank reconciliation statement when there is a positive bank balance. Exactly the same principles are followed when there is a bank overdraft. In this case, it is important to take great care with the arithmetic calculations and it is helpful to place brackets around overdrawn amounts. A bank overdraft will appear as a credit balance in the bank account in the cash book of the business and as a debit balance on the bank statement.

Walkthrough 14.2

On 31 July 20–8 the bank account in Fatima's cash book showed an overdrawn balance of $1 121. On the same date her bank statement showed a debit balance of $1 091.

When comparing the cash book and the bank statement it was found that the following items appeared only in the cash book:

1 A cheque paid to PJ Motors for $163 on 29 July.
2 Cash sales amounting to $1 010 paid into the bank on 31 July.

The following items appeared only on the bank statement and not in the cash book:

1 Rent received paid directly into the bank $190.
2 Bank charges of $213.
3 A credit balance on 1 July was shown as $2 100 instead of $1 200.

a Make any additional entries that are required in Fatima's cash book. Balance the bank account and bring down the balance on 1 May 20–8.

b Prepare a bank reconciliation statement at 31 July 20–8.

The comparison of the cash book with the bank statement has already been completed and the differences are shown, so it is possible to start with the updating of the cash book.

a

Cash book (bank columns only)									
Date	Details	Folio	$	Date	Details	Folio	$
20–8				20–8			
Aug 1	Rent received		190	Aug 1	Balance	b/d	1 121
	Balance	c/d	1 144		Bank charges		213
			1 334				1 334
				20–8			
				Aug 1	Balance	b/d	1 144

b

Fatima
Bank reconciliation statement at 31 July 20-8

	$
Balance shown on bank statement	(1 091)
Add Amounts not yet credited – Sales	1 010
	(81)
Less Cheques not yet presented – PJ Motors	163
	(244)
Less Bank error	900
Balance shown in cash book	(1 144)

14.5 Advantages of bank reconciliation

The advantages of reconciling the balance on the bank statement with that shown on the bank account in the cash book are:

1. After updating the bank account an accurate bank balance is available.
2. Errors in the bank account or on the bank statement can be identified.
3. It assists in discovering fraud and embezzlement.
4. Amounts not credited by the bank can be identified.
5. Cheques not yet presented can be identified.
6. Any 'stale' cheques (these are usually those which are over six months old, which will not be met by the bank) can be identified and written back into the bank account.

You can now answer Questions 1–6 at the end of this chapter.

Revision checklist

- The purpose of bank reconciliation is to explain the differences between the bank balance shown in the cash book and the balance on the bank statement.
- Most of the differences between the balances are caused by differences in the time at which items are recorded and because some items cannot be recorded in the cash book until the bank statement is received.
- The cash book should be updated by entering those items which appear on the bank statement but not in the cash book.
- The bank reconciliation statement shows the balance on the bank statement adjusted for amounts not yet credited, cheques not yet presented and any bank errors. The final figure should agree with the balance shown in the bank account in the cash book.

Chapter 14: Bank reconciliation statements

Exam-style questions

1. Which statement is correct about a bank reconciliation statement?

   A It contains bank charges and standing orders.
   B It is part of the double entry book-keeping records.
   C It is prepared by the bank.
   D It is prepared by the trader.

2. A bank reconciliation statement was prepared starting with the balance at bank shown on the bank statement. Which item would be deducted?

   A bank error resulting in the account being incorrectly debited
   B cash book error resulting in the balance being overstated
   C cheque not yet credited
   D cheque not yet presented

3. The bank column of a trader's cash book showed a debit balance of $952. This did not agree with the balance on the bank statement on the same date. The following differences were found:

	$
Cheque not yet presented	134
Bank charges	11
Rent paid by credit transfer	310

   What was the balance on the bank statement?

   A $765 credit   B $765 debit   C $1 139 credit   D $1 139 debit

4. Zafar is a trader. He maintains a three column cash book and compares this with his bank statement at the end of every month and prepares a bank reconciliation statement.

   a Suggest two reasons why it is useful for Zafar to reconcile his cash book with the bank statement every month.
   b Explain the difference between a cheque not credited and a cheque not presented.
   c Complete the following table by placing a tick in the correct column to indicate whether each item would be used to update the cash book or would appear in the bank reconciliation statement.

	Updating cash book	Bank reconciliation statement
unpresented cheque		
bank charges		
direct debit paid for electricity		
credit transfer from Waseem		
cash sales not yet credited		
bank error		
cheque from Adil dishonoured		

5 The cash book (bank columns) of Ella for the month of May 20–7 were as follows:

Cash book (bank columns only)

Date 20–7	Details	Folio	$	Date 20–7	Details	Folio	$
May 1	Balance	b/d	398	May 10	Lily		113
14	William		87	29	James		246
31	Sales		684	31	Balance	c/d	910
			1 169				1 269
20–7							
June 1	Balance	b/d	910				

Ella's bank statement for May 20–7 showed the following:

Date 20–7	Details	Debit $	Credit $	Balance $
May 1	Balance		398	398 Cr
18	Counter credit 99870		87	485 Cr
20	Cheque 404	113		372 Cr
24	Dishonoured cheque	87		285 Cr
30	SO Motor insurance company	36		249 Cr
31	Bank charges	12		237 Cr

The following errors were discovered:
1 Ella had overcast the debit side of her cash book by $100.
2 The bank should have charged the motor insurance to Ella's personal bank account not the business bank account.

a Update Ella's cash book. Bring down the updated balance on 1 June 20–7.
b Prepare a bank reconciliation statement for Ella at 31 May 20–7.
c Prepare a relevant extract from Ella's statement of financial position at 31 May 20–7 showing the entry for the bank balance.

6 Yatish is a trader. He compared his cash book with his bank statement on 30 June. The cash book showed an overdrawn balance of $2 356.
The following differences between the cash book and the bank statement were discovered:
1 Cheques not yet presented for payment

	$
Hemisha	428
Ben	910

2 Cash sales, $950, were not recorded on the bank statement.
3 The bank had debited $50 to the business bank account which should have been debited to Yatish's personal bank account.

a Prepare a bank reconciliation statement to show the balance on the bank statement.
b Explain the difference between a bank statement and a bank reconciliation statement.
c Explain why the entries on a bank statement are on the opposite side to where they appear in the cash book.

Chapter 15
Journal entries and correction of errors

Learning objectives

In this chapter you will learn to:

- explain the use of, and process accounting data in, the book of prime entry – the general journal   2.3
- post the ledger entries from the general journal   2.3
- prepare journal entries for the provision for depreciation   4.2
- prepare journal entries to record the sale of non-current assets   4.2
- prepare journal entries to record accrued and prepaid expenses   4.3
- prepare journal entries to record accrued and prepaid incomes   4.3
- prepare journal entries to record irrecoverable debts   4.4
- prepare journal entries to record the recovery of debts written off   4.4
- prepare journal entries to record the creation of, and adjustments to, a provision for doubtful debts   4.4
- correct errors by means of journal entries   3.2
- explain the use of a suspense account as a temporary measure to balance the trial balance   3.2
- correct errors by means of suspense accounts   3.2
- adjust a profit or loss for an accounting period after the correction of errors   3.2
- understand the effect of correction of errors on a statement of financial position.   3.2

Chapter 15: Journal entries and correction of errors

15.1 Introduction

The **journal** or general journal is a book of prime entry. Chapter 7 explained how all transactions are recorded in a book of prime entry **before** they are entered in the ledger.

The **journal** is not a part of the double entry book-keeping. It is regarded as a diary in which transactions are noted before they are entered in the ledger. **Anything which is not entered in one of the books of prime entry must be entered in the journal before being recorded in the ledger**.

A journal entry shows:

- the date of the transaction
- the name of the account to be debited and the amount
- the name of the account to be credited and the amount
- a narrative

The narrative consists of a brief explanation of what is being recorded and why the entry is being made. This is useful because it is impossible to remember the reason for every entry and the entries in the journal sometimes involve unusual transactions.

The layout of the journal is as follows:

Journal				
Date	Details	Folio	Debit $	Credit $

The items usually recorded in the journal are:

- opening entries
- purchase and sale of non-current assets
- non-regular transactions such as year-end transfers
- correction of errors

> **KEY TERM**
>
> The **journal** is a book of prime entry used to record transactions which cannot be recorded in any other book of prime entry.

> **LINK**
>
> You learned about the other books of prime entry in earlier chapters. In Chapters 4 and 5 you learned about cash books and petty cash books and in Chapter 7 you learned about sales, purchases and returns journals.

15.2 Opening journal entries

As the name suggests, opening journal entries are made when the business starts (or when the business first keeps accounting records). An opening journal entry lists the assets owned by the business (shown in the debit column), the liabilities owed by the business (shown in the credit column) and the capital of the business (also shown in the credit column).

After the journal entry has been prepared, the items are posted to the appropriate ledger accounts.

Walkthrough 15.1

Chandra started business on 1 November 20–4. He did not maintain any accounting records during his first year of trading.

On 1 November 20–5 he was able to provide the following information about his business:

Assets	Premises $56 000, fixtures $19 400, motor vehicles $12 500, inventory $3 100, trade receivables $4 700, cash $200
Liabilities	Trade payables $5 600, bank overdraft $2 300

Prepare an opening journal entry for Chandra at 1 November 20–5.

Make the appropriate entries in Chandra's ledger and cash book.

Chandra
Journal
Assets, liabilities and capital to open the books.

Date	Details	Folio	Debit $	Credit $
20–5				
Nov 1	Premises		56 000	
	Fixtures		19 400	
	Motor vehicles		12 500	
	Inventory		3 100	
	Trade receivables		4 700	
	Cash		200	
	Trade payables			5 600
	Bank			2 300
	Capital			88 000
			95 900	95 900

- It is usual to show the debit entries first.
- It is usual to slightly indent the credit entries.
- It is usual to draw a line after each separate journal entry.
- The capital was calculated as the difference between the assets and the liabilities.

Chandra
Nominal ledger
Premises account

Date	Details	Folio	$	Date	Details	Folio	$
20–5							
Nov 1	Balance		56 000				

Fixtures account

Date	Details	Folio	$	Date	Details	Folio	$
20–5							
Nov 1	Balance		19 400				

Chapter 15: Journal entries and correction of errors

Motor vehicle account

Date	Details	Folio	$	Date	Details	Folio	$
20–5							
Nov 1	Balance		12 500				

Inventory account

Date	Details	Folio	$	Date	Details	Folio	$
20–5							
Nov 1	Balance		3 100				

Capital account

Date	Details	Folio	$	Date	Details	Folio	$
				20–5			
				Nov 1	Balance		88 000

Cash Book

Date	Details	Cash $	Bank $	Date	Details	Cash $	Bank $
20–5				20–5			
Nov 1	Balance	200		Nov 1	Balance		2 300

- No names and amounts of individual credit customers and credit suppliers were provided in this question. In practice, these will be known.
- In the sales ledger an account will be opened for each credit customer and the account will be debited with the balance owed by that customer.
- In the purchases ledger an account will be opened for each credit supplier and the account will be credited with the balance owed to that supplier.

TEST YOURSELF 15.1

1. Name **three** transactions for which a journal entry would be made.
2. In connection with a journal entry:
   a. explain the meaning of a narrative
   b. explain why a narrative is necessary.

15.3 Purchase and sale of non-current assets

As the purchase and sale of non-current assets are not recorded in one of the other books of prime entry, they should be entered in the journal before being posted to the ledger.

After the journal entry has been completed, the transaction is posted to the appropriate ledger accounts.

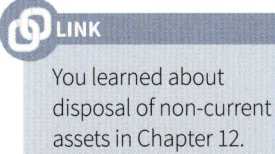

LINK

You learned about disposal of non-current assets in Chapter 12.

Walkthrough 15.2

Chandra's financial year ends on 31 October.

Prepare the journal entries to record the following transactions on 1 September 20–6.

- Purchased additional fixtures, $1 300, on credit from Office Supplies.
- Sold the motor vehicle (cost $12 500) for $7 400 on credit to Used Vehicles Ltd.

Chandra
Journal

Date	Details	Folio	Debit $	Credit $
20–6				
Sep 1	Fixtures		1 300	
	Office Supplies			1 300
	Purchase of fixtures on credit			
	Disposal of motor vehicle		12 500	
	Motor vehicles			12 500
	Used Vehicles Ltd		7 400	
	Disposal of motor vehicle			7 400
	Transfer of motor vehicle to disposal account and sale of motor on credit			
Oct 31	Income statement		5 100	
	Disposal of motor vehicle			5 100
	Loss on disposal transferred to income statement			

15.4 Non-regular transactions

As explained earlier, any transactions which cannot be recorded in another book of prime entry are recorded in the journal. These often consist of transactions which are not occurring regularly and year-end transfers to the income statement. The transaction is posted to the appropriate ledger accounts after the journal entry is completed.

Walkthrough 15.3

Chandra's financial year ends on 31 October. He provided the following information for the year ended 31 October 20–6.

- Irrecoverable debts written off up to 30 October 20–6 amounted to $140.
- On 31 October 20–6 it was decided to:

  Write off as irrecoverable a debt of $50 owing by Ansari Stores

  Create a provision for doubtful debts of $250

a Prepare journal entries to record the decisions made on 31 October 20–6 and any necessary year-end transfers.
b Show the appropriate ledger accounts after posting these entries.

a

Chandra
Journal

Date	Details	Folio	Debit $	Credit $
20–6				
Oct 31	Irrecoverable debts		50	
	Ansari Stores			50
	Writing off irrecoverable debt			
	Income statement		250	
	Provision for doubtful debts			250
	Creation of provision for doubtful debts			

b

Chandra
Sales ledger
Ansari Stores account

Date	Details	Folio	$	Date	Details	Folio	$
20–6				20–6			
Oct 1	Balance	b/d	50	Oct 31	Irrecoverable debts		50
			50				50

Nominal ledger
Irrecoverable debts account

Date	Details	Folio	$	Date	Details	Folio	$
20–6				20–6			
Oct 30	Debtors written off		140	Oct 31	Income statement		190
31	Ansari Stores		50				
			190				190

Provision for doubtful debts account

Date	Details	Folio	$	Date	Details	Folio	$
20-6				20-6			
Oct 31	Balance	c/d	250	Oct 31	Income statement		250
			250				250
				20-6			
				Nov 1	Balance	b/d	250

- On 31 October 20-7 Chandra:

    agreed to accept equipment valued at $100 from Khalid in settlement of a debt written off during the year ended 31 October 20-6.

    decided to increase the provision for doubtful debts to $310.

c Prepare journal entries to record the above information, including year-end transfers.

d Show the appropriate ledger accounts after posting these entries.

c

Chandra
Journal

Date	Details	Folio	Debit $	Credit $
20-7				
Jun 30	Equipment		100	
	Debts recovered			100
	Equipment accepted in settlement of debt previously written off			
Oct 31	Income statement		60	
	Provision for doubtful debts			60
	Adjustment to provision for doubtful debts			

d

Chandra
Nominal ledger
Debts recovered account

Date	Details	Folio	$	Date	Details	Folio	$
20-7				20-7			
Oct 31	Income statement		100	Jun 30	Equipment		100
			100				100

Chapter 15: Journal entries and correction of errors

Equipment account

Date	Details	Folio	$	Date	Details	Folio	$
20–7							
Oct 31	Debts recovered		100				

Provision for doubtful debts account

Date	Details	Folio	$	Date	Details	Folio	$
20–6				20–6			
Oct 31	Balance	c/d	250	Oct 31	Income statement		250
			250				250
20–7				20–6			
Oct 31	Balance	c/d	310	Nov 1	Balance	b/d	250
				20–7			
				Oct 31	Income statement		60
			310				310
				20–7			
				Nov 1	Balance	b/d	310

- The alternative ways of recording debts recovered are explained on Page 172:

Walkthrough 15.4

Chandra's financial year ends on 31 October. He provided the following information:

- At 31 October 20–6 Chandra's ledger accounts included the following:

    Purchases for the year $39 000
    Sales returns for the year $2 460
    Insurance $1 500, which included a prepayment of $300
    Inventory at 1 November 20–5 $3 100
    General expenses for the year $1 350
    Rent receivable $1 200 (part of the premises had been let to a tenant on 1 October 20–6 at an annual rent of $2 400)

- On 31 October 20–6:

    Inventory was valued at $3 900
    The motor vehicle should be depreciated by $2 500
    General expenses accrued amounted to $75

a Prepare journal entries to record the year-end transfers.
b Show the ledger accounts after posting these entries.

a

Chandra
Journal

Date	Details	Folio	Debit $	Credit $
20–6				
Oct 31	Income statement		39 000	
	Purchases			39 000
	Transfer of purchases for the year to the income statement			
	Income statement		2 460	
	Sales returns			2 460
	Transfer of sales returns for the year to the income statement			
	Income statement		1 200	
	Insurance			1 200
	Transfer of insurance for the year to the income statement			
	Income statement		3 100	
	Inventory			3 100
	Transfer of opening inventory to the income statement			
	Inventory		3 900	
	Income statement			3 900
	Transfer of closing inventory to the income statement			
	Income statement		1 425	
	General expenses			1 425
	Transfer of general expenses for the year to the income statement			
	Rent receivable		200	
	Income statement			200
	Transfer of rent receivable for the year to the income statement			
	Income statement		2 500	
	Provision for depreciation of motor vehicle			2 500
	Annual depreciation charge transferred to the income statement			

b

Chandra
Nominal ledger

Purchases account

Date	Details	Folio	$	Date	Details	Folio	$
20–6				20–6			
Oct 31	Total to date		39 000	Oct 31	Income statement		39 000
			39 000				39 000

Sales returns account

Date	Details	Folio	$	Date	Details	Folio	$
20–6				20–6			
Oct 31	Total to date		2 460	Oct 31	Income statement		2 460
			2 460				2 460

Insurance account

Date	Details	Folio	$	Date	Details	Folio	$
20–6				20–6			
Oct 31	Total paid		1 500	Oct 31	Income statement		1 200
					Balance	c/d	300
			1 500				1 500
20–6							
Nov 1	Balance	b/d	300				

Inventory account

Date	Details	Folio	$	Date	Details	Folio	$
20–5				20–6			
Nov 1	Balance		3 100	Oct 31	Income statement		3 100
			3 100				3 100
20–6				20–6			
Oct 31	Income statement		3 900	Oct 31	Balance	c/d	3 900
			3 900				3 900
20–6							
Nov 1	Balance		3 900				

General expenses account

Date	Details	Folio	$	Date	Details	Folio	$
20-6				20-6			
Oct 31	Total paid		1 350	Oct 31	Income statement		1 425
	Balance	c/d	75				
			1 425				1 425
				20-6			
				Nov 1	Balance	b/d	75

Rent receivable account

Date	Details	Folio	$	Date	Details	Folio	$
20-6				20-6			
Oct 31	Income statement		200	Oct 31	Total received		1 200
	Balance	c/d	1 000				
			1 200				1 200
				20-6			
				Nov 1	Balance	b/d	1 000

Provision for depreciation of motor vehicle account

Date	Details	Folio	$	Date	Details	Folio	$
20-6				20-6			
Oct 31	Balance	c/d	2 500	Oct 31	Income statement		2 500
			2 500				2 500
				20-6			
				Nov 1	Balance	b/d	2 500

Walkthrough 15.5

Chandra's financial year ends on 31 October. Prepare journal entries to record the following:

- On 30 September 20-6 he wrote off $50 owing by Ansari Stores as irrecoverable.
- At 31 October 20-6 Chandra's ledger accounts include the following:
  Purchases for the year $39 000
  Irrecoverable debts for the year $190
  Insurance, $1 500, which includes a prepayment of $300
  Inventory at 1 November 20-5 $3 100.

- On 31 October 20-6 Chandra's ledger accounts include the following:
  Inventory was valued at $3 900
  Fixtures are to be depreciated by $2 070
  A provision for doubtful debts is to be created of $250.

Chapter 15: Journal entries and correction of errors

Chandra
Journal

Date	Details	Folio	Debit $	Credit $
20–6				
Sept 30	Irrecoverable debts		50	
	Ansari Stores			50
	Writing off irrecoverable debt			
Oct 31	Income statement		39 000	
	Purchases			39 000
	Transfer of purchases for the year to the income statement			
	Income statement		190	
	Irrecoverable debts			190
	Transfer of total irrecoverable debts to the income statement			
	Income statement		1 200	
	Insurance			1 200
	Transfer of insurance for the year to the income statement			
	Income statement		3 100	
	Inventory			3 100
	Transfer of opening inventory to the income statement			
	Inventory		3 900	
	Income statement			3 900
	Transfer of closing inventory to the income statement			
	Income statement		2 070	
	Provision for depreciation of fixtures			2 070
	Annual depreciation charge transferred to the income statement			
	Income statement		250	
	Provision for doubtful debts			250
	Creation of provision for doubtful debts			

LINK

You learned about irrecoverable debts and provisions for doubtful debts in Chapter 13.

LINK

You learned about depreciation of non-current assets in Chapter 12.

LINK

You learned about other payables and other receivables in Chapter 11.

> **TEST YOURSELF 15.2**
>
> 1 Prepare a journal entry to record **each** of the following transactions:
>   a Goods costing $200 taken by the business owner for personal use.
>   b Drawings, $5 000, transferred from drawings account to capital account.
>   c The profit for the year, $15 000, transferred from the income statement to the capital account.

You can now answer Questions 1–3 at the end of this chapter.

15.5 Correction of errors

Errors made in the recording of the day-to-day transactions can be divided into those which are not revealed by the trial balance and those which result in the trial balance not balancing.

Errors which are not shown by a trial balance

There are six types of error which can be made which will not be revealed by the trial balance. These are:

Error of commission
Error or complete reversal
Error of omission
Error of original entry
Error of principle
Compensating errors

LINK

You learned about these errors in Chapter 3.

TIP

It is often helpful to prepare working notes in the form of ledger accounts before attempting more complex journal entries such as those to correct errors.

When such errors are discovered, they should be corrected by means of a journal entry before making entries in the appropriate ledger accounts.

Walkthrough 15.6

Chandra's financial year ends on 31 October.

The totals of the trial balance prepared on 31 October 20–7 agreed, but the following errors were later discovered.

a The purchase of stationery, $30, had been debited to the purchases account.
b A cheque, $500, received from K Singh had been credited to the account of H Singh.
c The wages account had been under-cast by $100 and the purchases account had been overcast by $100.

Prepare the necessary journal entries to correct these errors.

Chapter 15: Journal entries and correction of errors

Chandra
Journal

	Date	Details	Folio	Debit $	Credit $
	20–7				
a	Oct 31	Stationery		30	
		Purchases			30
		Error in posting stationery to purchases now corrected			
b		H Singh		500	
		K Singh			500
		Error in posting cheque to wrong personal account now corrected			
c		Wages		100	
		Purchases			100
		Wages under-cast and purchases over-cast, now corrected			

Errors which affect a trial balance

Some errors may occur that result in the totals of the trial balance not balancing.

If the errors are not found immediately, the trial balance is balanced by inserting the difference between the two sides in a **suspense account**. This is regarded as a temporary account in which the difference on the trial balance is held until the errors are discovered.

> **TIP**
> A suspense account ensures the balancing of the trial balance and allows draft financial statements to be prepared. It also allows errors to be corrected by using double entry and ensures that all errors are found.

As the errors are found, they are corrected by means of a journal entry. The appropriate entries are then made in the ledger accounts. When all the errors have been found and corrected, the suspense account will close automatically.

> **TIP**
> If all the errors affecting the balancing of a trial balance are discovered and corrected, the suspense account will automatically close. A balance remaining on a suspense account indicates that there are still some errors in the accounting records.

KEY TERM

A **suspense account** is a temporary account opened in order to make the totals of a trial balance agree.

LINK

You learned about the types of errors which result in the totals of a trial balance not balancing in Chapter 3.

Walkthrough 15.7

Chandra's financial year ends on 31 October.

The totals of the trial balance prepared on 31 October 20–8 failed to agree. The difference of $260 was a shortage on the debit side. This was entered in a suspense account.

The following errors were later discovered:

a The purchases account had been over-cast by $110.

b No entry had been made for office expenses, $20, paid in cash.

c Credit sales, $630, to Anil had been correctly entered in the sales account but debited as $360 in Anil's account.

d Capital introduced by Chandra, $5 000 (paid into the bank), has been debited to the capital account and credited to the bank account.

e A cheque, $200, received from a debtor, Yuvraj, has been correctly entered in the bank account, but no other entry has been made.

f Sales returns, $150, have been correctly entered in the credit customer's account but have been credited to the purchases returns account.

Prepare the necessary journal entries to correct these errors.

Write up the suspense account in Chandra's ledger.

Chandra

Journal

	Date	Details	Folio	Debit $	Credit $
	20–8				
a	Oct 31	Suspense		110	
		Purchases			110
		Purchases over-cast, now corrected			
b		Office expenses		20	
		Cash			20
		Omission of cash paid for office expenses, now corrected			
c		Anil		270	
		Suspense			270
		Sales, $630, incorrectly entered in Anil's account as $360, now corrected			
d		Bank		10 000	
		Capital			10 000
		Capital introduced debited to capital and credited to bank, now corrected			

e	Suspense	200	
	Yuvraj		200
	Cheque received from Yuvraj entered only in the bank, now corrected		
f	Sales returns	150	
	Purchases returns	150	
	Suspense		300
	Sales returns incorrectly credited to purchases returns, now corrected		

Chandra
Nominal ledger
Suspense account

Date	Details	Folio	$	Date	Details	Folio	$
20–8				20–8			
Oct 31	Difference on trial balance		260	Oct 31	Anil		270
	Purchases		110		Sales returns		150
	Yuvraj		200		Purchases returns		150
			570				570

- An entry was required in the suspense account to correct errors **a**, **c**, **e** and **f** as all these affected the balancing of the trial balance.
- No entry was required in the suspense account to correct errors **b** and **d** as these did not affect the balancing of the trial balance.
- Error **f** required two accounts to be debited – the sales returns and the purchases returns – with the corresponding credits in the suspense account in order to correct the error.
- Where an entry has been reversed (as in error **d**) it is necessary to double the amount of the error in order to correct it and to restore the accounts to the correct amount.

TEST YOURSELF 15.3

1. Explain when it is necessary to open a suspense account.
2. It is found that machinery repairs have been debited to the machinery account. Explain:
    a. the type of error that has been made
    b. whether a correcting entry is required in the suspense account, giving a reason.

You can now answer Questions 4–5 at the end of this chapter.

15.6 Effect on profit of correcting errors

If errors are discovered after the income statement has been prepared, it may be necessary to amend the profit figure. Any corrections made to items appearing in the trading section of the income statement will affect both the gross profit and the profit for the year. Any corrections made to items appearing in the profit and loss section of the income statement will affect the profit for the year.

Walkthrough 15.8

Chandra's financial year ends on 31 October.

The totals of the trial balance prepared on 31 October 20–8 failed to agree. The difference was entered in a suspense account and draft financial statements were prepared. The profit for the year was $15 000.

The following errors were later discovered:

a The purchases account had been over-cast by $110.
b No entry had been made for office expenses, $20, paid in cash.
c Credit sales, $630, to Anil had been correctly entered in the sales account but debited as $360 in Anil's account.
d Capital introduced by Chandra, $5 000 (paid into the bank), has been debited to the capital account and credited to the bank account.
e A cheque, $200, received from a credit customer, Yuvraj, has been correctly entered in the bank account, but no other entry has been made.
f Sales returns, $150, have been correctly entered in the credit customer's account but have been credited to the purchases returns account.

Prepare a statement to show the corrected profit for the year ended 31 October 20–8.

Chandra
Statement of corrected profit for the year ended 31 October 20–8

	$	$
Profit for the year from income statement		15 000
Add Purchases over-cast		110
		15 110
Less Office expenses omitted	20	
Sales returns understated	150	
Purchases returns overstated	150	320
Corrected profit for the year		14 790

- Errors **c**, **d** and **e** do not affect the calculation of the profit.
- If the purchases are over-cast, the profit will be understated and therefore $110 must be added.
- If expenses have been omitted, the profit will be overstated and therefore $20 must be deducted.

- If the sales returns have been understated, the profit will be overstated and so $150 must be deducted.
- If the purchases returns have been overstated, the profit will also be overstated and therefore $150 must be deducted.

15.7 Effect on statement of financial position of correcting errors

If errors are discovered and corrected after the preparation of financial statements, the statement of financial position may have to be amended. If the profit for the year has been corrected this will affect the capital section of the statement, but other items may also need to be amended.

Walkthrough 15.9

Chandra's financial year ends on 31 October.

The totals of the trial balance prepared on 31 October 20–8 failed to agree. The difference was entered in a suspense account and draft financial statements were prepared.

The following errors were later discovered:

a The purchases account had been over-cast by $110.
b No entry had been made for office expenses, $20, paid in cash.
c Credit sales, $630, to Anil had been correctly entered in the sales account but debited as $360 in Anil's account.
d Capital introduced by Chandra, $5 000 (paid into the bank), has been debited to the capital account and credited to the bank account.
e A cheque, $200, received from a credit customer, Yuvraj, has been correctly entered in the bank account, but no other entry has been made.
f Sales returns, $150, have been correctly entered in the credit customer's account but have been credited to the purchases returns account.

The corrected profit for the year ended 31 October 20–8 was $14 790.

Explain how correcting **each** of these errors will affect the statement of financial position at 31 October 20–8.

Errors **a**, **b**, and **f** do not affect items within the statement of financial position directly, but are used in the calculation of the corrected profit for the year. The profit which is added to the capital in the statement will need to be amended to the correct figure of $14 790.

To correct error **c** the figure for trade receivables in the current assets section of the statement will have to be increased by $270.

To correct error **d** the capital figure will have to be increased by $10 000. The figure for bank in the current assets section of the statement will also have to be increased by $10 000.

To correct error **e** the figure for trade receivables in the current assets section of the statement will have to be reduced by $200.

Cambridge IGCSE and O Level Accounting

> **TEST YOURSELF 15.4**
>
> No entries have been made for goods, $500, sold on credit to Mitali.
>
> 1 State the type of error made.
> 2 State what correcting entries are required.
> 3 State the effects on the profit for the year after correcting this error.

You can now answer Question 6 at the end of this chapter.

Revision checklist

- A journal can be regarded as a diary in which transactions are noted before they are entered in the ledger.
- A narrative is a brief explanation of what is being recorded in the journal entry and why the entry is being made.
- Journal entries are made to open the accounting records, to record the purchase and sale of non-current assets, to record non-regular transactions, and to correct errors.
- A suspense account is opened if a trial balance fails to balance. This means that the draft financial statements can be prepared.
- Errors affecting the balancing of the trial balance are corrected by making an entry in the suspense account.

Exam-style questions

1 Shayni's financial year ends on 31 May. She maintains a provision for doubtful debts at 4% of the trade receivables at the end of each financial year. On 1 June 20–2 Shayni's provision was $480. On 31 May 20–3 her trade receivables amounted to $10 800.

Which journal entry would Shayni make on 31 May 20–3?

		Debit $	Credit $
A	Income statement	48	
	Provision for doubtful debts		48
B	Income statement	432	
	Provision for doubtful debts		432
C	Provision for doubtful debts	48	
	Income statement		48
D	Provision for doubtful debts	432	
	Income statement		432

2 Shaheel's financial year ends on 31 March. On 1 April 20–7 he purchased furniture costing $4 400 for use in the office. He decided to depreciate the furniture using the reducing balance method at 15% per annum.

Which journal entry did Shaheel make on 31 March 20–9?

		Debit $	Credit $
A	Income statement	561	
	Provision for depreciation of furniture		561
B	Income statement	660	
	Provision for depreciation of furniture		660
C	Provision for depreciation of furniture	99	
	Furniture		99
D	Provision for depreciation of furniture	1 221	
	Depreciation of furniture		1 221

3 Jenny owns a retail store. Her financial year ends on 31 July. On 31 July 20–1:

Jenny purchased stationery, $112, on credit from AB Supplies

Jenny took goods, costing $130, for personal use

Jenny depreciated her shop fittings by $180.

a Prepare journal entries to record these items. Narratives are required.

On 31 July 20–1 the balances in Jenny's ledger included the following:

	$
Rent	3 120
Sales	95 600
Purchases returns	1 720

One quarter of the rent relates to Jenny's apartment above the shop.

b Prepare journal entries to adjust the rent and to record the year-end transfers to the income statement for the three accounts. Narratives are required.

4 Lindelwa discovered that goods sold on credit to Zack, $260, had been incorrectly credited to Zachary's account.

Which journal entry corrects this error?

		Debit $	Credit $
A	Suspense	520	
	Zachary		260
	Zack		260
B	Zachary	260	
	Zack	260	
	Suspense		520
C	Zachary	260	
	Zack		260
D	Zack	260	
	Zachary		260

5 At the end of his financial year on 31 July 20–4, Silas opened a suspense account with a credit balance of $70.

a Suggest one reason why this account was required.

After preparing draft financial statements Silas discovered the following errors:
1. The purchases returns journal was overcast by $100.
2. Carriage inwards, $195, had been debited to the carriage outwards account.
3. The total of the analysis column for travelling expenses in the petty cash book, $42, had not been transferred to the ledger.
4. $420 paid to Amina, a credit supplier, had been debited to the account of Amira, another credit supplier.
5. The balance of the petty cash book, $150, had not been entered in the trial balance.
6. The total of the discount received column in the cash book, $181, has been debited to the discount allowed account in the ledger.

b Prepare the suspense account. Balance or total the account as necessary.

c Prepare journal entries to correct the errors. Narratives are not required.

6 Alberto is a clothing wholesaler. His draft profit for the year ended 30 September 20–3 was $24 920. He then discovered the following errors:

1 One page of the sales journal had been overcast by $1 000.
2 Drawings by Alberto from the business bank account, $900, had been recorded as capital introduced.
3 No entry had been made for office expenses paid in cash, $40.
4 No entry had been made for the sale of a motor vehicle. This had originally cost $22 500 and had been depreciated by $10 980. A cheque was received for $12 000.
5 No entry had been made for cash discount, $50, received from Ted, a credit supplier.
6 $1 450 paid to Kaleem, a credit supplier, had been debited to the account of Kalid, another credit supplier.

Complete the statement of corrected profit for the year ended 30 September 20–3. Where an error does not affect the profit write 'no effect'.

Alberto		
Statement of corrected profit for the year ended 30 September 20–3		

	Effect on profit		
	Increase $	Decrease $	$
Draft profit for the year			_____
Error 1	_____	_____	
Error 2	_____	_____	
Error 3	_____	_____	
Error 4	_____	_____	
Error 5	_____	_____	
Error 6	=====	=====	
	_____	_____	_____
Corrected profit for the year			=====

Chapter 16
Control accounts

Learning objectives

In this chapter you will learn to:

- understand the purposes of purchases ledger and sales ledger control accounts   3.4
- identify the books of prime entry as sources of information for the control account entries   3.4
- prepare purchases ledger and sales ledger control accounts to include credit purchases and sales, receipts and payments, cash discounts, returns, irrecoverable debts, dishonoured cheques, interest on overdue accounts, contra entries, refunds, opening and closing balances (debit and credit within each account).   3.4

Chapter 16: Control accounts

16.1 Introduction

Control accounts are also known as **total accounts**. If the trial balance fails to balance and the error cannot be readily located, it is necessary to check all the accounting records. This can take a considerable amount of time. The checking process can be speeded up if a control account for the sales ledger (which contains the accounts of the debtors) and a control account for the purchases ledger (which contains the accounts of the creditors) have been prepared. These accounts act as a check on the individual accounts within these ledgers.

Like the trial balance, however, these accounts can only check the arithmetical accuracy: errors such as omission and commission will not be revealed by a control account.

LINK
You learned about the division of the ledger in Chapter 4.

LINK
You learned about the errors not revealed by a trial balance in Chapter 3.

16.2 Advantages of control accounts

Where a full set of accounting records is maintained, it is usual to prepare a **sales ledger control account** and a **purchases ledger control account**. The advantages of preparing these accounts are as follows:

1 They can assist in locating errors when the trial balance fails to balance.
2 They are proof of the arithmetical accuracy of the ledgers they control.
3 The balances on these accounts are regarded as being equal to the total of the trade receivables and the total of the trade payables, so this information is available immediately.
4 Draft financial statements can be prepared quickly because of the balances provided by the control accounts.
5 They help to reduce fraud as the control accounts are prepared by someone who has not been involved in making the entries in those particular ledgers.
6 They provide a summary of the transactions affecting the trade receivables and trade payables for each financial period.

KEY TERMS

A **sales ledger control account** is an account summarising all the accounts of the trade receivables and a **purchases ledger control account** is an account summarising all the accounts of the trade payables.

TEST YOURSELF 16.1

1 Name the account which summarises all the sales ledger accounts.
2 Name the account which summarises all the purchases ledger accounts.
3 State **three** reasons for preparing control accounts.

16.3 Sales ledger control account

This is also referred to as a **total trade receivables account**. This account resembles the account of a credit customer, but instead of containing transactions concerned with just one person or business it contains transactions relating to *all* the debtors. A typical sales ledger control account is shown here.

Nominal ledger							
Sales ledger control account							
Date	Details	Folio	$	Date	Details	Folio	$
	Balance	b/d			Sales returns		
	Sales				Cash		
	Bank				Bank		
	(dishonoured cheque)				Discount allowed		
	Bank/Cash (refunds)				Irrecoverable debts		
	Interest charged				Balance	c/d	
	Balance	b/d					

As this account acts as a check on the individual credit customers' accounts, it should be prepared independently and information in the individual accounts of the credit customers must **not** be used. (An error in the sales ledger would not be revealed if the control account is prepared from the accounts in that ledger.) **The information to prepare a sales ledger control account is obtained from the books of prime entry.** The sources of information are summarised as follows:

Item	Source of information
Sales	Sales journal
Sales returns	Sales returns journal
Receipts from credit customers	Cash book
Discounts allowed to credit customers	Cash book
Dishonoured cheques	Cash book
Refunds to credit customers	Cash book
Irrecoverable debts written off	Journal
Interest charged on overdue accounts	Journal

The sales ledger control account is drawn up at the end of the financial period (often monthly) and balanced. The total of the balances on all the individual credit customers' accounts should agree with the balance on the control account. If they differ, it indicates that there is an error in one of the customers' accounts or an error in the control account, so further checks are required.

TIP
A sales ledger account is a summary of the accounts of credit customers (trade receivables) so will not include items which do not appear in the account of a credit customer, such as cash sales and provision for doubtful debts.

Walkthrough 16.1

Shweta maintains a full set of accounting records and prepares control accounts at the end of each month.

She provided the following information:

			$
20–8 March 1	Sales ledger control account balance		1 200 debit
March 31	Totals for the month:		
	Sales journal		4 890
	Sales returns journal		250
	Cheques and bank transfers received from credit customers		3 892
	Discount allowed to credit customers		8
	Cash received from credit customers		120
	Cash refunds to credit customers		19
	Cheque received (included in the above figure) later dishonoured		80
	Irrecoverable debts written off		94

Prepare Shweta's sales ledger control account for the month of March 20–8.

Shweta
Nominal ledger
Sales ledger control account

Date	Details	Folio	$	Date	Details	Folio	$
20–8				20–8			
Mar 1	Balance	b/d	1 200	Mar 31	Sales returns		250
31	Sales		4 890		Cash		120
	Bank (dishonoured cheque)		80		Bank		3 892
					Discount allowed		8
	Cash (refunds)		19		Irrecoverable debts		94
					Balance	c/d	1 825
			6 189				6 189
20–8							
Apr 1	Balance	b/d	1 825				

16.4 Purchases ledger control account

This is also known as a **total trade payables account**. This account resembles the account of a credit supplier, but instead of containing transactions concerned with just one person or business it contains transactions relating to **all** the creditors. A typical purchases ledger control account is shown here.

Nominal ledger								
Purchases ledger control account								
Date	Details	Folio	$	Date	Details	Folio	$
	Purchases returns				Balance	b/d	
	Cash				Purchases		
	Bank				Interest charged		
	Discount received				Bank/Cash (refunds)		
	Balance	c/d					
					Balance	b/d	

> **TIP**
> The accounts in the sales and purchases ledgers are not used to provide information for preparing a control account otherwise errors in the ledgers would not be revealed.

This account serves a similar purpose to the sales ledger control account. It acts as a check on the individual credit suppliers' accounts and must be prepared independently and **not** from information in the individual accounts of the credit suppliers. **The information to prepare a purchases ledger control account is obtained from the books of prime entry.** The sources of information are summarised as follows:

Item	Source of information
Purchases	Purchases journal
Purchases returns	Purchases returns journal
Payments to credit suppliers	Cash book
Discounts received from credit suppliers	Cash book
Refunds from credit suppliers	Cash book
Interest charged on overdue accounts	Journal

Like the sales ledger control account, the purchases ledger control account is drawn up at the end of the financial period (often monthly) and balanced. The total of the balances on all the individual credit suppliers' accounts should agree with the balance on the control account. If they differ it indicates that there is an error in one of the suppliers' accounts or the control account, so further checks are required.

> **TIP**
> A purchases ledger account is a summary of the accounts of credit suppliers (trade payables) so will not include items which do not appear in the account of a credit supplier such as cash purchases.

Chapter 16: Control accounts

Walkthrough 16.2

Shweta maintains a full set of accounting records and prepares control accounts at the end of each month.

She provided the following information:

			$	
20–8	March 1	Purchases ledger control account balance	1 880	credit
	March 31	Totals for the month:		
		Purchases journal	4 230	
		Purchases returns journal	180	
		Cheques and bank transfers paid to credit suppliers	3 900	
		Discount received from credit suppliers	104	
		Cheque refunds from credit suppliers	100	
		Interest charged on overdue account	12	

Prepare Shweta's purchases ledger control account for the month of March 20–8.

Shweta
Nominal ledger
Purchases ledger control account

Date	Details	Folio	$	Date	Details	Folio	$
20–8				20–8			
Mar 31	Purchases returns		180	Mar 1	Balance		1 880
	Bank		3 900	31	Purchases		4 230
	Discount received		104		Bank (refunds)		100
	Balance	c/d	2 038		Interest charged		12
			6 222				6 222
				20–8			
				Apr 1	Balance	b/d	2 038

LINK

You will learn about the use of total accounts for calculating missing information in Chapter 17.

You can now answer Questions 1 and 2 at the end of this chapter.

TEST YOURSELF 16.2

1 Explain why the information used for preparing control accounts must be obtained from books of prime entry.
2 State the source of information for **each** of the following:
   a purchases returns
   b discount allowed
   c irrecoverable debts.

16.5 Balances on both sides of a control account

Occasionally a credit customer's account may show a credit balance. This may occur due to:

- an overpayment by the customer
- the customer returning goods after paying the account
- the customer paying in advance for the goods
- cash discount not being deducted before payment was made.

In the sales ledger control account it is usual to keep any credit balance separate from the debit balance. The control account will, therefore, have two balances – the usual debit balance representing money owing **by** credit customers, and the more unusual credit balance representing money owing **to** credit customers. Any credit balance is entered on the debit side of the control account and carried down as a credit balance. The account can then be balanced in the usual way.

Walkthrough 16.3

Shweta maintains a full set of accounting records and prepares control accounts at the end of each month.

She provided the following information:

			$
20–8	April 1	Sales ledger control account balance	1 825 debit
	April 30	Totals for the month:	
		Sales journal	4 910
		Sales returns journal	210
		Cheques and bank transfers received from credit customers	4 788
		Discount allowed to credit customers	12
		Interest charged on overdue account	10
	May 1	Sales ledger credit balances	115

Prepare Shweta's sales ledger control account for the month of April 20–8.

Shweta
Nominal ledger
Sales ledger control account

Date	Details	Folio	$	Date	Details	Folio	$
20–8				20–8			
Apl 1	Balance	b/d	1 825	Apl 30	Sales returns		210
30	Sales		4 910		Bank		4 788
	Interest charged		10		Discount allowed		12
	Balance	c/d	115		Balance	c/d	1 850
			6 860				6 860
20–8				20–8			
May 1	Balance	b/d	1 850	May 1	Balance	b/d	115

In a similar way, a credit supplier's account can show a debit balance. This may occur due to:

- an overpayment to the supplier
- returning goods to the supplier after paying the account
- paying the supplier in advance for the goods
- cash discount not being deducted before payment was made.

As in the sales ledger control account, the debit balance and the credit balance are shown separately in the purchases ledger control account. The purchases ledger control account will, therefore, have two balances – the usual credit balance representing money owing **to** credit suppliers, and the more unusual debit balance representing money owing **by** credit suppliers. Any debit balance is entered on the credit side of the control account and carried down as a debit balance. The account can then be balanced in the usual way.

> **TEST YOURSELF 16.3**
>
> 1   Explain how it is possible for a customer's account to have a credit balance.

You can now answer Questions 3 and 4 at the end of this chapter.

16.6 Contra entries in control accounts

Contra entries are also known as **inter-ledger transfers** or **set-offs**.

It may happen that a business sells goods to another business and also buys different goods from that business. This means that there will be two ledger accounts for that business – one in the sales ledger and the other in the purchases ledger.

Rather than each business sending the other a cheque to cover the amount due, they may agree to set one account off against the other. Any remaining amount will be settled by one business issuing a cheque.

KEY TERM

Contra entries may be referred to as inter-ledger transfers or set-offs and are when a transfer is made from an account in the sales ledger to an account of the same business/person in the purchases ledger.

Walkthrough 16.4

Shweta provided the following information:

20–8

May 15   Sold goods, $190, on credit to Mansingh Road Stores

22   Bought goods, $320, on credit from Mansingh Road Stores

30   The balances of the two accounts for Mansingh Road Stores were set-off and Shweta sent a cheque for the remaining balance.

Record these transactions in the account for Mansingh Road Stores in the sales ledger and the account for Mansingh Road Stores in the purchases ledger.

Shweta
Sales ledger
Mansingh Road Stores account

Date	Details	Folio	$	Date	Details	Folio	$
20–8				20–8			
May 15	Sales		190	May 30	Purchases ledger		190
			190				190

Cambridge IGCSE and O Level Accounting

Purchases ledger
Mansingh Road Stores account

Date	Details	Folio	$	Date	Details	Folio	$
20–8				20–8			
May 30	Sales ledger		190	May 22	Purchases		320
	Bank		130				
			320				320

> **TIP**
> A contra entry, sometimes known as an inter-ledger transfer or set-off, is recorded in both the sales ledger control account and the purchases ledger control account.

- A journal entry would be made for the transfer of $190 on 30 May as it is a non-regular transaction.
- As the transfer of $190 on 30 May affected both the accounts in sales ledger and purchases ledger, it would affect both the sales ledger control account and the purchases ledger control account. See Walkthrough 16.5.

Walkthrough 16.5

Shweta provided the following information for the month of May 20-8.

		$
20–8		
May 1	Sales ledger control account debit balance	1 850
	Sales ledger control account credit balance	115
	Purchases ledger control account credit balance	2 118
31	Totals for the month:	
	Sales journal	5 360
	Purchases journal	5 110
	Sales returns journal	134
	Purchases returns journal	216
	Cheques and bank transfers received from credit customers	4 965
	Cheques and bank transfers paid to credit suppliers	4 508
	Discount received from credit suppliers	92
	Irrecoverable debt written off	35
	Interest charged by credit supplier on overdue account	14
	Contra entry	190
June 1	Sales ledger control account debit balance	?
	Purchases ledger control account credit balance	?
	Purchases ledger control account debit balance	135

Prepare Shweta's sales ledger control account and purchases ledger control account for the month of May 20–8. Balance the accounts and bring down the balances on 1 June 20–8.

Shweta
Nominal ledger
Sales ledger control account

Date	Details	Folio	$	Date	Details	Folio	$
20–8				20–8			
May 1	Balance	b/d	1 850	May 1	Balance	b/d	115
31	Sales		5 360	31	Sales returns		134
					Bank		4 965
					Irrecoverable debt		35
					Contra entry		190
					Balance	c/d	1 771
			7 210				7 210
20–8							
June 1	Balance	b/d	1 771				

Shweta
Nominal ledger
Purchases ledger control account

Date	Details	Folio	$	Date	Details	Folio	$
20–8				20–8			
May 1	Purchases returns		216	May 1	Balance	b/d	2 118
	Bank		4 508	31	Purchases		5 110
	Discount received		92		Interest charged		14
	Contra entry		190		Balance	c/d	135
	Balance	c/d	2 371				
			7 377				7 377
20–8				20–8			
June 1	Balance	b/d	135	June 1	Balance	b/d	2 371

TEST YOURSELF 16.4

1 In connection with control accounts, explain the meaning of a contra entry.

You can now answer Questions 5 and 6 at the end of this chapter.

Revision checklist
- The main purpose of control accounts is to assist in locating errors in the sales ledger and the purchases ledger.
- A sales ledger control account resembles the account of a credit customer but contains transactions affecting all credit customers.
- A purchases ledger control account resembles the account of a credit supplier but contains transactions affecting all credit suppliers.
- The information to prepare control accounts is obtained from the books of prime entry.
- It is possible to have a balance on each side of a control account.
- If a business is both a customer and a supplier, a contra entry may be made to transfer a balance from the sales ledger account to the purchases ledger account.

Cambridge IGCSE and O Level Accounting

Exam-style questions

1. What is the purpose of preparing a sales ledger control account?
   - **A** to calculate the total credit sales for the period
   - **B** to calculate the total sales for the period
   - **C** to check the arithmetical accuracy of the sales account
   - **D** to check the arithmetical accuracy of the sales ledger accounts

2. What may appear on the debit side of a purchases ledger control account?
   - **A** credit purchases
   - **B** discount allowed
   - **C** payments to credit suppliers
   - **D** returns by credit customers

3. Shilpa's sales ledger control account had an opening credit balance. What does this mean?
   - **A** total amount owing by credit customers
   - **B** goods returned by credit customers
   - **C** interest charged on credit customers' accounts
   - **D** overpayment made by credit customers

4. Hamir is a trader who maintains full set of accounting records. He divides his ledger into three sections – nominal (general), sales and purchases.
   - **a** State **one** advantage of dividing the ledger into these sections.
   - **b** State **two** advantages of maintaining a purchases ledger control account.

   Hamir provided the following information for the month of May 20–1:

			$
May 1	Debit balances in purchases ledger		105
	Credit balances in purchases ledger		4 897
May 31	Totals for the month:		
	Credit purchases		5 424
	Purchases returns		657
	Payments to suppliers		4 312
	Discount received		88
	Interest charged by credit supplier		20
June 1	Debit balances in purchases ledger		76

   - **c** Prepare the purchases ledger control account for the month of May 20–1. Balance the account and bring down the balances on 1 June 20–1.
   - **d** Name the book of prime entry Hamir would use to provide information about:
     - **i** interest charged by credit supplier
     - **ii** purchases returns
     - **iii** discount received.

5 a Complete the following table to state where the items would appear in a purchases ledger control account. For each item name the book of prime entry from which the information would be obtained.

		Entry in purchases ledger control account		Source of information
		Debit	Credit	
i	payments to credit suppliers			
ii	cheques paid to credit suppliers later dishonoured			
iii	credit purchases			
iv	contra entry to sales ledger account			
v	discount received			
vi	interest charged by supplier on overdue account			
vii	returns to credit suppliers			

b Explain why the information required to prepare a purchases ledger control account is not obtained from the purchases ledger.

c Explain the contra entry to the sales ledger and why it was needed.

6 Eva is a trader who maintains a full set of accounting records and prepares control accounts at the end of each month. She provided the following information:

20–5		$
February 1	Debit balance in the sales ledger control account	2 470
	Credit balance in the sales ledger	110
	Provision for doubtful debts	100
February 28	Totals for the month:	
	Credit sales	3 480
	Cash sales	1 950
	Returns by credit customers	118
	Cheques received from credit customers	3 403
	Cheque received from credit customer (included in the cheques received above) later dishonoured	104
	Discount allowed	144
	Discount received	176
	Irrecoverable debts written off	200
	Contra entry	240
March 1	Debit balance in the sales ledger control account	?
	Credit balance in the sales ledger control account	95

a Select the relevant figures and prepare the sales ledger control account for the month of May 20–1. Balance the account and bring down the balances on 1 June 20–1.

b For each entry (excluding the balances) in the sales ledger control account prepared in **a** name the book of prime entry which would be used as a source of information.

c Select **two** items listed that should not appear in a sales ledger control account and explain why they do not appear.

d Suggest **two** reasons for the credit balance on the sales ledger control account on 1 March 20–1.

Chapter 17
Incomplete records

Learning objectives

In this chapter you will learn to:

- explain the disadvantages of not maintaining a full set of accounting records   5.6
- prepare opening and closing statements of affairs   5.6
- calculate profit for the year from changes in capital over time   5.6
- calculate sales, purchases, gross profit, trade receivables and trade payables and other figures from incomplete information   5.6
- prepare income statements and statements of financial position from incomplete records   5.6
- make adjustments to financial statements   5.6.6
- apply the techniques of mark-up, margin and inventory turnover to arrive at missing figures.   5.6

Cambridge IGCSE and O Level Accounting

17.1 Introduction

Sometimes businesses, small businesses in particular, do not maintain a full set of accounting records. This means that a trial balance cannot be drawn up and the financial statements cannot be prepared until a certain amount of preparatory calculations have been carried out. Much depends on the records and information available as to whether a full set of financial statements can be prepared.

17.2 Advantages of maintaining double entry records

Maintaining a full set of double entry record is important and provides many benefits. These include the following:

1. Full details are available about the assets, liabilities, revenues and expenses of the business.
2. The preparation of financial statements is relatively straightforward.
3. The calculation of the profit or loss for the year is likely to be reliable and accurate.
4. More informed decision-making is possible.
5. A greater degree of control over business activities can be exercised.
6. The possibility of fraud is reduced.
7. Comparisons with the results of previous years and with other businesses are possible.
8. Detailed records are available for reference purposes.
9. Information required by a bank or other lender is readily available.

KEY TERM

A **statement of affairs** is a summary of the financial position of a business on a certain date. It is prepared instead of a statement of financial position when double entry records have not been maintained.

LINK

You learned how to prepare a statement of financial position in Chapter 9.

17.3 Statement of affairs

If the only records available are those relating to the assets and liabilities of the business it is not possible to prepare an income statement. **These assets and liabilities are listed in a statement of affairs which is similar to a statement of financial position.**

When a list of assets and liabilities is prepared without the use of a set of double entry records it is known as a statement of affairs rather than a statement of financial position.

If the assets, liabilities and capital of the business are known and no further information is available, the only way in which the profit can be measured is to compare the change in the capital over the financial period. Capital increases when a profit is made and decreases when a loss is incurred. The basic formula for calculating profit is:

Closing capital – Opening capital = Profit

Part of the difference between the two capital figures may be caused by drawings made by the owner. If drawings have taken place during the period, the formula must be modified to:

Closing capital – Opening capital + Drawings = Profit

If additional capital has been introduced during the period, this will also account for some of the difference between the two capital figures. The formula must be modified to:

Closing capital – Opening capital + Drawings – Capital introduced = Profit

An alternative way to calculate profit is to construct a capital account and insert the missing figure of profit:

Chapter 17: Incomplete records

Capital account							
Date	Details	Folio	$	Date	Details	Folio	$
Year 1				Year 1			
Dec 31	Drawings		xxx	Jan 1	Balance	b/d	xxx
	Balance	c/d	xxx	Dec 31	Bank		xxx
					Profit		?
			—				xxx
			—				
				Year 2			
				Jan 1	Balance	b/d	xxx

- The dates of 1 January and 31 December have been used for convenience. The first and last days of the financial year of the particular business are used in practice.

Calculating profit by comparing the change in the capital is very unsatisfactory. Only an estimate of the profit for the year is possible: it is not possible to show details about gross profit, sales, purchases, expenses and so on. It is not possible to analyse the results and informed decisions about the future cannot be made.

> **TIP**
> The difference between the opening and closing capital (adjusted for capital introduced and drawings during the year) represents the profit (or loss) for the year.

TEST YOURSELF 17.1

1. Explain the meaning of a statement of affairs.
2. State the circumstances in which a statement of affairs is prepared.
3. State why it is not satisfactory to measure profit by changes in capital.

Walkthrough 17.1

Vijay is a sole trader. He has not kept a full set of double entry records, but is able to provide the following information about his assets and liabilities:

	1 May 20–8 $	30 April 20–9 $
Premises at cost	30 000	30 000
Equipment at cost	9 000	9 000
Motor vehicle at cost	8 000	8 000
Inventory	14 000	16 000
Trade receivables	8 500	9 400
Trade payables	8 000	9 200
Bank	1 200	–
Bank overdraft	–	900
Other payables	–	100
Other receivables	120	130

During the year ended 30 April 20–9 Vijay purchased additional equipment for the business, costing $7 000, out of his personal funds. This is in addition to the equipment listed. His cash drawings during the year amounted to $5 000, and he also took goods costing $3 000 for personal use.

On 30 April 20–9 it was decided that **all** the equipment should be depreciated by 10%, and the motor vehicle should be depreciated by 25%. It was also decided to create a provision for doubtful debts of 2% of the trade receivables.

a   Prepare a statement of affairs of Vijay at 1 May 20–8.
b   Prepare a statement of affairs of Vijay at 30 April 20–9.
c   Calculate Vijay's profit for the year ended 30 April 20–9.

a

Vijay
Statement of affairs at 31 May 20–8

	$	$	$
Non-current assets			Cost
Premises			30 000
Equipment			9 000
Motor vehicle			8 000
			47 000
Current assets			
Inventory			14 000
Trade receivables			8 500
Other receivables			120
Bank			1 200
			23 820
Total assets			70 820
Capital and liabilities			
Capital			
Balance			62 820
Current liabilities			
Trade payables			8 000
Total capital and liabilities			70 820

b

Vijay
Statement of affairs at 30 April 20–9

	$ Cost	$ Accumulated depreciation	$ Net book value
Non-current assets			
Premises	30 000		30 000
Equipment	16 000	1 600	14 400
Motor vehicles	8 000	2 000	6 000
	54 000	3 600	50 400
Current assets			
Inventory			16 000
Trade receivables		9 400	
Less Provision for doubtful debts		188	9 212
Other receivables			130
			25 342
Total assets			75 742
Capital and liabilities			
Capital			
Balance			65 542
Current liabilities			
Trade payables			9 200
Other payables			100
Bank overdraft			900
			10 200
Total capital and liabilities			75 742

- In **a** and **b** the capital figure has been inserted to make the statement of affairs balance.

c

Vijay
Calculation of profit for the year ended 30 April 20–9

	$	$
Capital at 30 April 20–9		65 542
Less Capital at 1 May 20–8		62 820
		2 722
Add Drawings: cash	5 000	
goods	3 000	8 000
		10 722
Less Capital introduced		7 000
Profit for the year		3 722

c   Alternative presentation

Vijay
Capital account

Date	Details	Folio	$	Date	Details	Folio	$
20–9				20–8			
Apr 30	Drawings		5 000	May 1	Balance		62 820
	Purchases		3 000	20–9			
	Balance	c/d	65 542	Apr 30	Equipment		7 000
					Profit		3 722
			73 542				73 542
				20–9			
				May 1	Balance	b/d	65 542

- The profit is inserted as a 'missing figure', in order to balance the account.

If no instructions are provided to the contrary, the profit calculation can be shown **within** the closing statement of affairs. In this case the profit for the year or the loss for the year will be inserted to make the statement of affairs balance.

Walkthrough 17.2

Vijay is a sole trader. He has not kept a full set of double entry records.

A statement of affairs on 1 May 20–8 was shown in **Walkthrough 17.1**.

Assume that the calculation of the profit is to be shown within the statement of affairs on 30 April 20–9. The first section of the statement of affairs on 30 April 20–9 would be as shown in **Walkthrough 17.1**. The capital section of the statement of affairs is shown as follows:

	$	$	$
Capital			
Opening balance			62 820
Add Capital introduced			7 000
Profit for the year			3 722
			73 542
Less Drawings (5 000 + 3 000)			8 000
			65 542

Chapter 17: Incomplete records

> **TEST YOURSELF 17.2**
>
> 1 Manan is a trader. The following information is provided:
>
> Capital 1 January 20–5 $40 000, capital 31 December 20–6 $50 000, profit for the year $8 500, capital introduced during the year $5 000.
>
> Calculate, by means of a capital account, Manan's drawings for the year.

You can now answer Questions 1 and 2 at the end of this chapter.

Even when a business has not maintained the double entry records it is sometimes able to provide information in addition to details of the assets and liabilities. If details of money received and paid are available, it is possible to calculate the sales, purchases and expenses. This means that, after various calculations, a set of financial statements can be prepared.

Walkthrough 17.3

Anjali is a sole trader. She maintains a bank account, but not a full set of double entry records. She provided the following information:

	1 July 20–4 $	30 June 20–5 $
Premises at cost	60 000	60 000
Equipment (cost $22 500)	18 000	?
Inventory	28 100	29 800
Trade receivables	23 800	26 800
Trade payables	19 700	20 200
Other payables (accrued general expenses)	200	–
Other receivables (prepaid general expenses)	–	340
Bank	12 700	?

Summary of receipts and payments for the year:

Receipts	$	Payments	$
Receipts from debtors	331 600	Payments to creditors	249 400
Cash sales	12 000	General expenses	19 620
		Drawings	38 400
		Wages	40 000
		Property tax	3 800
		Insurance	1 900
		Equipment	8 000

During the year ended 30 June 20–5 Anjali took goods costing $4 000 for her own use.

On 30 June 20–5 equipment should be depreciated by 10% on the cost of equipment owned at that date. On that date, it was decided to create a provision for doubtful debts of $2\frac{1}{2}$% of the trade receivables.

Prepare the income statement of Anjali for the year ended 30 June 20–5 and a statement of financial position at 30 June 20–5.

Before attempting to answer a question of this nature it is necessary to calculate the following:

1. Opening capital
2. Revenue for the year
3. Purchases for the year
4. Closing bank balance

Calculations

1. Opening capital

Statement of affairs at 1 July 20–4			
	$ Cost	$ Accumulated depreciation	$ Net book value
Non-current assets			
Premises	60 000		60 000
Equipment	22 500	4 500	18 000
	82 500	4 500	78 000
Current assets			
Inventory			28 100
Trade receivables			23 800
Bank			12 700
			64 600
Total assets			142 600
Capital and liabilities			
Capital			
Balance			122 700
Current liabilities			
Trade payables			19 700
Other payables			200
			19 900
Total capital and liabilities			142 600

2. Revenue for the year

   i Credit sales

   The amount received from the credit customers is not necessarily equal to the actual sales. Some of the money received is to settle the amount owed by credit customers at the start of the year (for goods sold in the previous financial year). Money is owed by the credit customers at the end of the year for goods sold during the present financial year.

The credit sales can be calculated as follows:

	$
Receipts from credit customers	331 600
Less Trade receivables 1 July 20–4	23 800
	307 800
Plus Trade receivables 30 June 20–5	26 800
Credit sales for the year	334 600

Alternatively, the credit sales can be calculated by inserting a 'missing figure' in a total trade receivables account:

Total trade receivables account								
Date	Details	Folio	$	Date	Details	Folio	$
20–4				20–5			
Jul 1	Balance	b/d	23 800	Jun 30	Bank		331 600
20–5					Balance	c/d	26 800
Jun 30	Sales*		334 600				
			358 400				358 400
20–5							
Jul 1	Balance	b/d	26 800				

ii Total revenue

	$
Credit sales	334 600
Cash sales	12 000
Total revenue	346 600

3 Purchases for the year

i Credit purchases

The amount paid to the credit suppliers is not necessarily equal to the actual purchases. Some of the money paid is to settle the amount owed to credit suppliers at the start of the year (for goods bought in the previous financial year). Money is owed to the credit suppliers at the end of the year for goods bought during the present financial year.

The credit purchases can be calculated as follows:

	$
Payments to credit suppliers	249 400
Less Trade payables 1 July 20–4	19 700
	229 700
Plus Trade payables 30 June 20–5	20 200
Credit purchases for the year	249 900

Alternatively, the credit purchases can be calculated by inserting a 'missing figure' in a total trade payables account:

Total trade payables account							
Date	Details	Folio	$	Date	Details	Folio	$
20–5				20–4			
Jun 30	Bank		249 400	Jul 1	Balance	b/d	19 700
	Balance	c/d	20 200	20–5			
				Jun 30	Purchases*		249 900
			269 600				269 600
				20–5			
				Jul 1	Balance	b/d	20 200

ii Total purchases

As there are no cash purchases the total purchases are equal to the credit purchases calculated.

4 Closing bank balance

The bank balance on 1 July 20–4 is given together with details of receipts and payments. A summary of the bank account can be prepared to calculate the closing bank balance. It is not usually necessary to itemise all the transactions.

Bank account							
Date	Details	Folio	$	Date	Details	Folio	$
20–4				20–5			
Jul 1	Balance	b/d	12 700	Jun 30	Total payments		361 120
20–5							
Jun 30	Total receipts		343 600				
	Balance	c/d	4 820				
			361 120				361 120
				20–5			
				Jul 1	Balance	b/d	4 820

Anjali
Income statement for the year ended 30 June 20–4

	$	$	$
Revenue			346 600
Less Cost of sales			
Opening inventory		28 100	
Purchases	249 900		
Less Goods for own use	4 000	245 900	
		274 000	
Less Closing inventory		29 800	244 200
Gross profit			102 400
Less General expenses		19 080	
Wages		40 000	
Property tax		3 800	
Insurance		1 900	
Provision for doubtful debts		670	
Depreciation of equipment		3 050	68 500
Profit for the year			33 900

- The figures for revenue and purchases have come from previous calculations.
- The general expenses have been calculated $19 620 – $200 – $340.
- The provision for doubtful debts has been calculated at $2\frac{1}{2}$% of $26 800.
- The depreciation of equipment has been calculated at 10% of ($22 500 + $8 000).

Cambridge IGCSE and O Level Accounting

TIP

Total accounts are prepared using the same principles as those used for control accounts which you learned about in Chapter 16.

Anjali
Statement of financial position at 30 June 20–5

	$ Cost	$ Accumulated depreciation	$ Net book value
Non-current assets			
Premises	60 000		60 000
Equipment	30 500	7 550	22 950
	90 500	7 550	82 950
Current assets			
Inventory			29 800
Trade receivables		26 800	
Less Provision for doubtful debts		670	26 130
Other receivables			340
			56 270
Total assets			139 220
Capital and liabilities			
Capital			
Opening balance			122 700
Plus Profit for the year			33 900
			156 600
Less Drawings			42 400
			114 200
Current liabilities			
Trade payables			20 200
Bank overdraft			4 820
			25 020
Total capital and liabilities			139 220

- The depreciation to date on equipment has been calculated $4 500 + $3 050.
- The figure for bank overdraft has come from a previous calculation.
- The drawings have been calculated $38 400 + $4 000.

TEST YOURSELF 17.3

1 A trader's financial year ends on 31 May. The following information is provided – Cash purchases $4 000, cheques paid to creditors $23 300, trade payables at 1 June 20–7 $2 500, trade payables at 31 May 20–8 $3 100. Calculate the purchases for the year.

When a business allows its credit customers a cash discount if the account is paid within the set time limit this will affect the calculation of the credit sales. Similarly, any discount received from credit suppliers will affect the calculation of the credit purchases.

LINK

You learned how to prepare a full set of financial statements with adjustments in Chapters 11, 12 and 13.

Chapter 17: Incomplete records

Walkthrough 17.4

Anjali is a sole trader. She maintains a bank account, but not a full set of double entry records. She provided the following information:

	1 July 20–4 $	30 June 20–5 $
Trade receivables	23 800	26 800
Trade payables	19 700	20 200

During the year ended 30 June 20–5 receipts from credit customers totalled $331 600 (after the deduction of $8 200 cash discount). $249 400 was paid to credit suppliers (after the deduction of $6 780 cash discount).

Calculate the credit sales and credit purchases for the year ended 30 June 20–5.

Total trade receivables account

Date	Details	Folio	$	Date	Details	Folio	$
20–4				20–5			
Jul 1	Balance	b/d	23 800	Jun 30	Bank		331 600
					Discount allowed		8 200
20–5					Balance	c/d	26 800
Jun 30	Sales*		342 800				
			366 600				366 600
20–5							
Jul 1	Balance	b/d	26 800				

Total trade payables account

Date	Details	Folio	$	Date	Details	Folio	$
20–5				20–4			
Jun 30	Bank		249 400	Jul 1	Balance	b/d	19 700
	Discount received		6 780	20–5			
	Balance	c/d	20 200	Jun 30	Purchases*		256 680
			276 380				276 380
				20–5			
				July 1	Balance	b/d	20 200

> **TIP**
> Cash discount allowed and received must be included in calculations of credit sales and credit purchases. The discounts must also be recorded in the profit and loss section of the income statement.

- The amounts shown for sales and purchases would appear in the trading account section of the income statement.
- The amounts for discount allowed and discount received would appear in the profit and loss account section of the income statement.

You can now answer Questions 3 and 4 at the end of this chapter.

17.5 Mark-up, margin and inventory turnover

When dealing with incomplete records, it is sometimes necessary to use percentages to calculate missing information.

> **KEY TERMS**
>
> **Mark-up** is the gross profit expressed as a percentage of cost price.
>
> **Margin** is the gross profit expressed as a percentage of the selling price.

Mark-up and margin

These both measure the gross profit as a percentage.

The **mark-up** is the gross profit measured as a percentage of the cost price.

The **margin** is the gross profit measured as a percentage of selling price.

Walkthrough 17.5

A trader's turnover for the year were $20 000 and the cost of goods sold was $15 000.

Calculate:

a the margin
b the mark-up.

a The margin $\dfrac{\text{Gross profit}}{\text{Sales}} \times \dfrac{100}{1} = \dfrac{\$5\,000}{\$20\,000} \times \dfrac{100}{1} = 25\%$

b The mark-up $\dfrac{\text{Gross profit}}{\text{Cost of sales}} \times \dfrac{100}{1} = \dfrac{\$5\,000}{\$15\,000} \times \dfrac{100}{1} = 33.33\%$

Applying either margin or mark-up, it is possible to calculate any one unknown figure in the trading account section of an income statement.

Walkthrough 17.6

The financial year of North West Traders ends on 30 November. The following information is provided:

	$
Inventory 1 December 20–3	4 600
Inventory 30 November 20–4	5 200
Revenue	72 000

The mark-up is at a standard rate of 25%.

Calculate, by means of a trading account section of an income statement, the purchases for the year ended 30 November 20–4.

Chapter 17: Incomplete records

North West Traders
Income statement for the year ended 30 November 20–4

	$	$
Revenue		72 000
Less Cost of sales		
Opening inventory	4 600	
Purchases	58 200 **d**	
	62 800 **c**	
Less Closing inventory	5 200	57 600 **b**
Gross profit		14 400 **a**

- An outline statement was prepared and the figures for revenue, opening inventory and closing inventory were inserted, with gaps left for purchases, cost of sales and gross profit.
- The gross profit was calculated. The mark-up is 25% so the gross profit is 25% of the cost of sales, so the selling price equals 125%. The gross profit is $\frac{25}{125}$ of the revenue which is $\frac{1}{5}$ or 20% of $72 000. The gross profit is, therefore, $14 400, **a**.
- The cost of sales was inserted as the difference between the revenue and the gross profit. Alternatively, it can be calculated at $\frac{100}{125}$ of the revenue which is $\frac{4}{5}$ or 80% of $72 000. The cost of sales is, therefore, $57 600, **b**.
- The purchases figure was calculated by working 'backwards' from the cost of sales. The cost of sales plus the opening inventory amounted to $62 800, **c**. This figure less the opening inventory equals the purchases of $58 200, **d**.

TEST YOURSELF 17.4

1. Explain the difference between margin and mark-up.
2. A trader purchased goods for $4 000 and sold them for $5 000. Calculate the percentage margin and the percentage mark-up.

LINK

You will learn about the importance of the rate of inventory turnover in Chapter 22.

Rate of inventory turnover

It is sometimes necessary to use calculations relating to the rate of inventory turnover in order to calculate an unknown figure in the trading account section of an income statement. The **rate of inventory turnover** is the number of times a business replaces its inventory in a given period of time.

The formula for calculating the rate of inventory turnover is:

$$\frac{\text{Cost of sales}}{\text{Average inventory}}$$

KEY TERM

The **rate of inventory turnover** is the number of times a business replaces its inventory in a given period of time.

Walkthrough 17.7

M Parmar is a trader. The financial year ends on 31 October. The following information is provided:

Inventory 1 November 20–1	$12 000
Inventory 31 October 20–2	$8 000

The margin is at a standard rate of 20%.

The rate of inventory turnover is 15 times a year.

Calculate, by means of the trading account section of an income statement, the purchases for the year ended 31 October 20–2.

M Parmar
Income statement for the year ended 31 October 20–2

	$	$	
Revenue		187 500	**e**
Less Cost of sales			
Opening inventory	12 000		
Purchases	146 000		**c**
	158 000		**b**
Less Closing inventory	8 000	150 000	**a**
Gross profit		37 500	**d**

- An outline of the statement was prepared and the figures of opening inventory and closing inventory were inserted, with gaps left for revenue, purchases, cost of sales and gross profit.

- The average inventory was calculated.

$$\text{Average inventory} = \frac{\text{Opening inventory} + \text{Closing inventory}}{2}$$

$$= \frac{12\,000 + 8\,000}{2} = \$10\,000$$

- The cost of sales was calculated:

$$\text{Rate of inventory turnover} = \frac{\text{Cost of sales}}{\text{Average inventory}}$$

$$= \frac{\text{Cost of sales}}{10\,000} = 15$$

The cost of sales is, therefore $150 000.

- The cost of sales was inserted in the statement, **a**.
- The purchases figure was calculated by working 'backwards' from the cost of sales, **b** and **c**.

- The gross profit was calculated. The margin is 20% so the gross profit is 20% of the revenue (sales). The selling price equals 100%, the gross profit equals 20%, so the cost of sales equals 80%. The gross profit is $\frac{20}{80}$ of the cost of sales which is $\frac{1}{4}$ or 25% of $150 000. The gross profit is $37 500, **d**.

- The revenue figure was calculated by working 'backwards'. The gross profit plus the cost of sales equals the sales (revenue), **e**.

You can now answer Questions 5 and 6 at the end of this chapter.

Revision checklist

- A statement of affairs is similar to a statement of financial position and is prepared when a full set of accounting records is not maintained.
- Profit can be measured from the change in the capital over a period of time, taking into consideration drawings and capital introduced.
- The amount received from credit customers does not necessarily equal the credit sales: the amount paid to credit suppliers does not necessarily equal the credit purchases.
- When a record of money paid and received is available as well as the assets and liabilities, it is possible to prepare a set of financial statements after calculating revenue and purchases (and possibly the capital and the bank balances).
- Gross profit can be expressed as margin (on selling price) and as mark-up (on cost price).
- The rate of inventory turnover is the number of times a business replaces its inventory in a given period of time.

Exam-style questions

1. Halina's capital on 1 January 20–7 was $25 900. On 31 December 20–7 her capital was $27 600. During the year she had invested a further $5 000 and had withdrawn goods costing $900 for personal use. How much was the profit or loss for the year?

   A $2 400 loss   B $2 400 profit   C $5 800 loss   D $5 800 profit

2. Leroy is a trader. He does not maintain a full set of accounting records, but was able to provide the following information on 1 June 20–8:

	$
Fixtures and fittings at valuation	6 000
Motor vehicle at cost	14 000
Inventory	3 800
Trade receivables	4 250
Trade payables	2 950
Long-term loan from Lenders Ltd	5 000
Other receivables	360
Bank overdraft	2 410

   During the year ended 31 May 20–9 he borrowed a further $3 500 from Lenders Ltd. He took $2 000 from the bank for personal use.

   On 31 May 20–9 it was decided that the motor vehicle should be depreciated by 20% on cost and that the fixtures and fittings should be valued at $5 600.

   On 31 May 20–9 the inventory was valued at $4 100, the trade receivables totalled $4 660, the trade payables totalled $3 140 and there was $380 in the bank.

   a Prepare a statement of affairs of Leroy on 1 June 20–8 showing the total capital at that date.

   b Prepare a statement of affairs of Leroy on 31 May 20–9 showing the total capital at that date.

   c Prepare a capital account for Leroy for the year ended 31 May 20–9 showing the profit or loss for the year.

3. Sally's financial year ends on 31 October. On 1 November 20–4 her trade receivables owed $5 840. During the year ended 31 October 20–5 she received $66 640 from trade receivables, after allowing cash discount of $1 360. Sales returns during the year totalled $2 430. On 31 October 20–5 the trade receivables owed $6 760.

   How much were the credit sales?

   A $65 490   B $69 510   C $69 990   D $71 350

Chapter 17: Incomplete records

4 Mohan is a sole trader who does not maintain a full set of accounting records. He was able to provide the following information:

On 1 May 20–8:

	$
Fixtures (cost $31 000)	24 800
Motor vehicle (cost $15 000)	9 000
Inventory	19 600
Trade receivables	17 300
Balance at bank	9 750
Trade payables	16 450

For the year ended 20 April 20–9:

		$
Receipts	– From trade receivables	458 800
Payments	– To trade payables	371 820
	For motor expenses	15 070
	For general expenses	25 500
	For new fixtures	4 000
	For Mohan's personal use	20 000

On 30 April 20–9:

	$
Inventory	23 080
Trade receivables	21 500
Trade payables	15 510

Fixtures should be depreciated by 10% per annum on the cost of fixtures held at the end of the year. The motor vehicle should be depreciated by 25% per annum on cost.

a Prepare the income statement of Mohan for the year ended 30 April 20–9.

b Prepare the statement of financial position of Mohan at 30 April 20–9.

Show all calculations.

5 Aisha applies a mark-up of 25% to obtain the selling price of her goods. She provided the following information:

	$
Opening inventory	4 800
Closing inventory	6 200
Revenue	70 000

How much were Aisha's purchases for the year?

A $51 100 **B** $53 900 **C** $54 600 **D** $57 400

6 Pradeep is a trader. He provided the following information:

	$
Inventory at cost on 1 August 20–5	1 600
For the year ended 31 July 20–6:	
Purchases	39 200
Revenue	48 000

On the evening of 31 July 20–6 a fire destroyed a quantity of goods. The cost of the goods salvaged from the fire was $700.

Pradeep marks up the goods by 25% on cost when calculating the selling price.

a Calculate, by means of a trading account section of an income statement, the cost of the goods which were destroyed.

b Explain the difference between mark-up and margin.

c Calculate Pradeep's rate of inventory turnover. Use the total inventory before the fire on 31 July 20–6 when calculating the average inventory.

d State what the answer to the calculation in **c** indicates.

Chapter 18
Accounts of clubs and societies

Learning objectives

In this chapter you will learn to:

- distinguish between receipts and payments accounts and income and expenditure accounts   5.4
- prepare receipts and payments accounts   5.4
- prepare accounts for revenue-generating activities, e.g. refreshments, subscriptions   5.4
- prepare income and expenditure accounts and statements of financial position   5.4
- make adjustments to financial statements   5.4
- define and calculate the accumulated fund.   5.4

Cambridge IGCSE and O Level Accounting

> **KEY TERMS**
>
> A **non-trading organisation** is an organisation formed to provide facilities and services for members. They are not formed with the aim of making a profit.
>
> **Subscriptions** are amounts members of an organisation pay, usually annually, to use the facilities provided by the club or society.
>
> A **receipts and payments account** is a summary of the cash book which is prepared annually by a non-trading organisation.

18.1 Introduction

This chapter concentrates on the accounts of **non-trading organisations** such as clubs and societies. The main aim of these organisations is to provide some facilities and services for their members; making a profit is not the main objective. Examples of such organisations include youth clubs, sports clubs, amateur dramatic groups, golf clubs, scout groups, etc.

In some cases a full set of double entry records is written up each year, but it is more usual to find that only a record of money received and paid is maintained.

The main source of income of a society is **subscriptions**. These are the amounts members pay, usually annually, to use the facilities provided by the club or society.

A person is appointed to act as treasurer and be responsible for collecting any money due to the society and for paying money owed by the society. At the end of the financial year the treasurer will usually present financial statements to the members. These financial statements may consist of a **receipts and payments account**, possibly a trading account section of an income statement, an income and expenditure account and a statement of financial position.

18.2 Preparation of a receipts and payments account

A receipts and payments account is regarded as a **summary of the cash book** for the financial year. All money received is debited and all money paid is credited. The account is balanced and the balance carried down to become the opening balance for the following financial year. This account does not usually distinguish between cash and bank transactions, so the balance may represent actual cash, money in the bank or a combination of the two. A debit balance is an asset and represents money owned by the society whereas a credit balance is a liability and represents a bank overdraft.

A receipts and payments account, just like a cash book, records all money received and paid. It is important to remember that:

- no adjustments are made for accruals and prepayments
- no distinction is made between capital receipts and revenue receipts
- no distinction is made between capital expenditure and revenue expenditure
- non-monetary items such as depreciation are not included.

Walkthrough 18.1

The Apollo Athletics Club was formed some years ago to provide various sporting facilities for its members. The club also has a shop where members can purchase sportswear.

On 1 August 20–7 the club had $2 200 in the bank. The treasurer provided the following list of receipts and payments for the year ended 31 July 20–8:

Chapter 18: Accounts of clubs and societies

	$
Subscriptions received	5 860
Receipts from shop sales	3 960
Purchases of goods for resale	2 130
Wages – shop assistant	1 300
athletics coach	2 700
Rates and insurance	328
General expenses	1 120
Purchase of new sports equipment	2 950
Athletics competition – entrance fees received	1 100
cost of prizes	660

All receipts are paid into the bank and all payments are made by cheque.

Prepare the receipts and payments account of the Apollo Athletics Club for the year ended 31 July 20–8.

Apollo Athletics Club
Receipts and payments account for the year ended 31 July 20–8

Receipts			$	Payments		$
20–7				20–8		
Aug 1	Balance	b/d	2 200	Jul 31 Purchases		2 130
20–8				Wages		
				shop assistant		1 300
Jul 31	Subscriptions		5 860	athletics coach		2 700
	Receipts from shop		3 960	Rates and insurance		328
	Competition			General expenses		1 120
	entrance fees		1 100	Sports equipment		2 950
				Competition prizes		660
				Balance	c/d	1 932
			13 120			13 120
20–8						
Aug 1	Balance	b/d	1 932			

> **TIP**
> A receipts and payments account includes all money paid and received, ignoring the year to which it relates, and includes both capital and revenue items.

TEST YOURSELF 18.1

1. Name **three** financial statements that the treasurer of a club may prepare at the end of the financial year.
2. Explain the term 'subscriptions' in connection with a club or society.
3. Explain the purpose of a receipts and payments account.

You can now answer Question 1 at the end of this chapter.

18.3 Preparation of an income statement of a club or society

Although buying and selling is not the main purpose of a club or society, many do carry out a trading activity. Many clubs operate a shop or a café where goods are bought and sold. At the end of the financial year **an income statement (trading section only)** should be prepared for each separate trading activity to show the profit earned on that activity.

The trading section of an income statement of a club or society is prepared in exactly the same way as that for a business. Any expenses which arise as a result of running the trading activity such as wages of café assistants, depreciation of café equipment and so on. should be added to the cost of the goods sold in order to calculate the correct profit or loss.

The profit on a trading activity is calculated in the income statement and then transferred to the income and expenditure account (see later in this chapter).

Walkthrough 18.2

The Apollo Athletics Club was formed some years ago to provide various sporting facilities for its members. The club also has a shop where members can purchase sportswear.

The treasurer provided the following information for the year ended 31 July 20–8:

	$
Receipts from shop sales	3 960
Purchases of goods for resale	2 130
Shop inventory 1 August 20–7	240
Shop inventory 31 July 20–8	310
Wages of shop assistant	1 300

Prepare the shop income statement of the Apollo Athletics Club for the year ended 31 July 20–8.

Apollo Athletics Club
Shop income statement for the year ended 31 July 20–8

	$	$
Revenue		3 960
Less Cost of sales		
Opening inventory	240	
Purchases	2 130	
	2 370	
Less Closing inventory	310	
Cost of goods sold	2 060	
Wages of shop assistant	1 300	3 360
Profit on shop (transferred to income and expenditure account)		600

> **TIP**
> Where an income statement is prepared for a particular activity, the profit or loss on that activity must be transferred from the income statement to the income and expenditure account.

Chapter 18: Accounts of clubs and societies

> **TEST YOURSELF 18.2**
>
> 1 Explain when it is necessary for a club or society to prepare a trading section of an income statement as part of the financial statements.

18.4 Preparation of an income and expenditure account

An **income and expenditure account** compares the gains of the club with the expenses of running the club. If the gains are more than the expenses the difference is referred to as a **surplus** or excess of income over expenditure (this is known as the profit for the year in a business). If the gains are less than the expenses the difference is referred to as a **deficit** or excess of expenditure over income (this is known as the loss for the year in a business).

An income and expenditure account is prepared using the same principles as those applied in the preparation of an income statement of a trading business.

It is important to remember that:

- adjustments must be made for accruals and prepayments
- capital receipts and capital expenditure are not included
- only revenue receipts and revenue expenditure are included
- non-monetary items such as depreciation are included
- assets and liabilities at the beginning and end of the financial year are not included.

Where the club or society holds a fundraising activity, the income and the expenses of that activity should be set off against each other in the income and expenditure account. In this way, the profit or loss on that particular activity can be calculated.

KEY TERMS

An **income and expenditure account** is prepared annually by a non-trading organisation. It compares the gains and the expenses to calculate the surplus or deficit.

A **surplus** arises when the gains of a non-trading organisation exceed the expenses.

A **deficit** arises when the expenses of a non-trading organisation exceed the gains.

LINK

You learned how to prepare an income statement of a business in Chapters 8, 11 and 12.

Walkthrough 18.3

The Apollo Athletics Club was formed some years ago to provide various sporting facilities for its members. The club also has a shop where members can purchase sportswear.

The following receipts and payments account was prepared for the year ended 31 July 20–8:

Apollo Athletics Club
Receipts and payments account for the year ended 31 July 20–8

Receipts			$	Payments		$
20–7				20–8		
Aug 1	Balance	b/d	2 200	Jul 31 Purchases		2 130
20–8				Wages		
				shop assistant		1 300
Jul 31	Subscriptions		5 860	athletics coach		2 700
	Receipts from shop		3 960	Rates and insurance		328
	Competition			General expenses		1 120
	entrance fees		1 100	Sports equipment		2 950
				Competition prizes		660
				Balance	c/d	1 932
			13 120			13 120
20–8						
Aug 1	Balance	b/d	1 932			

The treasurer also provided the following additional information:

1. On 31 July 20–8:
   - insurance prepaid amounts to $16
   - wages of athletics coach, outstanding amount of $400
   - 15 members still owe their annual subscription of $20 each for the current financial year
   - eight members have paid their annual subscription of $20 each for the following financial year
   - sports equipment is to be depreciated by $1 715.

2. The profit on the club's shop for the year ended 31 July 20–8 was $600 (calculated in the shop income statement).

Prepare the income and expenditure account of the Apollo Athletics Club for the year ended 31 July 20–8.

Apollo Athletics Club
Income and expenditure account for the year ended 31 July 20–8

	$	$
Income		
Subscriptions (5 860 + 300 – 160)		6 000
Profit on shop		600
Competition – entrance fees	1 100	
cost of prizes	660	440
		7 040
Expenditure		
Wages – athletics coach (2 700 + 400)	3 100	
Rates and insurance (328 – 16)	312	
General expenses	1 120	
Depreciation of equipment	1 715	6 247
Surplus for the year		793

TEST YOURSELF 18.3

1 State the equivalent term used by a business for **each** of the following terms used by a club:
 a deficit
 b income and expenditure account.
2 Explain why a club should set off the expenses of any fund-raising activity against the income from that activity.

You can now answer Question 2 at the end of this chapter.

18.5 Preparation of a statement of financial position of a club or society

The principles applied when preparing a statement of financial position of a club or society are similar to those applied in the preparation of a statement of financial position of a business. The statement of financial position of a club or society shows non-current assets, current assets, non-current liabilities and current liabilities in exactly the same way as a statement of financial position of a trading organisation.

The main difference is that there is **no capital in the statement of financial position of a club or society** whereas a business is usually financed by an investment of capital from the owner(s). Members of a club or society do not invest money in the same way as the proprietor of a business. Because of this, the members are not entitled to make any drawings if a club or society makes a surplus. This means that these surpluses will accumulate within the organisation to form a capital fund known as the **accumulated fund**. If the club makes a deficit then the accumulated fund will decrease. This **accumulated fund replaces capital in the statement of financial position of a club or society**.

> **LINK**
> You learned how to prepare a statement of financial position of a business in Chapters 9, 11 and 12.

> **KEY TERM**
> The **accumulated fund** consists of the surpluses (less any deficits) which have accumulated over the life of the organisation. It replaces capital in the statement of financial position of a club or society.

Walkthrough 18.4

The Apollo Athletics Club was formed some years ago to provide various sporting facilities for its members. The club also has a shop where members can purchase sportswear.

On 1 August 20–7 the following balances appeared in the books of the club:

	$
Premises at cost	20 000
Equipment at cost	14 200
Provision for depreciation of equipment	5 680
Balance at bank	2 200
Shop inventory	240
Accumulated fund	30 960

The income and expenditure account for the year ended 31 July 20–8 showed a surplus of $793.

During the year ended 31 July 20–8 new equipment costing $2 950 was purchased. The depreciation on equipment for the year amounted to $1 715.

On 31 July 20–8:

	$
Balance at bank	1 932
Shop inventory	310
Insurance prepaid	16
Wages of athletics coach outstanding	400
Subscriptions owing by members	300
Subscriptions paid in advance by members	160

Prepare the statement of financial position of the Apollo Athletics Club at 31 July 20–8.

Apollo Athletics Club
Statement of financial position at 31 July 20–8

	$ Cost	$ Accumulated depreciation	$ Net book value
Non-current assets			
Premises	20 000	–	20 000
Equipment	17 150	7 395	9 755
	37 150	7 395	29 755
Current assets			
Shop inventory		310	
Subscriptions accrued		300	
Other receivables		16	
Bank		1 932	
			2 558
Total assets			32 313
Accumulated fund and liabilities			
Accumulated fund			
Opening balance			30 960
Plus Surplus for the year			793
			31 753
Current liabilities			
Other payables			400
Subscriptions prepaid			160
			560
Total liabilities			32 313

- The subscriptions owing could have been included under other receivables and the subscriptions prepaid could have been included under the other payables. In this case a note to the statement of financial position would show the breakdown of these figures.

You can now answer Questions 3 and 4 at the end of this chapter.

18.6 Comparison of accounting terms used by a business and those used by a club or society

Business	Club or society
–	Receipts and payments account
Profit and loss account section of income statement	Income and expenditure account
Profit for the year	Surplus
Loss for the year	Deficit
Capital	Accumulated fund

> **TEST YOURSELF 18.4**
>
> 1 State the term used by a business to describe the equivalent of the accumulated fund in a club.
> 2 Explain how **each** of the following will affect the accumulated fund of a club.
>   a surplus
>   b deficit

18.7 Subscriptions

The receipts and payments account shows the amount of subscriptions **received** during the financial year, but the income and expenditure account shows the amount of subscriptions **relating** to the financial year. This means that the amount received must be adjusted for any subscriptions owed by members and any subscriptions paid in advance by members (see **Walkthrough 18.3**). The calculation of the amount relating to the financial year may be shown in the form of a ledger account known as a **subscriptions account**.

This may be regarded as the account of the members in the books of the organisation. Subscriptions owing by members will appear as a debit balance as they are a current asset to the club or society. Subscriptions paid in advance by members will appear as a credit balance as they are a current liability because the club or society has an obligation to provide a period of membership which has already been paid for. It is possible to have two balances on a subscriptions account as the account is for **all** the members and some may have paid subscriptions in advance and some may not have paid their subscription.

At the end of the financial year the account is closed by a transfer to the income and expenditure account of the amount relating to that financial year.

TIP
Subscriptions owing by members are a debit balance on the subscriptions account and a current asset in the statement of financial position. Subscriptions prepaid by members are a credit balance on the subscriptions account and a current liability in the statement of financial position.

Walkthrough 18.5

The Apollo Athletics Club was formed some years ago to provide various sporting facilities for its members.

On 1 August 20–7 there were no subscriptions owing by members and no members had paid their subscriptions in advance.

During the year ended 31 July 20–8 the club received subscriptions totalling $5 860 from members. This included subscriptions of $20 each from eight members for the following financial year. On 31 July 20–8 subscriptions of $20 each for the current financial year were still outstanding from 15 members.

During the year ended 31 July 20–9 the club received subscriptions from members totalling $6 020. On 31 July 20–9 there were subscriptions outstanding of $120.

Prepare the subscriptions account in the books of the Apollo Athletics Club for **each** of the **two** years ended 31 July 20–8 and 31 July 20–9.

Apollo Athletics Club
Subscriptions account

Date	Details	Folio	$	Date	Details	Folio	$
20–8				20–8			
July 31	Balance	c/d	160	July 31	Bank/cash		5 860
	Income & expenditure		6 000		Balance	c/d	300
			6 160				6 160
20–8				20–8			
Aug 1	Balance	b/d	300	Aug 1	Balance	b/d	160
20–9				20–9			
July 31	Income & expenditure		6 000	July 31	Bank/cash		6 020
					Balance	c/d	120
			6 300				6 300
20–9							
Aug 1	Balance	b/d	120				

A club may have a policy that subscriptions which remain unpaid after a certain period of time are written off. The entries a similar to those made when a business write off an irrecoverable debt. The subscriptions account is credited with the amount written off before the subscriptions for the year are transferred to the income and expenditure account. These irrecoverable debts will be included in the expenses in the income and expenditure account.

TEST YOURSELF 18.5

1. Explain why the amount received from members appears on the credit of a subscriptions account.
2. Explain why subscriptions prepaid by members are a current liability of a club.
3. Explain why the amount shown for subscriptions in a receipts and payments account is not necessarily the same as that shown in an income and expenditure account.

18.8 Calculation of sales and purchases

As the accounts of a club or society are often incomplete it is often necessary to calculate credit purchases (and sometimes credit sales if goods are sold on credit) before the preparation of the income statement.

The same principles applied when calculating these figures for a business which has not got a complete set of accounting records are followed.

LINK

You learned how to calculate purchases and sales for businesses which do not have complete accounting records in Chapter 17.

Walkthrough 18.6

The Apollo Athletics Club has a shop where members can purchase sportswear. All the sales are made for cash and all purchases are made on credit terms.

The treasurer provided the following information:

	$
Trade payables 1 August 20–5	155
Trade payables 31 July 20–6	215
Amount paid to credit suppliers during the year ended 31 July 20–6	2 980

Calculate the purchases for the year ended 31 July 20–6.

Apollo Athletics Club
Total trade payables account

Date	Details	Folio	$	Date	Details	Folio	$
20–6				20–5			
July 31	Bank		2 980	Aug 1	Balance	b/d	155
	Balance	c/d	215	20–6			
				July 31	Purchases		3 040*
			3 195				3 195
				20–6			
				Aug 1	Balance	b/d	215

* This represents the purchases for the year and will appear in the shop income statement.

You can now answer Question 5 at the end of this chapter.

18.9 Calculation of accumulated fund

It is sometimes necessary to calculate the accumulated fund of a club or society. This can be calculated by applying the same formula used to calculate the capital of a business.

| In a business | Assets = Capital + Liabilities |
| In a club or society | Assets = Accumulated fund + Liabilities |

Walkthrough 18.7

On 1 August 20–6 the assets and liabilities of the Apollo Athletics Club were as follows:

	$
Premises at cost	20 000
Equipment at cost	14 200
Provision for depreciation of equipment	4 260
Balance at bank	1 700
Shop inventory	285
Trade payables for shop supplies	215

Calculate the accumulated fund on 1 August 20–7.

Calculation of accumulated fund on 1 August 20–6			
		$	$
Assets	Premises at cost		20 000
	Equipment at cost	14 200	
	Less Provision for depreciation	4 260	9 940
	Balance at bank		1 700
	Shop inventory		285
			31 925
Liabilities	Trade payables		215
Accumulated fund			31 710

> **TEST YOURSELF 18.6**
>
> 1 Explain why the amount shown for purchases in the café income statement of a club is not necessarily equal to the amount paid to credit suppliers.
> 2 State the formula for calculating accumulated fund.

You can now answer Question 6 at the end of this chapter.

Revision checklist

- A club or society is often referred to as a non-trading organisation.
- At the end of the financial year a club will usually prepare a receipts and payments account which is a summary of the cash book.
- If a club carries out a trading activity it may be necessary to prepare a trading section of an income statement at the end of the financial year.
- At the end of the financial year a club will prepare an income and expenditure account which is similar to the profit and loss section of the income statement.
- The statement of financial position of a club is very similar to that of a business except that the capital is replaced by the accumulated fund.
- The main source of income for a club is the subscriptions received from its members for the use of the facilities provided by the club.

Exam-style questions

1 The treasurer of the YY Club provided the following information:

	$
Bank balance 1 May 20–7	4 734 overdraft
Subscriptions received:	
for the year ended 30 April 20–7	1 200
for the year ended 30 April 20–8	12 000
for the year ending 30 April 20–9	800
Profit on sale of old sports equipment	
(book value $520: proceeds of sale $580)	60
Cost of new sports equipment	3 100
Rent paid for 15 months to 31 July 20–8	3 000
Insurance	520
Loan from a member of the club	4 000
Running expenses	?
Bank balance 1 May 20–8	3 324 debit

Prepare a receipts and payments account for the year ended 30 April 20–8 showing the amount paid for running expenses during the year.

2 A club provided the following information:

	$
Subscriptions outstanding at the start of year	250
Subscriptions received during the year	2 450
Subscriptions prepaid at the end of the year	200

How much was included for subscriptions in the income and expenditure account?

A $2 000 **B** $2 250 **C** $2 400 **D** $2 500

3 A sports club was formed on 1 January 20–4. During the year ended 31 December 20–4 the club purchased sports equipment by cheque.
In which of the financial statement would this be included?

	Receipts and payments account	Income and expenditure account	Statement of financial position
A	✓	✓	✓
B	✓	✓	
C	✓		✓
D		✓	✓

4 The WS Music Club was formed on 1 June 20–8. The following information was provided for the year ended 31 May 20–9:

		$
Receipts	Subscriptions	12 100
	Tickets for concert	1 400
	Loan from AB Music Group	1 000
Payments	Rent of rehearsal rooms	5 000
	Insurance (15 months to 31 August 20–9)	600
	General expenses	1 720
	Concert expenses	990
	Musical instruments	3 000

Additional information:

1 The club has 240 members. The annual subscription is $50. On 31 May 20–9 eight members had not paid their subscription and ten members had paid their subscription in advance for the following year.
2 On 31 May 20–9 general expenses accrued amounted to $30 and rent accrued amounted to $200.
3 A ten-year loan from the AB Music Group was received on 1 December 20–8. Interest is payable at 5% per annum.
5 Musical instruments are to be depreciated at the rate of 10% per annum based on the cost of instruments owned at the end of the financial year.

a Prepare the income and expenditure account for the year ended 31 May 20–9.
b Prepare a statement of financial position at 31 May 20–9.

5 In addition to providing sports facilities for members, the HJ Club also has a shop selling sports clothing to members and guests. All purchases are made on credit terms and all sales are made for cash.

The following information is available:

	1 July 20-4 $	30 June 20-5 $
Shop inventory	1 030	1 680
Subscriptions owing by members	200	–
Subscriptions prepaid by members	–	300
Rent payable accrued	–	450
Amounts owing to credit suppliers	920	870
Sports equipment at cost	18 200	?
Provision for depreciation of sports equipment	7 280	?

During the year ended 30 June 20-5:

		$
Receipts	Subscriptions	15 500
	Receipts from shop sales	14 100
	Competition entrance fees	1 350
Payments	New sports equipment	2 000
	Credit suppliers to shop	8 520
	Rent	3 150
	Competition prizes	1 220
	Wages – shop assistant	4 500
	sports trainer	3 630
	General expenses	5 470

The sports equipment is being depreciated at the rate of 20% per annum using the straight line method. A full year's depreciation is charged in the year of purchase.

a Prepare the shop income statement for the year ended 30 June 20-5.
b Prepare the income and expenditure account for the year ended 30 June 20-5.

6 On 1 January 20-4 the accumulated fund of a club amounted to $14 240. The only item of income during the year was subscriptions of $9 500. The expenses for the year included running costs of $9 360 and deprecation of $830. How much was the accumulated fund on 1 January 20-5?

A $13 550   B $14 100   C $14 380   D $14 930

Chapter 19
Partnerships

Learning objectives

In this chapter you will learn to:

- explain the advantages and disadvantages of forming a partnership   5.2
- outline the importance and contents of a partnership agreement   5.2
- explain the purpose of an appropriation account   5.2
- prepare income statements, appropriation accounts and statements of financial position   5.2
- record interest on partners' loans, interest on capital, interest on drawings, partners' salaries and the division of the balance of profit or loss   5.2
- make adjustments to financial statements   5.2
- explain the uses of, and differences between, capital and current accounts   5.2
- draw up partners' capital and current accounts in ledger account form and as part of a statement of financial position.   5.2

KEY TERM

A **partnership** is a business in which two or more people work together as owners with a view to making profits.

LINK

You learned about financial statements of sole traders in Chapters 8 and 9.

LINK

You learned about the advantages and disadvantages of sole trader businesses in Chapter 8.

19.1 Introduction

The earlier chapters (except Chapter 18) related to businesses which were owned by only one person (a sole trader). Another very common form of business is a **partnership**. A **partnership is a business in which two or more people work together as owners with a view to making profits**. Normally, there cannot be more than 20 partners in a business.

Professional people such as accountants and solicitors often operate as partnerships. A large number of family businesses also run as partnerships. Sometimes a new business is formed as a partnership, sometimes a partnership is formed when a sole trader wishes to expand his/her business, sometimes a partnership is formed when two or more sole traders agree to amalgamate their businesses.

A partnership business will maintain double entry records in the same way as a sole trader. At the end of the financial year, an income statement and a statement of financial position are prepared. However, a partnership will prepare an extra account after the income statement. This is known as a **profit and loss appropriation account**.

19.2 The advantages and disadvantages of partnership businesses

Before agreeing to enter into a partnership business a person must consider the likely advantages and disadvantages of such an arrangement. The advantages and disadvantages are summarised as follows:

Advantages	Disadvantages
Additional finance is available.	Profits have to be shared among the partners.
Additional knowledge, experience and skills are available.	Decisions have to be recognised by all partners.
The responsibilities are shared.	Decisions may take longer to put into effect.
The risks are shared.	One partner's actions on behalf of the business are binding on all the partners.
Discussions can take place before decisions are taken.	Disagreements can occur.
	All partners are responsible for the debts of the business.

TEST YOURSELF 19.1

1. Define a partnership.
2. Rahul is a sole trader. He forms a partnership with Anuradha. State:
   a **two** benefits this may have for Rahul
   b **two** drawbacks this may have for Rahul.

19.3 Partnership agreement

Although it is not legally necessary to draw up a **partnership agreement** when forming a partnership, it is advisable to do so. Drawing up an agreement can avoid misunderstandings and arguments later. The clauses of a partnership agreement cover many aspects of the business. Those relating to the accounting usually include the following:

Amount of capital invested by each partner	Partners do not need to invest equal amounts.
How profits and losses are to be shared	Profits and losses may be shared equally, in proportion to capital invested or in some other ratio.
If interest on partners' capital is to be paid, and if so, at what rate	This interest is a reward for investing in the business rather than elsewhere. If all partners invest the same amount it may not be necessary to pay interest. Where partners invest different amounts, interest can be a form of compensation to the person who has invested most capital.
If partners' salaries are to be paid, and if so, what amount	If all partners share the work and responsibilities equally it may be not necessary to pay salaries. A salary can be a form of compensation where one partner has a greater share of the work and responsibilities.
If an upper limit is to be placed on partners' drawings, and if so, what amount	The business will benefit if partners keep drawings as low as possible.
If interest on partners' drawings is to be charged, and if so, at what rate	This is a method of discouraging partners from making drawings from the business (especially early in the financial year). Interest on the amount withdrawn is calculated from the date of withdrawal until the end of the financial year.
If interest on partners' loans is to be paid, and if so, at what rate	If extra finance is required a partner may make a loan to the business. To compensate for the loss of interest they could otherwise earn, interest on the loan may be paid.

> **KEY TERM**
>
> A **partnership agreement** is a document setting out the rules under which the partners will operate the business, including profit-sharing arrangements.

19.4 Loans from partners

A partnership may borrow money from one of the partners if extra finance is required (particularly if it is needed for a fixed period of time). Loans from partners are **not** part of the capital of the business and are treated in the same way as any other loan. Unlike investing additional capital, money lent to a partnership business by a partner will be repaid at an agreed time. Interest on the loan is a business expense and is not affected by the amount of profit or loss.

TIP

Interest on a loan from a partner is an expense in the income statement; it is not an appropriation of profit.

When a loan is obtained from a partner

Debit bank account   Credit loan from partner X account

When a loan is repaid to a partner

Debit loan from partner X account   Credit bank account

The loan account appears as a non-current liability in the statement of financial position

Interest on loan paid

Debit interest on loan account   Credit bank account

Interest on loan due but not paid

Debit interest on loan account   Credit partner X current account*

The interest on loan account is transferred to the debit of the income statement

*See Section 19.6.

19.5 Preparation of a profit and loss appropriation account of a partnership business

The profit and loss **appropriation account** for the financial year is prepared after the income statement and shows how the profit for the year is shared between the partners.

The profit for the year is transferred to this account from the income statement. Any interest on drawings charged to the partners increases the amount available to share and this must be added to the profit. The **appropriations** (profit shares) detailed in the partnership agreement for interest on capital and partners' salaries are deducted. The remaining figure is known as the **residual profit** and is shared between the partners in the agreed profit-sharing ratio.

KEY TERMS

A partnership **appropriation account** is part of the year-end financial statements. It shows the division of the profit or loss between the partners.

The **residual profit** is the profit remaining after adjusting the profit for the year for interest on drawings, interest on capital and partners' salaries. It is divided between the partners in the agreed profit-sharing ratio.

Walkthrough 19.1

Sumit and Padma are in partnership. Their financial year ends on 31 May. They provide the following information:

		$
Capital on 1 June 20–8	Sumit	40 000
	Padma	20 000
Drawings for the year ended 31 May 20–9	Sumit	11 000
	Padma	8 000
Profit for the year ended 31 May 20–9		24 680

The partnership agreement includes the following terms:

- Interest on capital is allowed at 5% per annum
- Interest on drawings is charged at 3%
- Padma is entitled to a partnership salary of $9 500 per annum
- Residual profits are shared in proportion to capital invested

Prepare the profit and loss appropriation account for the year ended 31 May 20–9.

Sumit and Padma
Profit and loss appropriation account for the year ended 31 May 20–9

		$	$	$
Profit for the year				24 680
Add Interest on drawings	Sumit		330	
	Padma		240	570
				25 250
Less Interest on capital	Sumit	2 000		
	Padma	1 000	3 000	
Partner's salary	Padma		9 500	12 500
				12 750
Profit shares*	Sumit		8 500	
	Padma		4 250	12 750

*The profit shares are calculated.

Sumit $\dfrac{40\,000}{60\,000} \times \dfrac{12\,750}{1}$ Padma $\dfrac{20\,000}{60\,000} \times \dfrac{12\,750}{1}$

TEST YOURSELF 19.2

1. Explain why partners may agree to charge interest on drawings.
2. Explain why partners may agree to allow interest on capital.
3. Explain the term residual profit.

You can now answer Questions 1 and 2 at the end of this chapter.

19.6 Partners' ledger accounts

Capital accounts
Similar to a sole trader each member of the partnership business has their own capital account in the nominal ledger. These usually record permanent increases or decreases in the capital invested by the individual partner. Capital accounts prepared in this way are referred to as **fixed capital accounts**.

A capital account has a credit balance as the business owes this to the partner.

Current accounts
Each member of a partnership business also has a current account. Anything which the partner becomes entitled to such as interest on capital, interest on loan, partner's salary and profit share is credited to this account. Anything which the partner is charged with, such as drawings and interest on drawings, is debited to this account.

A credit balance on a current account represents the amount owed to the partner and a debit balance represents the amount owed by the partner to the business. If a partner's drawings are more than his/her total share of profit, the current account will have a debit balance as the partner owes this to the business. If a partner's drawings are less than his/her total share of profit, the current account will have a credit balance as the business owes this to the partner.

If current accounts are not maintained, interest on capital, partners' salaries, profit share, drawings and interest on drawings are recorded in the capital account.

TIP

Only permanent increases and decreases in capital are entered in a partner's capital account. Anything to which a partner becomes entitled, or is charged with, during the year is entered in the partner's current account.

Drawings accounts

A drawings account is maintained for each partner. The total of this account is transferred to the partner's current account at the end of the financial year.

Walkthrough 19.2

Sumit and Padma are in partnership. Their financial year ends on 31 May. They provide the following information:

	Sumit $	Padma $
On 1 June 20–8:		
Capital account	40 000	20 000
Current account	130 cr	910 dr
For the year ended 31 May 20–9:		
Drawings	11 000	8 000
Interest on drawings	330	240
Interest on capital	2 000	1 000
Partner's salary		9 500
Profit share	8 500	4 250

Prepare the capital account and the current account of Sumit for the year ended 31 May 20–9.

Sumit and Padma
Sumit capital account

Date	Details	Folio	$	Date	Details	Folio	$
				20–8			
				Jun 1	Balance	b/d	40 000

Sumit current account

Date	Details	Folio	$	Date	Details	Folio	$
20–9				20–8			
May 31	Drawings		11 000	Jun 1	Balance	b/d	130
	Interest on drawings		330	20–9			
				May 31	Interest on capital		2 000
					Profit share		8 500
					Balance	c/d	700
			11 330				11 330
20–9							
Jun 1	Balance	b/d	700				

It saves time to show partners' capital accounts and current accounts side-by-side using a column for each partner.

> **TIP**
> Maintaining both a capital account and a current account for each partner means it is easy to see the amount invested and to calculate the interest on capital. The current account shows the profit retained and whether the drawings exceed the total profit share.

Walkthrough 19.3

Using the information in **Walkthrough 19.2** prepare the capital and current accounts of Sumit and Padma for the year ended 31 May 20–9. Prepare the accounts in columnar format.

Sumit and Padma
Capital accounts

Date	Details	Fo	Sumit $	Padma $	Date	Details	Fo	Sumit $	Padma $
					20–8				
					Jun 1	Balance	b/d	40 000	20 000

Cambridge IGCSE and O Level Accounting

			Sumit	Padma				Sumit	Padma
Date	Details	Fo	$	$	Date	Details	Fo	$	$
20–8					20–8				
Jun 1	Balance	b/d		910	Jun 1	Balance	b/d	130	
20–9					20–9				
May 31	Drawings		11 000	8 000	May 31	Interest on			
	Interest on					capital		2 000	1 000
	drawings		330	240		Salary			9 500
	Balance	c/d		5 600		Profit share		8 500	4 250
						Balance	c/d	700	
			11 330	14 750				11 330	14 750
20–9					20–9				
Jun 1	Balance	b/d	700		Jun 1	Balance	b/d		5 600

Current accounts

You can now answer Questions 3–5 at the end of this chapter.

TEST YOURSELF 19.3

1 A partner has a debit balance on her current account.
   a Explain what may have caused this.
   b Explain whether it represents money owed by the business to the partner or by the partner to the business.

19.7 Preparation of a statement of financial position of a partnership business

A statement of financial position of a partnership is same as that of a sole trader with the exception of the capital section. This must show that the capital account and current account balances for each partner separately.

It is not necessary to show all the details of the transactions affecting the current accounts. It is adequate to show the closing balance on each account.

Walkthrough 19.4

Sumit and Padma are in partnership. Their financial year ends on 31 May. Their current accounts are shown in **Walkthrough 19.3**.

Prepare a relevant extract from the statement of financial position of Sumit and Padma at 31 May 20–9.

Sumit and Padma
Extract from statement of financial position at 31 May 20–9

	Sumit $	Padma $	Total $
Capital accounts	40 000	20 000	60 000
Current accounts	(700)*	5 600	4 900
	39 300	25 600	64 900

* The debit balance on Sumit's current account is shown as a minus, which reduces the amount owed by the business to Sumit.

Sometimes the partners may wish to show the full details of the current accounts in the statement of financial position.

Walkthrough 19.5

Sumit and Padma are in partnership. Their financial year ends on 31 May. Their current accounts are shown in **Walkthrough 19.3**.

Prepare a relevant extract from the statement of financial position of Sumit and Padma on 31 May 20–9 showing full details of their current accounts.

Sumit and Padma
Extract from statement of financial position at 31 May 20–9

	Sumit $	Padma $	Total $
Capital accounts	40 000	20 000	60 000
Current accounts			
Opening balance	130	(910)	
Interest on capital	2 000	1 000	
Partner's salary		9 500	
Profit share	8 500	4 250	
	10 630	13 840	
Less Drawings	11 000	8 000	
Interest on drawings	330	240	
	11 330	8 240	
	(700)	5 600	4 900
			64 900

You can now answer Question 6 at the end of this chapter.

Revision checklist

- A partnership is a business in which two or more people work together as owners with a view to making profits.
- There are both advantages and disadvantages of being a member of a partnership business.
- It is advisable to draw up a partnership agreement when the partnership is formed.
- A partner may make a loan to the business. This is treated in a similar way to all other loans.
- A profit and loss appropriation account is prepared after the income statement to share out the profit between the partners.
- Each partner usually has a capital account and a current account.
- In the statement of financial position of a partnership the balances on each partner's capital account and current account must be shown separately.

Chapter 19: Partnerships

Exam-style questions

1. Cindy is a sole trader. She is considering forming a partnership with Lora. What is a disadvantage of being a partner?

   A additional capital is available
   B additional skills are available
   C profits are shared
   D risks are shared

2. Which items may appear as deductions from the profit for the year in the appropriation account of a partnership?

	Drawings	Interest on capital	Interest on loan	Partner's salary
A	✓	✓		
B	✓	✓	✓	
C				✓
D			✓	✓

3. Hao and Quan are partners. Hao's capital is $100 000 and Quan's is $50 000. The partnership agreement provides for interest on capital at 3% per annum and an annual salary for Quan of $6 000. Profits and losses are shared in proportion to capital invested.

   The profit for the year ended 31 December 20–5 was $18 900. How much was credited to Quan's current account on 31 December 20–5?

   A $6 300   B $10 300   C $11 700   D $13 800

4. Diksha and Padmaja are in partnership. Their financial year ends on 31 July. Their partnership agreement provides for:

   - interest on capital at 4% per annum
   - an annual salary of $4 000 for Padmaja
   - interest on drawings at $2\frac{1}{2}\%$
   - residual profits and losses to be shared in the ratio of 2:1.

   The following information is available:

	Diksha $	Padmaja $
Capital account at 1 August 20–4	50 000	40 000
Current account at 1 August 20–4	4 200 (Cr)	200 (Dr)
Drawings during the year	3 000	5 000

   The profit for the year ended 31 July 20–5 was $11 240.

a Prepare the profit and loss appropriation account for the year ended 31 July 20–5.

b Write up Padmaja's current account for the year ended 31 July 20–5. Balance the account and bring down the balance on 1 August 20–5.

c Suggest **two** reasons why partners maintain both a capital and a current account for each partner.

5 Beth and Kate are in partnership. Their financial year ends on 31 December. On 1 January 20–5 their capitals were: Beth $90 000 and Kate $70 000. The uncompleted current accounts for the year ended 31 December 20–5 were as follows.

			Beth $	Kate $				Beth $	Kate $
20–5					20–5				
Jan 1	Balance	b/d		9 000	Jan 1	Balance	b/d	5 000	
Dec 31	Drawings		16 000	8 000		Capital			10 000
	Interest on drawings			160	Dec 31	Salary		9 000	
				320					
	Share of loss		6 300	4 200		Interest on capital		4 500	3 000
						Interest on loan			200

a Explain the entry on 1 January 'Capital $10 000'.

b Calculate the profit or loss for the year before appropriations.

c Calculate the percentage rate of interest on capital the partners received.

d Calculate the ratio in which the partners shared the loss.

e State the balance on each partner's current account on 1 January 20–6, indicating whether each balance is debit or credit.

f Explain what a credit balance on a partner's current account means.

g Explain how a debit balance on a partner's current account may arise.

h Suggest one reason why Beth made a loan to the business instead of investing additional capital.

6 Manu and Zahur are in partnership. The total capital of the business is $600 000, which was contributed by Manu and Zahur in the ratio of 2:1. Profits and losses are shared in the same ratio. Interest on capital is allowed at 5% per annum. Zahur is entitled to an annual salary of $14 000.

The following information is available:

		$
Current account 1 May 20–7	Manu	9 000 credit
	Zahur	1 000 debit
Drawings during the year ended 30 April 20–8	Manu	30 000
	Zahur	29 600
Profit for the year ended 30 April 20–8		59 000
At 30 April 20–8:		
Premises at cost		400 000
Plant and machinery at book value		190 000
Fixtures and fittings at book value		34 000
10% Loan from CFU Limited		25 000
Trade payables		37 450
Trade receivables		26 170
Other payables		320
Other receivables		450
Inventory		29 350
Bank		9 800 credit

a Prepare the profit and loss appropriation account for the year ended 30 April 20–8.
b Prepare the statement of financial position at 30 April 20–8 (showing the current accounts in full).

Chapter 20
Manufacturing accounts

Learning objectives

In this chapter you will learn to:

- distinguish between direct and indirect costs   5.5
- understand direct material, direct labour, prime cost and factory overheads   5.5
- understand and make adjustments for work in progress   5.5
- calculate factory cost of production   5.5
- prepare manufacturing accounts, income statements and statements of financial position   5.5
- make adjustments to financial statements   5.5

Chapter 20: Manufacturing accounts

20.1 Introduction

The previous chapters (except Chapter 18) relate to businesses which are involved in trading (such as wholesale or retail businesses which buy goods and sell them without changing the goods in any way) or service businesses. There are, of course, manufacturing businesses which buy raw materials and convert these into finished products which they then sell.

A manufacturing business will maintain double entry records similar to those of retail and wholesale businesses. At the end of the financial year, in addition to an income statement (and possibly an appropriation account) and statement of financial position, a manufacturing business will also prepare a **manufacturing account**. The purpose of preparing this account is to calculate how much it has cost the business to manufacture the goods produced in the financial year.

> **LINK**
> You learned about income statements and statements of financial position in Chapters 8 and 9.

> **KEY TERM**
> A **manufacturing account** is part of the annual financial statements and is used to calculate the cost of goods produced.

20.2 The elements of cost

The cost of manufacture is made up of four main elements. These are outlined below.

Direct material

The first thing a manufacturer needs is raw material to make the finished goods. This raw material takes many forms depending on the type of business – a baker will need flour, a furniture maker will need wood, a car maker will need steel and so on.

Direct labour

The next essential cost for a manufacturer is the cost of the wages of the people who are employed in the factory making the goods. Depending on the type of business, these may be bakers, carpenters, machine operators and so on. This cost is sometimes referred to as **direct wages**.

The term direct labour includes only those people who are actually involved in the production of the finished goods. It does not include the wages of supervisors, maintenance staff, factory cleaners and so on. These people have an important role to play within the factory, but are regarded as indirect labour.

Direct expenses

These are any expenses which a manufacturer can directly link with the product being manufactured. It may be that for every item produced, a manufacturer has to pay a fee (known as a **royalty**) to the person who originally invented the product. A manufacturer may have to hire a special piece of equipment to complete the manufacturing process. Such expenses are regarded as direct expenses.

Factory overheads

These are sometimes referred to as **indirect factory expenses**. They include all the costs involved in operating the factory which cannot be directly linked with the product being manufactured. Expenses such as factory rent and rates, factory heat and light, factory machinery repairs, depreciation of factory machinery, indirect factory wages and so on are all regarded as factory overheads.

> **TEST YOURSELF 20.1**
>
> 1. Explain the difference between direct factory wages and indirect factory wages.
> 2. Give **two** examples of direct expenses.
> 3. For **each** of the following state whether it is direct material, direct labour or a factory overhead of a clothing factory:
>   a. electricity used in the factory
>   b. purchase of suiting fabric
>   c. wages of factory supervisors
>   d. wages of sewing machinists
>   e. purchase of spare parts for machine
>   f. purchase of buttons and threads

20.3 Preparation of a manufacturing account

The cost of manufacturing the goods produced is calculated in the manufacturing account.

The first item in a manufacturing account is **direct material**. The cost of the raw material used during the year is calculated in a similar way to that in which a retailer calculates the cost of goods sold. The cost of raw material actually used during the year is calculated as:

  Opening inventory of raw material
+ Purchases of raw material
+ Carriage inwards on raw material
− Closing inventory of raw material

The cost of the **direct labour** is then added to the direct material. Any **direct expenses** are then added.

The total of these three elements of cost is known as the **prime cost**.

  Direct material + Direct labour + Direct expenses = Prime cost

The total **cost of production** is found by adding the **factory overheads** to the prime cost.

  Prime cost + Factory overheads = Cost of production

KEY TERMS

Prime cost is the total of the direct materials, direct labour and direct expenses. It is the cost of the essentials necessary for production.

Cost of production is prime cost plus factory overheads, adjusted for any work in progress at the start and at the end of the year. It is the total cost of manufacturing the goods completed.

Chapter 20: Manufacturing accounts

Walkthrough 20.1

The following information was provided by the Kapoor Manufacturing Company on 30 April 20–6:

		$
Raw materials	– Inventory 1 May 20–5	14 900
	Inventory 30 April 20–6	15 300
	Purchases	181 200
	Carriage on purchases	3 300
Factory wages	– Direct	166 100
	Indirect	93 800
Royalties		10 000
Factory insurance		2 070
Factory rent and rates		2 930
Factory general expenses		6 350
Depreciation of factory machinery		9 500

Prepare the manufacturing account of the Kapoor Manufacturing Company for the year ended 30 April 20–6.

Kapoor Manufacturing Company
Manufacturing account for the year ended 30 April 20–6

	$	$
Cost of material consumed		
Opening inventory of raw material	14 900	
Purchases of raw material	181 200	
Carriage on purchases	3 300	
	199 400	
Less Closing inventory of raw material	15 300	184 100
Direct wages		166 100
Direct expenses		
Royalties		10 000
Prime cost		360 200
Factory overheads		
Indirect wages	93 800	
Insurance	2 070	
Rent and rates	2 930	
General expenses	6 350	
Depreciation of machinery	9 500	114 650
Cost of production		474 850

TIP
It is important to remember that revenue does not appear in a manufacturing account. Only costs relevant to the manufacture of goods are included.

TIP
The factory overheads must be added to the prime cost.

> **TEST YOURSELF 20.2**
>
> 1. Explain the term prime cost.
> 2. State an alternative term for factory overheads.

20.4 Work in progress

Goods which are partly completed at the end of the financial year are known as **work in progress**. The work in progress is excluded from the cost of production as these goods cannot be sold until they are completed. They do have some value however, as it has cost something to get them to their present condition – some material has been used and some direct wages have been incurred and so on. It is therefore necessary to place a value on the work in progress.

The partly-made goods at the end of the financial year are known as **closing work in progress**. These goods will, of course, become the **opening work in progress** at the start of the following financial year.

In a manufacturing account, it is necessary to adjust the cost of production so that it represents only the cost of goods actually completed in the year. This adjustment is done in the same way as for any other type of inventory – the opening inventory is added and the closing inventory is deducted.

> **KEY TERM**
>
> **Work in progress** is the goods which are partly completed at the end of the financial year.

Walkthrough 20.2

The following information was provided by the Kapoor Manufacturing Company on 30 April 20–6.

	$
Prime cost	360 200
Factory overheads	114 650
Work in progress – Inventory 1 May 20–5	8 790
Inventory 30 April 20–6	8 640

Prepare the manufacturing account of the Kapoor Manufacturing Company for the year ended 30 April 20–6.

Kapoor Manufacturing Company
Manufacturing account for the year ended 30 April 20–6

	$	$
Prime cost*		360 200
Factory overheads*		114 650
		474 850
Add Opening work in progress		8 790
		483 640
Less Closing work in progress		8 640
Cost of production		475 000

* Full details would be shown as in **Walkthrough 20.1**.

> **TEST YOURSELF 20.3**
>
> 1 Explain the term 'work in progress'.
> 2 State why it is necessary to adjust the cost of production for work in progress.

20.5 Calculation of unit cost

Where a manufacturer makes only one type of identical product, the cost of making one article can be found by dividing the cost of goods completed by the number of articles manufactured.

> **Walkthrough 20.3**
>
> The Kapoor Manufacturing Company makes one type of identical product. The cost of production during the year ended 30 April 20–6 was $475 000, and a total of 20 000 articles were completed.
>
> Calculate the unit cost.
>
> $$\text{Unit cost} \frac{\text{Cost of production}}{\text{Number of units produced}} = \frac{\$475\,000}{20\,000} = \$23.75$$

20.6 Preparation of a trading section of an income statement of a manufacturing business

The gross profit of a manufacturing business is calculated in the trading section of the income statement. This is very similar to that prepared by a wholesale or retail business. The main difference is that because the business actually makes the goods it sells, the item for purchases is replaced by the production cost of goods completed. Sometimes, however, a manufacturing business may purchase some finished goods which it does not manufacture itself. This may occur:

- when production does not meet demand
- when it is cheaper to buy the goods rather than make them
- when those particular items cannot be made by the business.

Purchases of finished goods are added to the production cost of goods completed in the income statement.

In the trading section of the income statement the proceeds from the sale of finished goods is compared with the cost of those finished goods. This means that the inventories included are the inventories of finished goods held by the manufacturer at the start and end of the financial year.

Walkthrough 20.4

The following information was provided by the Kapoor Manufacturing Company on 30 April 20–6:

	$
Cost of production*	475 000
Revenue	661 500
Finished goods – Inventory 1 May 20–5	31 000
Inventory 30 April 20–6	23 250
Purchases	15 500

*Calculated in the manufacturing account.

Prepare the trading section of the income statement of the Kapoor Manufacturing Company for the year ended 30 April 20–6.

Kapoor Manufacturing Company
Income statement for the year ended 30 April 20–6

	$	$
Revenue		661 500
Less Cost of sales		
Opening inventory of finished goods	31 000	
Cost of production	475 000	
Purchases of finished goods	15 500	
	521 500	
Less Closing inventory of finished goods	23 250	498 250
Gross profit		163 250

TEST YOURSELF 20.4

1. Explain why the cost of production of goods completed appears in a trading section of the income statement of a manufacturing business.
2. Explain why a manufacturer may sometimes purchase finished goods from another manufacturer.

20.7 Preparation of a profit and loss section of an income statement of a manufacturing business

The profit for the year of a manufacturing business is calculated in the profit and loss section of the income statement. This is very similar to that prepared by a wholesale or retail business. Expenses relating to the manufacturing process have already been entered in the manufacturing account, so only administration expenses, selling and distribution expenses, and financial expenses will appear in the profit and loss section of the income statement.

Where an expense relates to the whole of the business it may be necessary to share this out between the factory and the offices. Expenses such as insurance of buildings, rent and rates, and heat and light often have to be apportioned in this way. For example, the insurance of the buildings may be apportioned $\frac{2}{3}$ to the factory and $\frac{1}{3}$ to the offices. This means that if the total cost of insurance was $900 an amount of $600 would be included in the manufacturing account and $300 in the profit and loss section of the income statement.

20.8 Preparation of a statement of financial position of a manufacturing business

The statement of financial position of a manufacturing business is similar to that prepared by a wholesale or retail business. There is only one main difference which is that a manufacturer may have three different inventories – raw material, work in progress and finished goods. It is usual to show each of these inventories separately in the current asset section of the statement of financial position.

Walkthrough 20.5

On 30 April 20–6 the Kapoor Manufacturing Company had inventories valued as follows:

	$
Raw material	15 300
Work in progress	8 640
Finished goods	23 250

Prepare a relevant extract from the statement of financial position of the Kapoor Manufacturing Company at 30 April 20–6.

Kapoor Manufacturing Company		
Extract from statement of financial position at 30 April 20–6		
	$	$
Current assets		
Inventories – Raw materials	15 300	
Work in progress	8 640	
Finished goods	23 250	47 190

20.9 Year-end adjustments

This chapter has concentrated on the difference between the financial statements of a manufacturing business and those of a trading business. In order to emphasise these differences none of the examples included year-end adjustments. A manufacturer may well have to make year-end adjustments for such things as accruals, prepayments, provision for doubtful debts and so on.

You can now answer Questions 1–6 at the end of this chapter.

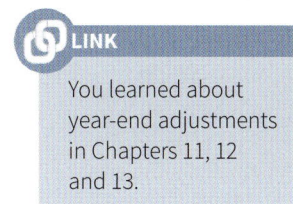

LINK

You learned about year-end adjustments in Chapters 11, 12 and 13.

Revision checklist

- A manufacturing account is used to calculate the cost of making goods produced in the financial year. It consists of direct materials + direct labour + direct expenses + factory overheads.
- Direct materials + direct labour + direct expenses = prime cost.
- The cost of production may have to be amended for the goods partly made at the end of the financial year (known as work in progress).
- In the trading section of the income statement of a manufacturer, the cost of production is included together with any purchases of finished goods.
- In the statement of financial position of a manufacturer, it may be necessary to show three different inventories.

Exam-style questions

1. How is cost of production calculated?
   - **A** prime cost + factory overheads + increase in work in progress
   - **B** prime cost + factory overheads − increase in work in progress
   - **C** prime cost − factory overheads + increase in work in progress
   - **D** prime cost − factory overheads − increase in work in progress

2. What may be included in prime cost?
   1. salary of factory manager
   2. salary of supervisor of production workers
   3. wages of machine maintenance workers
   4. wages of production workers

   - **A** 1, 2 and 3
   - **B** 2, 3 and 4
   - **C** 3 and 4
   - **D** 4 only

3. A manufacturer provided the following information:

	$
Prime cost	132 000
Factory overheads	17 000
Opening work in progress	11 000
Closing work in progress	13 000

   How much was the cost of production?

   - **A** $113 000
   - **B** $117 000
   - **C** $147 000
   - **D** $151 000

4. The financial year of Leeford Manufacturers Ltd ends on 30 September. They supplied the following information:

	$
At 1 October 20–7:	
Inventory – raw materials	41 800
finished goods	62 300
work in progress	18 600
For the year ended 30 September 20–8:	
Purchases of raw materials	495 800
Purchases of finished goods	4 300
Revenue	824 000
Wages – factory direct wages	52 750
factory indirect salaries	29 760
office and sales salaries	36 890
Factory expenses	41 840
At 30 September 20–8:	
Inventory – raw materials	43 200
finished goods	60 750
work in progress	17 850

a Select the relevant figures and prepare the manufacturing account of Leeford Manufacturers Ltd for the year ended 30 September 20–8.

b Select **two** of the items in this list which should **not** appear in a manufacturing account and explain why they are not included.

5 a Explain the difference between:
   i direct costs and indirect costs
   ii prime cost and cost of production.

b Explain the meaning of the term 'work in progress'.

c Explain why a manufacturer may purchase finished goods as well as raw materials.

Iftikhar is a manufacturer. He provided the following information for the year ended 31 May 20–9:

		$
1 June 20–8	Inventory of raw materials	4 750
	Inventory of work in progress	5 600
31 May 20–9	Inventory of raw materials	4 850
	Inventory of work in progress	4 300

For the year ended 31 May 20–9:
	$
Purchases of raw materials	49 590
Direct factory wages	61 940
Indirect factory wages	29 660
Carriage on raw materials	3 710
Factory direct expenses	2 960
Factory indirect expenses	48 930

d i Calculate the prime cost.
  ii Calculate the cost of production.

6 Farouk started a manufacturing business on 1 April 20–5. He provided the following information:

	$
On 1 April 20–5:	
Cost of factory machinery	28 000
Cost of factory hand tools	800
Cost of office fixtures and fittings	6 500
For the year ended 31 March 20–6:	
Purchases of raw materials	22 800
Purchases of finished goods	12 200
Carriage on raw materials	1 300
Revenue	100 400
Wages and salaries – factory operatives	27 200
office staff	15 400
factory supervisors	10 400
General expenses	4 800
Rent and rates	5 100
At 31 March 20–6:	
Inventory – raw materials	2 520
work in progress	2 140
finished goods	5 210
Value of factory hand tools	650

Additional information:

1 The rent and rates and the general expenses are to be apportioned $\frac{2}{3}$ to the factory and $\frac{1}{3}$ to the office.
2 The factory machinery is to be deprecated at 25% per annum on cost and the office fixtures and fittings by 10% per annum on cost. No additional non-current assets were purchased during the year.

a Prepare the manufacturing account for the year ended 31 March 20–6.
b Prepare the income statement for the year ended 31 March 20–6.

Chapter 21
Limited companies

Learning objectives

In this chapter you will learn to:

- explain the advantages and disadvantages of operating as a limited company   5.3
- understand the meaning of the term limited liability   5.3
- understand the meaning of the term equity   5.3
- understand the capital structure of a limited company comprising preference share capital, ordinary share capital, general reserve and retained earnings   5.3
- understand and distinguish between issued, called-up and paid-up share capital   5.3
- understand and distinguish between share capital (preference shares and ordinary shares) and loan capital (debentures)   5.3
- prepare income statements, statements of changes in equity and statements of financial position   5.3
- make adjustments to financial statements.   5.3

21.1 Introduction

A **limited company** is a legal entity which has a separate identity from its shareholders, whose liability for the company's debts is limited.

Sometimes a new business is formed as a limited company; sometimes a limited company is formed when a sole trader or partnership wishes to expand their business.

21.2 The nature of a limited company

One person acting alone can form a limited company and there is no maximum number of members. The **capital of a company is divided into units known as shares** which can be of any monetary amount. The **members (shareholders) of the company are only liable for the debts of the company up to the amount they agree to pay for their shares**. Since a company can have a large number of members whose liability is limited, a large amount of capital can be raised. The shares of a company have a face value (par value) such as $5, $1, $0.50, etc. **Profits are distributed among the members in the form of dividends** which are often stated in terms of a percentage of the face value of the shares.

KEY TERM

A **limited company** is a legal entity which has a separate identity from its shareholders, whose liability for the company's debts is limited.

Walkthrough 21.1

Dass Limited has a total capital of 200 000 shares of $2 each and decides to pay the shareholders a dividend of 10%.

a What is the total amount payable?

b What is the amount payable per share?

a Total amount payable is $40 000 ($400 000 × 10%).

b Amount payable per share is $0.20 (10% of $2).

There are two types of limited company – a **public limited company** which may offer its shares to the public and a **private limited company** which is usually a smaller company and is not allowed to offer its shares to the public.

From the viewpoint of the individual, the main benefit of being a member of a limited company is the fact that the liability for the debts of the company is limited to the amount the member agreed to contribute. It is also beneficial that a limited company has a separate legal entity to its shareholders so legal actions are taken against the company not the individual shareholders. Apart from very small limited companies, it is not usually practical for shareholders to take an active part in the running of the business, so a board of directors is appointed to run the business on a daily basis. If shares are held in a public limited company, it is easy to buy and sell shares.

From the viewpoint of the business, being a limited company means that it is possible to access greater capital than is possible for a sole trader or partnership business. Loans can often be obtained more easily by a limited company than by a sole trader or a partnership business. A company has continuity of existence, unlike a sole trader or a partnership business. However, there are many legal requirements in relation to forming and running a limited company and annual financial statements must be prepared and provided to shareholders.

Cambridge IGCSE and O Level Accounting

> **TEST YOURSELF 21.1**
>
> 1. Define a limited liability company.
> 2. 'A member of a company has limited liability'. Explain.
> 3. Name **two** types of limited company.
> 4. State the name for profits distributed to members of a limited company.

KEY TERMS

Issued share capital is the amount of capital issued to the shareholders.

Called up capital is that part of the issued share capital for which payment has been requested from shareholders.

Paid up capital is that part of the called up share capital for which the company has received payment from shareholders.

21.3 Share capital

When a limited company is formed the amount of share capital required will be issued to the shareholders (members) and this is known as the **issued share capital**. If more capital is required at a later date, further shares can be issued.

A company may not immediately require all the money due on the shares it issues. In this case shareholders may be allowed to pay in 'instalments' at times and amounts fixed by the company. The total amount a company has requested from the shareholders is known as the **called up capital**. This may be less than the issued capital as a company may only 'call up' the amount it actually requires at that date. The term **paid up capital** refers to that part of the called up capital for which a company has actually received cash from its shareholders.

Walkthrough 21.2

Mishra Limited was formed on 1 January 20–8. A total of 300 000 $1 shares were issued immediately and shareholders were asked to pay 50% of the sum due immediately and the other 50% in January 20–9.

By 1 May 20–8 holders of 290 000 shares had paid the amount due.

State:

a   The issued capital of Mishra Limited on 1 May 20–8.
b   The called up capital of Mishra Limited on 1 May 20–8.
c   The paid up capital of Mishra Limited on 1 May 20–8.

a   The issued capital is $300 000 consisting of 300 000 shares of $1 each.
b   The called up capital is $150 000 consisting of $0.50 called up on 300 000 shares.
c   The paid up capital is $145 000 consisting of $0.50 paid up on 290 000 shares.

21.4 Types of shares

The share capital of a limited company may be divided into different types of shares. The most common ones are **preference shares** and **ordinary shares**.

Preference shares

As the name implies, these get preference over the ordinary shares. They receive a fixed rate of dividend (based on the face value of the shares) which is payable before any dividend is payable to the ordinary shareholders. The dividend is the same every year (provided that the profit of the company is enough to cover this amount). If a company is wound up (closed down) any money left after paying outside liabilities is used to pay back the preference shareholders before anything is returned to the ordinary shareholders. Preference shareholders are not usually entitled to vote at shareholders' meetings.

There are several types of preference shares, and most of these are outside the scope of this book. However, it is necessary to understand the difference between redeemable and non-**redeemable preference shares** as this affects the treatment of dividend and how the shares appear in the statement of financial position. If the preference shares are redeemable, the dividend is included as a finance cost in the profit and loss section of the income statement (with any accrued dividend appearing in the current liabilities in the statement of financial position). The preference shares are shown as a non-current liability in the statement of financial positon. If the preference shares are non-redeemable, the dividend paid is included in the statement of changes in equity (see Section 21.7) and the preference shares are included in the equity and reserves section (see Section 21.8) of the statement of financial position.

Ordinary shares

These are also known as **equity** shares. The dividend on ordinary shares is only payable after that on the preference shares has been accounted for. The dividend is not a fixed amount, but can vary according to the profits of the company. If the trading results are poor the ordinary shareholders may receive no dividend at all, but if trading results are good they may be awarded high dividends. If a company is wound up, the outside liabilities and the preference shareholders are repaid before any monies are returned to the ordinary shareholders. This may result in very little being returned to the ordinary shareholders if the company was short of funds. However, the ordinary shareholders may receive a return higher than their original capital investment if the company had adequate funds. Ordinary shareholders are usually entitled to vote at shareholders' meetings on the basis of one vote per share.

KEY TERMS

Redeemable preference shares are those preference shares which must be bought back by the company at an agreed date and for an agreed price.

Equity is the total funds provided by the shareholders of the company.

A **debenture** is a long-term loan which has a fixed rate of interest, payable irrespective of the profit of the company.

21.5 Debentures (Loan notes)

In addition to the funds provided by the owners (shareholders), a company may also obtain funds from **debentures**, which are long-term loans. Like most loans, debentures carry a fixed rate of interest, which is payable whether or not the company makes a profit. This loan interest appears as a finance cost in the profit and loss section of the income statement. If the company is wound up, the debenture holders will be repaid before any capital is repaid to shareholders. Debenture holders are not members of the company and so are not entitled to vote at shareholders' meetings.

> **TEST YOURSELF 21.2**
>
> 1 State **three** differences between preference shares and ordinary shares.
> 2 State **three** differences between ordinary shares and debentures.

TIP

Debenture interest appears in the income statement under 'finance costs'.

You can now answer Question 1 at the end of this chapter.

21.6 Income statement of a limited company

An annual income statement is prepared for a limited company in exactly the same way as it is prepared for a sole trader or a partnership business. The only different is that in the finance costs there may be debenture interest and dividend on redeemable preference shares.

21.7 Statement of changes in equity

Chapter 19 explained how it was necessary to prepare a profit and loss appropriation account for a partnership business to show how the profit was divided between the partners. In a similar way, a limited company must prepare a statement showing how the profit for the year is used. This statement is known as a **statement of changes in equity**. It summarises the changes during the year to the ordinary share capital, non-redeemable preference share capital, retained earnings and general reserve.

It has already been explained that profits are distributed to the shareholders of a limited company in the form of dividends. Any ordinary share dividend (and any dividend on non-redeemable preference shares) which has actually been paid during the financial year is recorded in the statement of changes in equity for that particular year.

Sometimes the directors will recommend an interim dividend (half way dividend) to be paid during the year on ordinary shares (and also on non-redeemable preference shares). This will appear in the statement of changes in equity for that particular year.

At the end of each financial year the directors of a company propose that ordinary share dividends (and possibly dividends on non-redeemable preference shares) are paid and these will be paid early in the following year. These proposed dividends are not included in the financial statements for the current year (but may appear as a note). They are included in the statement of changes in equity in the year in which they are actually paid. Very often limited companies do not distribute the whole of the profit for the year as dividends. Even if a limited company wished to distribute the whole profit it would not be possible if there was not enough cash available. Any profit that is not appropriated for dividends is carried forward to the following year. This is known as **retained earnings** and will appear in the equity and reserves section of the statement of financial position

In addition to leaving a balance of retained earnings, many companies will transfer an amount from the profit for the year to a general reserve. This is another means of **ploughing back profits** into the company to help it grow. The general reserve also appears in the equity and reserves section of the statement of financial position.

Walkthrough 21.3

Anand Limited was formed on 1 July 20–3. By 30 June 20–6 a total of 200 000 5% redeemable preference shares of $1 each and 600 000 ordinary shares of $0.50 each had been issued and were fully paid.

The following information is provided:

1. The profit for the year ended 30 June 20–6 **before** the preference share dividend was $58 000.
2. On 1 July 20–5 the retained earnings brought forward amounted to $41 000 and the general reserve amounted to $45 000.
3. Half of the preference share dividend was paid on 31 December 20–5. On 30 June 20–6 the remaining preference share dividend was outstanding.
4. The proposed final ordinary share dividend of $30 000 for the year ended 30 June 20–5 was paid on 30 September 20–5.
5. An interim dividend of $24 000 was paid on 31 March 20–6.
6. On 30 June 20–6 the directors recommended a transfer of $8 000 to the general reserve and the payment of an ordinary share dividend of 8%.

Prepare a statement of changes in equity of Anand Limited for the year ended 30 June 20–6.

Anand Limited
Statement of changes in equity for the year ended 30 June 20–6

	Ordinary share capital $	General reserve $	Retained earnings $	Total $
Balance at 1 July 20–5	300 000	45 000	41 000	386 000
Profit for the year			48 000	48 000
Divided paid (final)			(30 000)	(30 000)
Dividend paid (interim)			(24 000)	(24 000)
Transfer to general reserve		8 000	(8 000)	
Balance at 30 June 20–6	300 000	53 000	27 000	380 000

TIP

Check the arithmetic in a statement of changes in equity by adding each column vertically and then cross-checking by adding the totals of the columns horizontally.

- After entering the opening balances, each item is entered in the appropriate column and also in the total column.
- The profit for the year of $58 0000 was reduced by the preference share dividend for the year of $10 000.
- The final dividend paid relates to the previous year but is entered in the statement as the dividend was paid during the current year.
- The interim dividend is entered on the statement as it was paid in the year.
- The dividend proposed at the end of the current year does not appear as it has not yet been paid.
- A figure in brackets indicates that it is reducing the amount in that column.
- The totals should be added vertically and then cross-checked horizontally.

You can now answer Questions 2–3 at the end of this chapter.

TEST YOURSELF 21.3

1. Explain the term retained earnings.
2. Explain the term interim dividend.
3. Explain the difference between dividends paid and dividends proposed.

21.8 Statement of financial position of a limited company

In the statement of financial position of a limited company the assets section and the current liabilities section are presented in exactly the same way as for a sole trader or a partnership.

The non-current liabilities section may include redeemable preference shares, debentures and any other non-current liabilities. The capital section has to be modified so that it shows details of the shares and reserves of the company. The general reserve and the retained earnings are added to the share capital as they represent profits which have been retained in the company, and, as such, belong to the ordinary shareholders.

LINK

You learned about statements of financial position of sole traders in Chapter 9.

Walkthrough 21.4

Using the information and the statement of changes in equity provided in **Walkthrough 21.3**, prepare an appropriate extract from the statement of financial position of Anand Limited at 30 June showing the capital and reserves.

Anand Limited
Extract from statement of financial position at 30 June 20–6

	$
Equity and liabilities	
Equity	
Ordinary share capital	300 000
General reserve	53 000
Retained earnings	27 000
	380 000

- The amounts for share capital, general reserve and retained earnings are obtained from the statement of changes in equity (see **Walkthrough 21.3**).
- The preference shares are redeemable so would appear in the non-current liabilities section.

> **TIP**
> The totals of the columns in the statement of changes in equity are used to enter the items in the equity and reserves section of the statement of financial position.

TEST YOURSELF 21.4

1. State how debentures are recorded in the statement of financial position of a limited company.
2. Explain why reserves such as general reserve and retained earnings are added to the ordinary share capital in the statement of financial position of a limited company.

You can now answer Questions 4–6 at the end of this chapter.

Revision checklist

- A limited company is a legal entity which has a separate identity from its shareholders, whose liability is limited.
- The share capital actually issued to shareholders is known as the issued capital.
- There are two main types of shares – preference shares and ordinary shares.
- Debentures are a form of long-term loan.
- A statement of changes in equity summarises the changes during the year to ordinary share capital, non-redeemable preference share capital, retained earnings and general reserve.

Exam-style questions

1 Which statement about debentures is correct?

  A Debentures carry a fixed rate of dividend.
  B Debentures carry a fixed rate of interest.
  C Debentures are part of the equity of a limited company.
  D Debenture holders are allowed to vote at shareholders' meetings.

2 XZ Limited was formed on 1 August 20–1. Which items may appear in the statement of changes in equity for the year ended 31 July 20–2?

	Debenture interest paid	Ordinary share dividend paid	Ordinary share dividend proposed	Transfer to general reserve
A	✓	✓	✓	
B	✓			✓
C		✓	✓	✓
D		✓		✓

3 a Explain the difference between the following:

  i called-up share capital and paid-up share capital
  ii preference shares and ordinary shares
  iii ordinary share dividend paid relating to the current financial year and ordinary share dividend proposed relating to the current year.

Silsford Ltd provided the following information:

	$
6% redeemable preference shares of $1 each	50 000
Ordinary shares of $1 each	80 000
Retained earnings	14 300

During the financial year ended 31 December 20–9 an interim dividend of $2 400 was paid on the ordinary shares.

The profit for the year ended 31 December 20–9 before preference share dividend was $33 000.

On 31 December 20–9 it was decided to:

- pay the dividend due on the redeemable preference shares
- pay a final dividend of 5% on the ordinary shares
- transfer $5 000 to general reserve.

b Calculate:

  i the profit for the year after preference share dividend
  ii the retained earnings at 31 December 20–9.

Cambridge IGCSE and O Level Accounting

4   Which items are included in the equity section of the statement of financial position of a limited company?

1   bank overdraft
2   debentures
3   general reserve
4   ordinary shares

A 1 and 2   **B** 1 and 3   **C** 2 and 4   **D** 3 and 4

5   Tiwari & Company Ltd have issued 100 000 5% redeemable preference shares of $1 each and 600 000 ordinary shares of $0.50 each. All the shares are fully paid.

Tiwari and Company Ltd provided the following information relating to the year ended 30 June 20–8:

			$
20–7			
July 1	Retained earnings		9 500
	General reserve		12 000
Dec 31	Dividends paid:		
	Half year dividend on preference shares		
	Interim dividend of 5% on ordinary shares		
20–8			
June 30	Profit for the year before preference share dividend		59 000
	Dividend paid:		
	Half year dividend on preference shares		

On 30 June 20–8 it was decided to transfer $10 000 to the general reserve and to pay a final dividend of 10% on the ordinary shares.

a   Calculate the profit for the year ended 30 June 20–8 after the preference share dividend. Show your workings.

b   Prepare the statement of changes in equity of Tiwari & Company Ltd for the year ended 30 June 20–8.

c   Prepare a relevant extract from the statement of financial position of Tiwari & Company Ltd at 30 June 2008 showing the equity and reserves section.

d   Explain which dividends (if any) would appear in the statement of financial position of Tiwari and Company Ltd at 30 June 20–8. Give reasons for your answer.

6   AK Limited provided the following information:

	$
On 1 May 20–4:	
Ordinary share capital	400 000
General reserve	20 000
Retained earnings	51 500
On 1 August 20–4 the final ordinary share for the year ended 30 April 20–4 was paid	16 000
On 1 November 20–4 an interim ordinary share dividend for the year ended 30 April 20–5 was paid	10 000
Profit for the year ended 30 April 20–5	79 500

On 30 April 20–5 the directors decided to:
- transfer 17 500 to general reserve
- proposed an final ordinary share dividend of 3%.

Additional information at 30 April 20–5:

	$
Premises at cost	425 000
Equipment at cost	124 000
Motor vehicles at cost	80 000
Provision for depreciation of equipment	93 000
Provision for depreciation of motor vehicles	25 000
Trade payables	38 700
Trade receivables	32 000
Other payables	770
Other receivables	1 520
Provision for doubtful debts	800
5% debentures	30 000
Balance at bank	15 000
Inventory	35 750

a Prepare the statement of changes in equity for the year ended 30 April 20–5.

b Prepare the statement of financial position at 30 April 20–5.

Chapter 22
Analysis and interpretation

Learning objectives

In this chapter you will learn to:

- calculate and explain the importance of the following ratios: gross margin, profit margin, return on capital employed, current ratio, liquid (acid test) ratio, rate of inventory turnover, trade receivables turnover, trade payables turnover   6.1
- prepare and comment on simple statements showing comparison of results for different years   6.2
- make recommendations and suggestions for improving profitability and working capital   6.2
- understand the significance of the difference between the gross margin and the profit margin as an indicator of a business's efficiency   6.2
- explain the relationship of gross profit and profit for the year to the valuation of inventory, rate of turnover, revenue, expenses and equity   6.2
- understand the problems of inter-firm comparison   6.3
- apply accounting ratios to inter-firm comparison   6.3
- explain the uses of accounting information by interested parties for decision making   6.4
- recognise the limitations of accounting statements.   6.5

Chapter 22: Analysis and interpretation

22.1 Introduction

It is necessary to analyse and interpret the financial statements of a business in order to assess its performance and progress. **Analysis** consists of a detailed examination of the information in a set of financial statements of a business. The results of this analysis are then interpreted in order to assess the performance of the business. **Interpretation** can include comparing to the results of other similar businesses and also comparing within the business (with the results for previous years and with targets and budgets).

To enable this comparison to be carried out in a meaningful way the results are usually expressed as accounting ratios. This is a general term which includes calculations in the form of ratios, percentages and time periods. Ratios are usually divided into two main groups – profitability ratios and liquidity ratios.

Working capital is the difference between the current assets and the current liabilities and is the amount available for the day-to-day running of the business (it is also known as **net current assets**). **Capital owned** is the amount owed by a business to the owner(s) of the business on a certain date. **Capital employed** is the total funds which are being used by a business. This may be calculated as the owner's capital plus any non-current liabilities (alternatively, it may be calculated as non-current assets plus net current assets). Capital employed can be defined in several ways: the figure at the start of the year, the figure at the end of the year, or an average of the two.

> **LINK**
> You learned about the main types of assets and liabilities in Chapter 9.

> **TEST YOURSELF 22.1**
>
> 1. Name the two main groups of ratios.
> 2. Define working capital.
> 3. State what is meant by capital owned.
> 4. State **two** ways in which capital employed can be calculated.

> **LINK**
> You learned about the financial statements of a sole trader in Chapters 8 and 9.

Walkthrough 22.1

Arun is a trader who has been in business for several years. His financial year ends on 31 December.

The following financial statements will be used in **Walkthrough 22.2** to **Walkthrough 22.10**.

Arun
Income statement for the year ended 31 December 20–7

		$	$
Revenue –	Cash sales	10 000	
	Credit sales	110 000	120 000
Less	Cost of sales		
	Opening inventory	7 500	
	Purchases (all on credit)	97 000	
		104 500	
	Less Closing inventory	8 500	96 000
Gross profit			24 000
Less Administration and selling expenses			8 000
Profit from operations			16 000
Less Loan interest			1 000
Profit for the year			15 000

Arun
Statement of financial position at 31 December 20–7

	$	$
Non-current assets (at book value)		124 250
Current assets		
Inventory		8 500
Trade receivables		10 500
Bank		12 250
		31 250
Total assets		155 500
Capital and liabilities		
Capital		
Opening balance		130 000
Plus Profit for the year		15 000
		145 000
Less Drawings		22 000
		123 000
Non-current liabilities		
Loan – AB Finance Ltd		20 000
Current liabilities		
Trade payables		12 500
Total liabilities		155 500

Chapter 22: Analysis and interpretation

22.2 Profitability ratios

Profitability ratios are used to relate the profit figures to other figures within the same set of financial statements.

> **KEY TERM**
>
> **Profitability ratios** measure the performance of the business by comparing the profit to other figures in the same set of financial statements.

Return on Capital Employed (ROCE)

This is calculated using the following formula:

$$\frac{\text{Profit for the year before interest}}{\text{Capital employed}} \times \frac{100}{1}$$

Walkthrough 22.2

Using the financial statements shown in **Walkthrough 22.1** calculate Arun's return on capital employed.

Assume that capital employed equals the total of capital owned and non-current liabilities on 31 December 20–7.

$$\frac{\$16\,000}{\$143\,000} \times \frac{100}{1} = 11.19\%$$

This is a very important ratio as it shows the profit earned for every $100 used in the business in order to earn that profit. The total funds used in the business are the capital of the owner(s) plus the non-current liabilities. The higher the return, the more efficiently the capital is being employed within the business.

Gross margin

This is calculated using the following formula:

$$\frac{\text{Gross profit}}{\text{Revenue}} \times \frac{100}{1}$$

Walkthrough 22.3

Using the financial statements shown in **Walkthrough 22.1** calculate Arun's **gross margin**.

$$\frac{\$24\,000}{\$120\,000} \times \frac{100}{1} = 20\%$$

This is also called gross profit as a percentage of turnover (turnover equals net sales less sales returns). This ratio shows the gross profit earned for every $100 of sales. Different types of industries and trades tend to have different gross profit percentages. The same business may have a similar gross margin from year-to-year. The higher the return, the more profitable is the business. However, by reducing selling prices slightly (and so reducing the gross margin), a business may achieve a higher monetary gross profit.

The gross margin can be improved by measures such as:

- increasing selling prices
- obtaining cheaper supplies
- changing the proportions of different types of goods sold.

However, these measures may have some adverse effects. For example, increasing the selling price may result in customers going elsewhere, obtaining cheaper goods may result in a lower quality of goods, and so on.

If the gross margin changes significantly from one year to another the cause should be investigated. A fall in the gross margin may be caused by:

- increasing the rate of trade discount
- selling goods at cheaper prices
- not passing on increased costs to customers.

Profit margin

This is calculated using the following formula:

$$\frac{\text{Profit for the year}}{\text{Revenue}} \times \frac{100}{1}$$

Walkthrough 22.4

Using the financial statements shown in **Walkthrough 22.1** calculate Arun's profit margin.

$$\frac{\$15\,000}{\$120\,000} \times \frac{100}{1} = 12.50\%$$

This ratio shows the profit earned for every $100 of revenue. The higher the return, the more profitable is the business. This ratio acts as an indicator of how well a business is able to control its expenses. If the profit margin of a business increases, it indicates that the operating expenses are being controlled. This ratio will be influenced by the different types of expense: some expenses increase in proportion to the sales (e.g. commission paid on sales made) but other expenses remain the same whatever the sales are (e.g. insurance of buildings). Any change in the gross margin will also affect the profit margin.

The profit margin can be improved by measures such as:

- increasing the gross margin
- controlling expenses
- increasing other income.

A fall in the profit margin may be caused by:

- a decrease in the gross profit
- an increase in expenses
- a decrease in other income
- a change in the type of expense.

The difference between the gross margin and the profit margin represents the percentage of the expenses to the revenue. This indicates the ability of the business to control its expenses.

> **TEST YOURSELF 22.2**
>
> 1. Explain what is shown by the rate of return on capital employed.
> 2. State **two** factors which may increase the gross margin.
> 3. State the expenses as a percentage of the revenue if the gross margin is 25% and the profit margin is 14%.

22.3 Liquidity ratios

In business, the term 'liquidity' relates to money and **liquidity ratios** measure the ease and speed with which assets can be turned into cash.

KEY TERM

Liquidity ratios measure the ability of the business to turn assets into cash to pay its short term debts.

Current ratio

This is calculated using the following formula:

Current assets : Current liabilities

> **Walkthrough 22.5**
>
> Using the financial statements shown in **Walkthrough 22.1** calculate Arun's **current ratio**.
>
> $31 250 : $12 500 = 2.50 : 1

This is also referred to as the **working capital ratio**. It compares the assets which are in the form of cash, or which can be turned into cash relatively easily within the next 12 months, with the liabilities which are due for repayment within that period of time. This measures the ability of a business to meet its current liabilities when they fall due.

Ratios between 1.5 : 1 and 2 : 1 are generally regarded as satisfactory, but it is important to consider the size and type of business. Some businesses necessarily need a large amount of non-current assets whereas other businesses have a higher proportion of current assets; some businesses always purchase goods on credit whereas others always pay cash; some businesses obtain long-term loans whereas others make use of short-term loans or a bank overdraft. If the current ratio is over 2 : 1 it may indicate poor management of the current assets.

The working capital of a business must be adequate to finance the day-to-day trading activities. A business which is short of working capital may encounter the following problems:

- cannot meet immediate liabilities when they are due
- experience difficulties in obtaining further supplies on credit
- cannot take advantage of cash discounts
- cannot take advantage of business opportunities when they arise.

Ways to improve the working capital position include:

- introduction of further capital by the owner(s)
- obtaining long-term loans/non-current liabilities
- selling surplus non-current assets
- delaying purchasing non-current assets
- increasing profit
- reducing drawings by the owner(s) (or reduction in dividends).

The actual cash position can also be improved by measures such as delaying payments to credit suppliers, increasing the proportion of cash sales, and reducing the period of credit allowed to credit customers. These measures may also have some adverse effects such as the refusal of further supplies on credit, customers moving to other suppliers where longer credit is allowed, and so on.

Liquid (acid test) ratio

This is calculated using the following formula:

Current assets − Inventory : Current liabilities

Walkthrough 22.6

Using the financial statements shown in **Walkthrough 22.1** calculate Arun's liquid (acid test) ratio.

($31 250 − $8 500) : $12 500 = 1.82 : 1

The liquid (acid test) ratio compares the assets which are in the form of money, or which will convert into money quickly, with the liabilities which are due for repayment in the near future. This is a similar calculation to the current ratio, but the liquid (acid test) ratio excludes inventory as this is not regarded as a liquid asset. Inventory is two stages away from being money: the goods have to be sold and then the money has to be collected from the debtors.

Ratios between 0.7 : 1 and 1 : 1 are usually regarded as satisfactory, but, as with the current ratio, the size and type of business should also be considered. A ratio of 1 : 1 indicates that the immediate liabilities can be met out of the liquid assets without having to sell inventory. (Where inventory has to be sold immediately it can sometimes only be done at a reduced price.) If the liquid (acid test) ratio is over 1 : 1 it may indicate poor management of liquid assets such as having too high a balance on a bank current account.

You can now answer Questions 1–2 at the end of this chapter.

TEST YOURSELF 22.3

1. State **two** disadvantages of a shortage of working capital.
2. State **two** ways of improving the working capital.
3. Explain the difference between the current ratio and the liquid (acid test) ratio.

Rate of inventory turnover

This is calculated using the following formula:

$$\frac{\text{Cost of sales}}{\text{Average inventory}}$$

This gives the number of times inventory is sold and replaced in the period.

An alternative calculation uses the following formula:

$$\frac{\text{Average inventory}}{\text{Cost of sales}} \times \frac{365}{1}$$

This gives the number of days on average the inventory is held before being sold.

Walkthrough 22.7

Using the financial statements shown in **Walkthrough 22.1**, calculate Arun's rate of inventory turnover to show the following:

a the number of times in the year inventory is replaced

b the number of days inventory is held before being sold.

a $\dfrac{\$96\,000}{(\$7\,500 + \$8\,500) \div 2} = 12$ times

b $\dfrac{\$8\,000}{\$96\,000} \times \dfrac{365}{1} = 30.42$ days $= 31$ days

> **LINK**
> You learned about the effects of an incorrect inventory valuation in Chapter 10.

The rate of inventory turnover is sometimes referred to as **inventory turnover**. This ratio calculates the number of times a business sells and replaces its inventory in a given period of time. The rate of inventory turnover will obviously vary according to the type of business. Businesses selling luxury goods such as expensive jewellery and private jet planes will have a low rate of inventory turnover whereas businesses selling low value 'everyday' requirements such as fresh bread and newspapers will have a high rate of inventory turnover. The same business may have a similar rate of inventory turnover from year-to-year. If the rate increases it may indicate improved efficiency; if the rate decreases if may indicate that the business has too much inventory or that the sales are slowing down. The quicker the rate of inventory turnover, the less time funds are tied up in inventory which is regarded as the least liquid of the current assets.

> **LINK**
> You learned about the rate of inventory turnover in Chapter 17.

The rate of inventory turnover can affect the profit of the business. If business activity slows down both the gross profit and the profit for the year will be adversely affected.

A lower rate of inventory turnover can be caused by factors such as:

- lower sales (resulting in higher inventory levels)
- inventory over-purchased
- too high selling prices
- falling demand
- business activity slowing down
- business inefficiency.

Trade receivables turnover

This is calculated using the following formula:

$$\frac{\text{Trade receivables}}{\text{Credit sales}} \times \frac{365}{1} \text{ to give an answer in days}$$

Using alternative formulae, an answer can be obtained in weeks or months:

$$\frac{\text{Trade receivables}}{\text{Credit sales}} \times \frac{52}{1} \text{ to give an answer in weeks}$$

$$\frac{\text{Trade receivables}}{\text{Credit sales}} \times \frac{12}{1} \text{ to give an answer in months}$$

Walkthrough 22.8

Using the financial statements shown in **Walkthrough 22.1**, calculate (to the nearest whole day) Arun's trade receivables turnover.

$$\frac{\$10\,500}{\$110\,000} \times \frac{365}{1} = 34.84 \text{ days} = 35 \text{ days}$$

> **LINK**
>
> You learned about irrecoverable debts in Chapter 13.

This may also be referred to as the **trade receivables/sales ratio**. It measures the average time the credit customers take to pay their accounts. The answer to this calculation – the length of time credit customers actually take to pay their accounts – should be compared with the term of credit allowed to them. The quicker the customers pay their accounts, the better it is; the money can then be used for other purposes within the business. The longer a business has to wait for a debt to be paid the greater the risk of it becoming irrecoverable.

The same business may have a similar trade receivables turnover from year-to-year. If the period decreases it may indicate that the credit control policy is being applied more effectively: if the period increases it may indicate that the credit control policy is inefficient, or that longer credit terms are being allowed in order to maintain the quantity of credit sales.

The rate of the trade receivables turnover can be improved by measures such as:

- improving credit control policy (sending regular statements of account, 'chasing' overdue accounts and so on)
- offering cash discount for early settlement
- charging interest on overdue accounts
- refusing further supplies until any outstanding debt is paid
- invoice discounting and debt factoring.*

*For a fee, a debt factor will maintain the sales ledger, collect the debts and advance money against those debts. For a fee, a discounter will advance money against certain debts, but does not maintain the sales ledger.

Chapter 22: Analysis and interpretation

Trade payables turnover

This is calculated using the following formula:

$$\frac{\text{Trade payables}}{\text{Credit purchases}} \times \frac{365}{1} \text{ to give an answer in days}$$

Using alternative formulae, an answer can be obtained in weeks or months:

$$\frac{\text{Trade payables}}{\text{Credit purchases}} \times \frac{52}{1} \text{ to give an answer in weeks}$$

$$\frac{\text{Trade payables}}{\text{Credit purchases}} \times \frac{12}{1} \text{ to give an answer in months}$$

Walkthrough 22.9

Using the financial statements shown in **Walkthrough 22.1**, calculate (to the nearest whole day) Arun's trade payables turnover.

$$\frac{\$12\,500}{\$97\,000} \times \frac{365}{1} = 47.04 \text{ days} = 48 \text{ days}$$

This may also be referred to as the **trade payables/purchases ratio**. It measures the average time taken to pay the accounts of credit suppliers. The answer to this calculation should be compared with the term of credit allowed by the suppliers.

The same business may have a similar trade payables turnover from year-to-year. If the period decreases, the business is paying the suppliers more quickly; if the period increases it may indicate that the business is short of immediate funds and is finding it difficult to meet debts when they fall due. This ratio can also be influenced by the trade receivables turnover: if the credit customers do not settle their accounts promptly the business may not be able to pay the credit suppliers promptly. Taking longer to pay the suppliers means that the business can use the funds for other purposes, but there can be adverse effects such as:

- the supplier refusing credit in the future
- the supplier refusing further supplies
- the loss of any cash discount for early settlement
- damage to the relationship with the supplier.

You can now answer Question 3 at the end of this chapter.

TIP
When attempting questions which require the calculation of ratios it is advisable to show workings. In this way some of the available marks may be earned even if the final answer is incorrect.

TEST YOURSELF 22.4

1. State the formula for calculating rate of inventory turnover.
2. State **two** reasons why the rate of inventory turnover may fall.
3. State the formula for calculating trade receivables turnover.
4. A trader allows his credit customers 30 days credit. The trade receivables turnover is 40 days. State whether the trader will be satisfied. Give a reason for your answer.
5. A trader's credit suppliers allow him 45 days credit. State **one** advantage and **one** disadvantage to the trader if he pays after 45 days.

TIP
When stating the answer to a ratio calculation the figure should be accompanied by the appropriate description such as %, 'times' and 'days'.

22.4 Inter-firm comparison

Comparing the ratios calculated for the current financial year with those of previous years can measure the progress and performance of a business and indicate the trends in profitability, liquidity and so on.

Another useful comparison is to compare the ratios with those of a similar business.

Walkthrough 22.10

Arun is a trader who has been in business for several years. Renu started a similar business in another town two years ago. The financial year for both businesses ends on 31 December.

Renu allows Arun access to her financial records. The following information is available:

	Arun $	Renu $
On 1 January 20–7:		
Inventory	7 500	5 100
For the year ended 31 December 20–7:		
Revenue – cash sales	10 000	–
credit sales	110 000	100 000
Purchases – cash	–	26 600
credit	97 000	50 000
Cost of sales	96 000	76 000
Administration and selling expenses	8 000	13 000
Finance costs	1 000	500
On 31 December 20–7:		
Inventory	8 500	5 700
Trade receivables	10 500	10 900
Bank	12 250	–
Bank overdraft	–	6 600
Trade payables	12 500	5 000
Capital employed	143 000	115 000

a For **each** business calculate the following ratios:
  i   return on capital employed
  ii gross margin
  iii profit margin
  iv current ratio
  v   liquid (acid test) ratio
  vi rate of inventory turnover
  vii trade receivables turnover
  viii trade payables turnover.

b Using the ratios calculated in **a**, compare the performance of the two businesses.

Chapter 22: Analysis and interpretation

a

		Arun $	Renu $
i	Return on capital employed	11.19%	$\dfrac{\$11\,000}{\$115\,000} \times \dfrac{100}{1} = 9.57\%$
ii	Gross margin	20%	$\dfrac{\$24\,000}{\$100\,000} \times \dfrac{100}{1} = 24\%$
iii	Profit margin	12.50%	$\dfrac{\$10\,500}{\$100\,000} \times \dfrac{100}{1} = 10.50\%$
iv	Current ratio	2.50 : 1	$16\,600 : \$11\,600 = 1.43 : 1$
v	Liquid (acid test) ratio	1.82 : 1	$10\,900 : \$11\,600 = 0.94 : 1$
vi	Rate of inventory turnover	12 times	$\dfrac{\$76\,000}{\$5400} = 14.07$ times
vii	Trade receivables turnover	35 days	$\dfrac{\$10\,900}{\$100\,000} \times \dfrac{365}{1} = 40$ days
viii	Trade payables turnover	48 days	$\dfrac{\$5000}{\$50\,000} \times \dfrac{365}{1} = 37$ days

- The detailed calculations for Arun's business have been shown earlier in this chapter.

b Comparison of the ratios:

Profitability

Arun is employing more capital and has a higher return on capital employed than Renu. For every $100 of capital employed Arun had a return of 11.19%, whereas Renu only achieved $9.57. This may indicate that Renu is not employing the capital in the most effective way.

Both businesses earned the same amount of gross profit, but Renu achieved a higher gross margin. It may be that Arun failed to pass on increased costs, or sold goods at cheaper prices in order to achieve greater sales. Renu may have been selling the goods at higher prices or buying goods at a cheaper price than Arun.

Despite both businesses earning the same amount of gross profit, Arun achieved a higher amount of profit for the year by controlling his expenses. Arun's expenses as a percentage of revenue were 8.50% compared with 13.50% for Renu. This resulted in Arun having a higher profit margin.

Liquidity

Arun's current ratio of 2.50 : 1 is quite satisfactory as his current assets are two and a half times the current liabilities. Renu's current ratio of 1.43: 1 may be regarded as too low as her current assets are only 1.43 times greater than her current liabilities. Renu may find it difficult to meet her current liabilities when they fall due and may not be able to take advantage of cash discounts or business opportunities when they arise. The introduction of additional capital or a long-term loan to replace part (or all) of the bank overdraft would improve her working capital position.

Arun's liquid (acid test) ratio is also satisfactory (some may even regard it as a little too high). Renu's liquid (acid test) ratio is quite reasonable as her liquid assets and her current liabilities are almost equal. However, her only liquid asset is trade receivables, so

TIP

When comparing the ratios of two businesses, offer suggestions on how the difference has occurred and the consequences of low or high ratios. Do not limit the answer to basic comments such as 'X had a higher ratio than Y'.

she is dependent on credit customers paying their accounts before she is able to pay her current liabilities.

Renu has achieved a slightly quicker rate of inventory turnover than Arun. This may indicate that Renu is more efficient. Arun could consider reducing his inventory levels and try to increase his rate of sales.

Arun's credit sales are only slightly higher than Renu's. The amount of trade receivables of each business is very similar. Arun's credit customers are paying their accounts in an average of 35 days, Renu's credit customers are taking an average of 40 days to pay their accounts. It may be that Renu's credit control policy is inefficient or that she is not offering cash discounts. To be more meaningful, these figures should be compared to the credit allowed by each business.

The amount of Arun's credit purchases was much higher than that of Renu. The total of Arun's trade payables is much greater than that owed by Renu. Arun's credit suppliers are being paid in an average of 48 days, Renu takes an average of 37 days to pay her credit suppliers. This may be linked to the fact that Renu is relying on a bank overdraft for short-term finance, and her trade payables much less than Arun's.

22.5 Problems of inter-firm comparison

A business can often obtain valuable information by comparing their accounting ratios with those of another business, but the business must be aware of the limitations of such a comparison. Every business is different and has different requirements and accounting policies. A comparison is only meaningful if it is between two or more businesses of the same type, of the same size and in the same trade. The problems of comparison include the following:

- The businesses may apply different accounting policies, for example they may use different methods of depreciation.

- The businesses may apply different operating policies such as renting premises or purchasing premises, obtaining long-term finance from capital only or using capital and long-term loans. Such policies will affect both the profit for the year and the statement of financial position.

- Non-monetary items such as the skill of the workforce, the goodwill of the business and so on do not appear in the accounting records, but are very important in the success of the business.

- It is not always possible to obtain all the information about another business which is needed to make a true comparison. For example, the inventory shown in the financial statements may not represent the average amount held during the year; the financial statements do not show the age of the non-current assets and when they need replacing.

- The information relating to other businesses may be for one financial year only, so it is not possible to calculate business trends. That particular year may also not be a 'typical' year.

- The financial years may end on different dates which can make comparison difficult. For example, the year end for one business may be at a time when inventories are particularly low; the year end for another business may be when inventories are particularly high.

- The accounts are based on historic cost and do not show the effects of inflation.

You can now answer Question 4 at the end of this chapter.

Chapter 22: Analysis and interpretation

> **TEST YOURSELF 22.5**
>
> 1 State and explain **four** problems of inter-firm comparison.

22.6 Users of accounting statements

It is not only the owner who is interested in analysing and interpreting the financial statements of an organisation. Various other people are also interested in different aspects of the accounts. The users of accounting statements can be divided into two main groups – internal users and external users.

Internal users

1 **Owner(s)**
   The owners of a business such as a sole trader or partners will be interested in all aspects of the business, both profitability and liquidity, in order to assess the business's performance and progress. Any potential partners are interested in the profitability of the business. The shareholders and potential shareholders of a limited company are interested in the profitability of the company and also in various investment ratios (which are outside the scope of this book).

2 **Manager(s)**
   In many small businesses, the owners manage the business. In some cases, management may be carried out by an employee. Like the owners, managers are interested in all aspects of the business. They may use ratios to assess past performance, plan for the future and take remedial action where necessary.

External users

1 **Bank manager**
   If a business requests a bank loan or an overdraft facility the bank manager will require the financial statements of the business. The bank manager will need to know whether there is adequate security to cover the amount of the loan or overdraft, whether it can be repaid when due, and whether interest can be paid when due.

2 **Other lenders**
   Anyone who has made a loan to a business (and any potential lenders) will be interested in the security available, the repayment of the loan when due and the payment of interest when due.

3 **Trade payables**
   Anyone who has supplied a business with goods on credit terms (and any potential credit supplier) is interested in the liquidity position and the trade payables turnover. These factors may be considered when determining the credit limit and the length of credit allowed. In practice, it may not be possible to obtain the accounts of sole traders and partnership businesses, so other means of checking creditworthiness are employed.

4 **Potential buyers of the business**
   Anyone with an interest in purchasing the business or making a takeover bid will be interested in the profitability of the business and the market value of the assets of the business.

TIP
In addition to naming the users of financial statements you must be able to explain the reason for their interest in the statements.

5 **Customers**
Customers of the business are interested in ensuring the continuity of supplies.

6 **Employees and trade unions**
Employees and trade unions want to know that the company is able to continue operating, and so maintain jobs and continue to pay adequate wages (and, in some cases, contribute to pension schemes).

7 **Government departments**
Government department may want information for purposes such as compiling business statistics and checking that the correct amount of tax is being paid.

8 **Club members**
The members of a club or society want to know that the club is being well-managed financially so that it will be able to continue in existence and provide the facilities to members.

You can now answer Questions 5 and 6 at the end of this chapter.

22.7 Limitations of accounting statements

Accounting statements and the ratios calculated from them provide valuable information about a business. They do, however, have limitations and are not able to provide a complete picture of the performance and position of a business. Their limitations include the following.

Time factor
The accounting statements are a record of what has happened in the past, not a guide to the future. Additionally, there is a gap between the end of the financial year and the preparation of the accounting statements. In that time significant events such as changes in inventory levels and purchasing of non-current assets may have taken place.

Historic cost
The only way to record financial transactions is to use the actual cost price. However, comparing transactions taking place at different times can be difficult because of the effect of inflation. For example, in times of inflation, it would cost more to buy a machine in 20–8 identical to one purchased in 20–1.

Accounting policies
All businesses should apply the accounting principles of **prudence** and **consistency** which should help in making comparisons. However, there are several acceptable accounting policies which may be applied, for example there are several different methods of calculating depreciation. Where businesses have used different accounting policies it is difficult to make a meaningful comparison of their results. Similarly, where a business changes its policy, a comparison with the results of previous years is difficult.

LINK
You learned about the principles of prudence and consistency in Chapter 10.

Different definitions
Where a business has borrowed money, for example in the form of loans or debentures, the income statement may show the profit from operations and then deduct the finance costs to give the profit for the year. Another business may not show this distinction. Businesses may use a different definition of 'profit' when calculating profitability ratios.

A comparison of profit and profitability ratios is only meaningful if 'like is compared with like' and the same definitions are applied.

Money measurement

Accounts only record information which can be expressed in monetary terms. This means that there are many important factors which influence the performance of a business which will not appear in the accounting statements.

The factors which are within the control of the business include the quality of management, the skill and reliability of the workforce, the goodwill of the business, the age and condition of the non-current assets and the ability to adapt in response to changing market conditions.

Other factors are outside the control of the business. These include government policies, competition, impact of new technology, and future long-term prospects for the particular trade or industry.

LINK

You learned about historic cost and money measurement in Chapter 10.

> **TEST YOURSELF 22.6**
>
> 1 Name **three** business people who would be interested in the accounts of a sole trader. Explain the reason for their interest in each case.
> 2 Explain **three** limitations of the accounting statements of a business.

Revision checklist

- There are three ratios which measure profitability: return on capital employed, gross margin and profit margin.
- There are five ratios which measure liquidity: current ratio, liquid (acid test) ratio, rate of inventory turnover, trade receivables turnover and trade payables turnover.
- Ratios can be used to compare the current year with previous years and with other similar businesses. Problems can arise when making inter-firm comparisons.
- Certain aspects of the accounting statements of a business are of interest to users such as owner(s), managers, lenders, trade payables, potential buyers, customers, employees and trade unions, and government departments.
- Accounting statements and the ratios calculated from them provide valuable information, but they have limitations and are not able to provide a complete picture of the performance and position of a business.

Cambridge IGCSE and O Level Accounting

Exam-style questions

1 A trader provided the following information about his current ratio:

Year 1	Year 2	Year 3
1.45 : 1	1.75 : 1	2.00 : 1

What would explain the change in this ratio?

- **A** decrease in cash at bank
- **B** decrease in inventory
- **C** decrease in trade payables
- **D** decrease in trade receivables

2 Rizwan is a trader. His financial year ends on 31 January. He provided the following information on 1 February 20–4:

	$
Inventory	4 620
Trade payables	4 150
Trade receivables	5 340
Bank overdraft	2 110
Loan from Haziq repayable 31 December 20–4	2 000
Loan from Amar repayable 31 January 20–6	5 000

a Calculate Rizwan's working capital.

b Suggest two problems Rizwan may encounter if his working capital is inadequate.

Rizwan is considering adopting one of four possible courses of action aimed at increasing his working capital.

c Explain the effect on the working capital of each of the following proposals:

- Proposal 1 Introduce an additional $5 000 capital.
- Proposal 2 Convert the loan from Haziq into a bank loan repayable on the same date.
- Proposal 3 Sell one third of the inventory to a cash customer at cost price.
- Proposal 4 Pay the trade payables immediately and earn a 2% cash discount.

d Suggest **two** other ways Rizwan could consider to increase his working capital.

3 Samira provided the following information at the end of her first year of trading:

	$	$
Sales for the year – cash	4 800	
credit	38 200	43 000
Trade receivables at year end		3 700

The account of a customer to whom Samira sold goods on credit, $700, should be written off as an irrecoverable debt.

What was the trade receivables turnover?

- **A** 26 days
- **B** 29 days
- **C** 32 days
- **D** 36 days

Chapter 22: Analysis and interpretation

4 Vijay runs a wholesale furniture business. All goods are sold on credit terms. He provided the following information at the end of his third year of trading:

	$
On 1 January 20–2:	
Inventory	5 600
Capital employed	130 000
For the year ended 31 December 20–2:	
Revenue	66 000
Cost of sales	48 840
Loan interest	1 500
Profit for the year	5 610
At 31 December 20–2:	
Inventory	6 200
Trade receivables	5 120

Vijay decided to compare his results with those of AK Limited, an old-established food wholesaler.

a Complete the following table to show the ratios for Vijay's business for the year ended 31 December 20–2. The answers should be correct to two decimal places.

	Vijay	AK Limited
Gross margin		17.50%
Profit margin		9.25%
Return on capital employed		6.76%
Rate of inventory turnover		16.44

b Suggest **two** reasons for the difference in the gross margin.
c State which business has better control of its expenses. Give a reason for your answer.
d Suggest **two** reasons for the difference in the rate of inventory turnover.
e Suggest **four** factors which Vijay should consider when comparing his results with those of AK Limited.

5 Why may John, a credit supplier, be interested in the financial statements of Paul, a new customer?

  A to calculate Paul's current assets
  B to calculate Paul's trade payables turnover
  C to set the rate of trade discount to be allowed to Paul
  D to set the rate of cash discount to be allowed to Paul.

6 Rita is a trader. She provided the following information on 31 July 20–2:

	$
Inventory	3 140
Cash at bank	2 650
Trade payables	3 670
Trade receivables	2 960
Loan repayable 30 September 20–2	2 500

a State the formula for the calculation of the liquid (acid test) ratio.
b Calculate the liquid (acid test) ratio.
c Comment on your answer to **b**.
d State why the liquid (acid test) ratio is a more reliable indicator of liquidity than the current ratio.
e Complete the table by stating the effect of each of the following on Rita's current ratio and liquid (acid test) ratio. The first one has been completed as an example.

	Current ratio	Liquid (acid test) ratio
Sold old inventory at cost price to credit customer	*no effect*	*increase*
Purchased a new machine paying by cheque		
Purchased inventory on credit		
Arranged for loan repayment date to be extended for two years		

f Name **four** interested parties, apart from Rita, who may wish to look at the financial statements of Rita. Give a reason in each case.

Section 4: Practice questions

1. A trader's cash book had a credit balance of $480. On the same date, his bank statement showed a credit balance of $389. The difference in the balances was caused by bank charges, $25, which appeared only on the bank statement, and a cheque not yet presented.

   What was the amount of the unpresented cheque?

   A $66 **B** $116 **C** $848 **D** $894

2. Goods returned by Zeena, $100, were debited to her account as $1 000.

   What entries are required to correct this error?

	Account to be debited	$	Account to be credited	$
A	suspense	900	Zeena	900
B	suspense	1 100	Zeena	1 100
C	Zeena	900	suspense	900
D	Zeena	1 100	suspense	1 100

3. Gary is both a customer and a supplier to Leroy. On 28 June Leroy's account in Gary's purchases ledger had a credit balance of $275, and his account in Gary's sales ledger had a debit balance of $140. A contra entry was made to set the balance of one account against the balance of the other account.

   What entry will be made in the control accounts prepared on 30 June?

	Debited	$	Credited	$
A	purchases ledger control account	135	sales ledger control account	135
B	purchases ledger control account	140	sales ledger control account	140
C	sales ledger control account	135	purchases ledger control account	135
D	sales ledger control account	140	purchases ledger control account	140

4. A sports club provided the following information at the end of its first financial year:

	$
Subscriptions received for the current year	9 750
Subscriptions received in advance for the following year	150
Expenses of sports competition	2 040
Rates and insurance	1 986
General expenses	787
General expenses accrued at the end of the year	103
Balance at bank at the end of the year	7 403
Receipts from sports competition entry fees	?

   How much was received from the sports competition entry fees?

   A $2 316 **B** $2 466 **C** $3 103 **D** $3 253

5 In addition to purchasing raw materials a manufacturer also purchased a quantity of finished goods. The cost of carriage inwards on the raw materials was incorrectly recorded as carriage inwards on finished goods.

How did this error affect the cost of production and the gross profit?

	Cost of production			Gross profit		
	Overstated	Understated	No effect	Overstated	Understated	No effect
A	✓				✓	
B		✓			✓	
C		✓				✓
D			✓	✓		

6 Omar maintains a three column cash book. On 1 March 20–4 he had a cash balance of $150 and a bank overdraft of $3 940.

Omar's transactions for March 20–4 included the following:

March 8 Withdrew $1 500 from the bank for personal use
14 Cash sales paid directly into the bank, $2 310
18 Paid Mariam a cheque to settle her account of $320, less $2\frac{1}{2}$% cash discount
21 Abdul paid his account of $110 by credit transfer
25 Zaffar paid $490 by cheque in full settlement of his account of $500
29 Cash sales, $2 462
30 Paid operating expenses in cash, $242
31 Paid all cash into bank except $200

Omar received his bank statement for March. He compared the two records and found the following differences:

1 Item appearing on the bank statement but not recorded in the cash book:

$
Bank charges 21

2 The bank had not recorded the transactions which took place on the following dates:
25 March
31 March

3 The bank had made an error and recorded the cash paid in on 14 March as $3 210.

a Write up Omar's cash book, including all relevant entries, for March 20–4. Balance the cash book and bring down the balances on 1 April 20–4.

b Prepare a bank reconciliation statement at 31 March 20–4 showing the balance on the bank statement at that date.

7 Darren started a business on 1 February 20–8. He transferred $120 000 from his private bank account to a business bank account. He obtained a long-term loan from his family of $50 000 which was also paid into the business bank account.

On the same date he purchased premises, $125 000, shop fittings, $17 500, and inventory, $5 320, all of which were paid by credit transfer.

  a Prepare the opening journal entry on 1 February 20–8. A narrative is required.

  The following transactions took place in August 20–8:
  August 1   Darren took goods, $440, from the business for personal use.
          12 Darren transferred his personal motor vehicle to the business at a valuation of $16 250.

  b Prepare journal entries to record these transactions. Narratives are required.

  Darren made year-end transfers to the income statement on 31 January 20–9 and also made some year-end adjustments.

  c Prepare journal entries to record the following. Narratives are required.
   1 Writing off a debt of $150 owed by Paula as irrecoverable.
   2 Transferring the balance of the irrecoverable debts account to the income statement.
   3 Transferring the balance of the purchases returns account, $1 075, to the income statement.
   4 Transferring the balance of the operating expenses account, $13 620, to the income statement.
   5 Creating a provision for doubtful debts of $550.
   6 Depreciating shop fittings by 10% on cost.

8 Uzma's trial balance drawn up at the end of her financial year did not balance, but she proceeded to prepare draft financial statements. The statement of financial position she prepared is provided.

Draft statement of financial position at 31 October 20–6	
	$
Non-current assets at book value	26 000
Inventory	8 500
Trade receivables	6 270
Bank	700
	41 470
Capital	
Opening balance	28 000
Plus draft profit for the year	2 860
	30 860
Less Drawings	12 900
	17 960
Long-term loan	15 000
Trade payables	10 150
	43 110
Less Suspense account	1 640
	41 470

The following errors were later discovered:
1 No adjustment had been made for prepaid rent at 31 October 20–6 of $480.
2 The balance of the petty cash book, $120, had been omitted from the trial balance.
3 $200 paid to a credit supplier by bank transfer had been recorded in the cash book but not in the supplier's account.
4 Purchases on credit, $990, have not been entered in the accounting records.
5 The sales journal was overcast by $1 000.
6 The total of the discount allowed account, $320, had been omitted from the trial balance (and consequently omitted from the income statement).

a Write up the suspense account. Close or balance the account as necessary.
b Calculate the correct profit for the year.
c Prepare a corrected statement of financial position at 31 October 20–6.

9 Violetta is a trader. She maintains a full set of accounting records and prepares monthly control accounts.

a State **two** advantages to Violetta of preparing a monthly sales ledger control account.

b Explain the meaning of the word 'contra' in connection with control accounts and explain when such an entry is required.

Violetta provided the following information:

	$
On 1 May 20–1:	
Debit balances in sales ledger	3 020
Credit balances in sales ledger	35
Totals for the month of May 20–1:	
Credit sales	3 965
Cash sales	1 400
Receipts from credit customers	2 695
Returns by credit customers	166
Returns to credit suppliers	205
Discount allowed	55
Discount received	79
Irrecoverable debts	114
Provision for doubtful debts	120
Interest charged by credit supplier	14
Interest charged to credit customer	10
Contra entry	150
On 31 May 20–1:	
Debit balances in sales ledger	?
Credit balances in sales ledger	20

c Select the relevant figures and prepare the sales ledger control account for May 20–1. Balance the account and bring down the balances on 1 June 20–1.

On 10 May Violetta had the following transactions:
1. Wrote off $95 owing by Wilma as irrecoverable.
2. Transferred the balance of $200 on Jim's account in the sales ledger to his account in the purchases ledger.

d Prepare journal entries to record these transactions. Narratives are required.

10 Veena's financial year ends on 30 November. All sales are made on credit terms and the selling price is calculated by marking-up the cost price by 20%.

He does not maintain a full set of double entry records but was able to provide the following information:

	$
On 1 December 20–0:	
Trade receivables	3 620
During the year ended 30 November 20–1:	
Amounts received from trade receivables	36 750
Discount allowed to trade receivables	750
Irrecoverable debts	860
On 30 November 20–1:	
Trade receivables	4 020

a Calculate the credit sales for the year ended 30 November 20–1.
b Calculate the gross profit for the year ended 30 November 20–1.
c Calculate the cost of sales for the year ended 30 November 20–1.
d Suggest to Veena three advantages of maintaining a full set of double entry records.

11 Jamal is a trader. He does not maintain a full set of accounting records. All money received is banked and all payments are made by credit transfer.

Jamal provided the following information:

	$
On 1 October 20–3:	
Balance at bank	11 440
Trade receivables	3 166
Trade payables	4 095
During the year ended 30 September 20–4:	
Receipts from credit customers	34 125
Cash sales	19 420
Payments to credit suppliers	?
Credit purchases	49 420
Credit sales	?
Irrecoverable debts	134
Discount allowed to credit customers	875
Discount received from credit suppliers	1 452
Returns from credit customers	2 066
Purchase of non-current assets	12 600
Operating expenses	?

On 30 September 20–4:

Bank overdraft	1 340
Trade receivables	3 256
Trade payables	5 115

a Prepare a total trade receivables account to calculate the credit sales.
b Prepare a total trade payables account to calculate the payments to credit suppliers.
c Prepare a bank account to calculate the operating expenses paid.

12 The CK Club was formed some years ago. The club has 200 members and the annual subscription is $120. The financial year ends on 31 December.

The treasurer of the CK Club provided the following information:

On 1 January 20–7:
  14 members still owed their subscription for 20–6
  Five members had paid their subscription for 20–7 in advance

During the year ended 31 December 20–7:
  Ten members had paid their outstanding subscription for 20–6
  187 members had paid their subscription for 20–7
  Six members had paid their subscription for 20–8

On 31 December 20–7 it was decided to write off the subscriptions still outstanding for 20–6 as irrecoverable.

a Prepare the subscriptions account for the year ended 31 December 20–7. Balance the account and bring down the balances on 1 January 20–8.
b Explain the meaning of each of the following terms:
  i subscriptions
  ii income and expenditure account
  iii receipts and payments account
  iv accumulated fund
c Explain why it may be necessary for an income statement to be prepared for a club.

13 Hamid and Waheed are in partnership. Their financial year ends on 31 August. The partnership agreement provides for the following:

  Interest on capital at 4% per annum
  Interest on drawings at 3%
  Partnership salary for Waheed at $5 000 per annum
  Residual profits and losses to be shared 3:2

The balances on the partners' accounts on 1 September 20–5 were:

	Hamid	Waheed
	$	$
Capital account	90 000	70 000
Current account	1 950 debit	12 050 credit

Hamid invested $20 000 additional capital on 1 March 20–6. On the same date the partners decided to amend the partnership agreement to increase Waheed's salary to $7 000 per annum.

During the year ended 31 August 20–6 the partners' drawings were: Hamid $4 200 and Waheed $7 200.

Profit for the year ended 31 August 20–6 was $19 463.

a Prepare the profit and loss appropriation account for the year ended 31 August 20–6.

b Prepare the partners' current accounts for the year ended 31 August 20–5. Balance the accounts and bring down the balances on 1 September 20–5.

c Prepare an extract from the statement of financial position at 31 August 20–6 to show the capital and current accounts of the partners. Full details of the current accounts are not required.

Waheed transferred $10 000 from his current account to his capital account on 1 September 20–6. On the same date he transferred office equipment, $2 000, to the business.

d Prepare journal entries to record these transactions. Narratives are required.

14 Beth and Zara are in partnership. They provide office services to local businesses. Their financial year ends on 31 August. They share profits and losses in the ratio of 3:2 respectively.

The balances on the partners' accounts on 1 September 20–1 were:

	Beth	Zara
	$	$
Capital account	36 000	24 000
Current account	4 000 credit	1 500 debit

During the year ended 31 August 20–2 the partners made the following drawings:

	Beth	Zara
	$	$
	3 000	4 000

The partially completed profit and loss appropriation account for the year ended 31 August 20–2 showed the following:

		$	$
Profit for the year			5 460
Interest on drawings –	Beth	60	
	Zara	80	140
			5 600
Interest on capital –	Beth	1 440	
	Zara	960	
		2 400	
Salary – Zara		5 000	7 400
Residual profit available for distribution			(1 800)

On 31 August 20–2 the following balances remained in the books of the partnership:

	$
Office furniture and equipment	36 850
Motor vehicles	18 250
Trade payables	4 200
Trade receivables	6 120
Other payables	150
Other receivables	310
Balance at bank	3 780

a Prepare the statement of financial position at 31 August 20–2. Full details of the current accounts should be shown within the statement.

b i Calculate the rate of interest which has been charged on partners' drawings.
  ii Calculate the rate of interest allowed on partners' capital.

Beth and Zara are considering converting their partnership into a limited company.

c i State **one** advantage to Beth and Zara of converting the partnership to a limited company.
  ii State **one** disadvantage to Beth and Zara of converting the partnership to a limited company.

As an alternative to converting to a limited company, Beth is considering making a loan to the partnership.

d Suggest **two** advantages to Beth of making a 5% five year loan to the partnership rather than investing additional capital.

15 Pierre is a furniture manufacturer. His financial year ends on 31 March. He provided the following information:

	At 1 April 20–5 $	At 31 March 20–6 $
Inventory – raw materials	30 460	31 850
work in progress	18 020	17 470
finished goods	62 000	71 060
Factory machinery at cost	154 000	?
Provision for depreciation of factory machinery	61 600	?
Office equipment at cost	32 000	?
Provision for depreciation of office equipment	8 880	?

	$
For the year ended 31 March 20–6:	
Revenue	1 036 500
Purchases of raw materials	364 510
Purchases of finished goods	38 720
Carriage on purchases of raw materials	9 430
Carriage on purchases of finished goods	1 240
Rent, rates and insurance	28 480
Operating expenses	33 780
Wages – factory operatives	296 770
factory supervisors	87 400
office and sales staff	82 300

Additional information:

1 At 31 March 20–6 wages of factory operatives accrued amounted to $1 830.
2 At 31 March 20–6 rates and insurance prepaid amounted to $1 040.
3 Rent, rates and insurance are apportioned $\frac{3}{4}$ to the factory and $\frac{1}{4}$ to the offices.
4 Operating expenses are apportioned $\frac{2}{3}$ to the factory and $\frac{1}{3}$ to the offices.
5 Factory machinery, $18 000, was purchased on 1 October 20–5. No machinery was disposed of during the year. Factory machinery is being depreciated at 20% per annum on cost, from the date of purchase.
6 Office equipment is being depreciated at 15% per annum using the reducing balance method.

a Prepare the manufacturing account for the year ended 31 March 20–6.

b Prepare the income statement for the year ended 31 March 20–6.

c Name the accounting principle Pierre is observing by valuing his inventories at the lower of cost and net realisable value.

d Explain how Pierre is observing the principle of matching by making an adjustment for the prepaid rates and insurance.

e Name the accounting principles Pierre is observing by depreciating his non-current assets.

Section 4: Practice questions

16 The financial year of LS Limited ends on 30 June. The income statement for the year ended 30 June 20–3 showed a profit for the year of $7 300.

a Complete the following partially prepared statement of changes in equity for the year ended 30 June 20–3.

	Ordinary share capital $	General reserve $	Retained earnings $	Total $
On 1 July 20–2	100 000	15 000	8 900	123 900
Issue of ordinary shares	20 000	………….	………….	………….
Profit for the year	………….	………….	………….	7 300
Ordinary share dividend for year ended 30 June 20–3	………….	………….	………….	(5 000)
Transfer to general reserve	………….	3 000	………….	………….
On 30 June 20–3	………….	………….	………….	………….

The following additional information is provided on 30 June 20–3:

	$
Land and building at cost	98 000
Fixtures and equipment at cost	50 000
Motor vehicles at cost	36 000
Trade payables	8 450
Trade receivables	16 800
Other payables	870
Other receivables	650
Inventory	15 680
Provision for doubtful debts	420
Provision for depreciation of fixtures and equipment	13 550
Provision for depreciation of motor vehicles	22 500
5% debentures (repayable in 10 years)	20 000
Bank overdraft	5 140

b Prepare the statement of financial position at 30 June 20–3.

The directors of LS Limited are hoping to expand the business and estimate that $45 000 will be required. They discussed whether to issue ordinary shares or 5% debentures and decided to issue 5% debentures.

The directors do not expect the expansion to have any impact on the operating profit for the first three years. After that the annual operating profit is expected to increase by 10%.

c State **two** features of ordinary shares.

d State **two** features of debentures.

e Calculate the annual profit after interest the company is expected to earn over each of the next three years.

f Calculate the annual profit after interest the company is expected to earn in Year 4.

g Suggest how the ordinary shareholders may be affected if it is decided to issue debentures rather than additional ordinary shares.

17 DC Limited was formed some years ago. The financial year ends on 30 April.
The following information is available:

	$
On 1 May 20–8:	
Ordinary share capital (300 000 shares of $0.50 each)	150 000
General reserve	35 000
Retained earnings	13 500
On 31 August 20–8:	
Ordinary share dividend of $0.05 was paid	
On 1 November 20–8:	
An issue of 5% debentures was made	40 000
For the year ended 30 April 20–9:	
Operating profit for the year	65 500

On 30 April 20–9:
The directors recommended a transfer to general reserve of $6 000 and the payment of an ordinary share dividend of $0.10.

a Explain each of the following terms:
  i issued share capital
  ii called-up share capital
  iii paid-up share capital.
b State **two** differences between ordinary shares and debentures.
c Explain why DC Limited retains some profit each year.
d State **one** reason why DC Limited pays a dividend to ordinary shareholders.
e Calculate the profit for the year ended 30 April 20–9.
f Calculate the retained earnings on 30 April 20–9.
g Prepare an extract from the statement of financial position on 30 April 20–9 to show the capital and reserves section.

18 Marcus is a trader selling and buying on both cash and credit terms.
He provided the following information on 28 February 20–9:

	$
Inventory	7 600
Trade payables	5 460
Trade receivables	6 150
Loan repayable 30 September 20–9	4 000
Balance at bank	650

The total sales for the year ended 28 February 20–9 amounted to $110 000, of which $36 800 represented cash sales. Marcus allows his credit customers 30 days' credit.

The total purchases for the year ended 28 February 20–9 amounted to $88 800, of which one quarter represented cash purchases. Marcus is allowed 21 days credit by his credit suppliers.

a i State the formula for the calculation of the current ratio.

   ii Calculate the current ratio.

   iii Comment on your answer to **ii**.

b i State the formula for the calculation of the liquid (acid test) ratio.

   ii Calculate the liquid (acid test) ratio.

   iii Comment on your answer to **ii**.

c i State the formula for the calculation of the trade receivables turnover.

   ii Calculate the trade receivables turnover.

   iii Comment on your answer to **ii**.

   iv Suggest **two** ways in which the trade receivables turnover may be improved.

d i State the formula for the calculation of the trade payables turnover.

   ii Calculate the trade payables turnover.

   iii Suggest **one** advantage to the credit suppliers of your answer to **ii**.

   iv Suggest **one** disadvantage to the credit suppliers of your answer to **ii**.

19 The financial year of YZ Limited ends on 30 November. The capital consists of ordinary shares of $1 each. No additional shares were issued during the year ended 30 November 20–7. The company has no non-current liabilities.

The following information is available:

For the year ended 30 November 20–6:

Gross margin	23.50%
Profit margin	9.25%
Return on capital employed	5.54%

For the year ended 30 November 20–7:

	$
Revenue	360 000
Expenses	44 500
Gross margin	20.00%

On 30 November 20–7:

	$
Non-current assets	543 000
Current assets	119 500
Current liabilities	92 500

a Suggest **two** reasons for the change in the gross margin over the two years.

b i Calculate the profit for the year ended 30 November 20–7.

ii Calculate the profit margin (to two decimal places) for the year ended 30 November 20–7.

iii State in which year the company had better control of the expenses. Give a reason for your answer.

c i Calculate the return on capital employed.

ii Comment on the change in the return on capital employed over the two years.

iii State, giving reasons, how each of the following transactions would affect the return on capital employed:

Transaction 1 Sale for cash of surplus non-current assets at book value.

Transaction 2 Issue of additional ordinary shares.

Transaction 3 Receipt of a long-term loan.

Glossary

Accounting is using book-keeping records to prepare financial statements and to assist in decision-making.

Accrued expense is an expense relating to a particular accounting period which is unpaid at the end of that period.

Accrued income is income relating to a particular accounting period which has not been received at the end of that period.

Accumulated fund consists of the surpluses (less any deficits) which have accumulated over the life of the organisation. It replaces capital in the statement of financial position of a club or society.

Analysis columns are used to divide the payments into different categories.

Assets represent anything owed by or owing to the business.

Balance on a ledger account is the difference between the debit side and the credit side.

Bank overdraft occurs when more has been paid out of the bank than was put into the bank account.

Bank reconciliation statement is a document prepared by a business to explain why the updated bank balance in the cash book does not agree with the balance on the bank statement.

Bank statement is a copy of a customer's account in the books of the bank which is sent to the customer at regular intervals.

Book of prime entry is one in which transactions are recorded before being entered in the ledger.

Book-keeping is the detailed recording of all the financial transactions of a business.

Business entity principle means that the business is treated as being completely separate from the owner of the business.

Called up capital is that part of the issued share capital for which payment has been requested from shareholders.

Capital is the total resources provided by the owner and represents what the business owes the owner.

Capital expenditure is money spent on purchasing, improving or extending non-current assets.

Capital receipt is money received by a business from a source other than the normal trading activities.

Carriage inwards is the cost of bringing the goods to the business.

Carriage is the cost of transporting goods.

Carriage outwards is the cost of delivering the goods to the customer.

Cash discount is an allowance given to a customer when an account is settled within a time limit set by the supplier.

Cheque is a written order to a bank to pay a stated sum of money to the person or business named on the order.

Consistency principle means that accounting methods must be used consistently from one accounting period to the next.

Contra entries may be referred to as inter-ledger transfers or set-offs and are when a transfer is made from an account in the sales ledger to an account of the same business/person in the purchases ledger.

Contra entry is one which appears on both sides of the cash book.

Cost of production is prime cost plus factory overheads, adjusted for any work in progress at the start and at the end of the year. It is the total cost of manufacturing the goods completed.

Credit note is a document issued by a seller of goods on credit to notify of a reduction in an invoice previously issued.

Current assets are short-term assets whose amounts are constantly changing.

Current liabilities are amounts owed which are due for repayment within the next 12 months.

Debenture is a long-term loan which has a fixed rate of interest, payable irrespective of the profit of the company.

Debit note is a document issued by a purchaser of goods on credit to request a reduction in the invoice received.

Debt written off may be recovered if a credit customer pays some, or all, the amount owed, after the amount was written off.

Deficit arises when the expenses of a non-trading organisation exceed the gains.

Depreciation is an estimate of the loss in value of a non-current asset over its expected working life.

Dishonoured cheque is a cheque received which the debtor's bank refuses to pay.

Double entry book-keeping is the process of making a debit entry and a credit entry for each transaction.

Drawings represent any value taken from the business by the owner of that business.

Equity is the total funds provided by the shareholders of the company.

Going concern principle means that the accounting records are maintained on the basis that the business will continue to operate for an indefinite period of time.

Goodwill is the amount by which the value of a business as a whole exceeds the value of the separate assets and liabilities.

Gross profit is the difference between the selling price and the cost of those goods.

Historic cost principle means that all assets and expenses are initially recorded at their actual cost.

Imprest system of petty cash is where the amount spent each period is restored so that the petty cashier starts each period with the same amount.

Income and expenditure account is prepared annually by a non-trading organisation. It compares the gains and the expenses to calculate the surplus or deficit.

Income statement is a statement prepared for a trading period to show the gross profit and profit for the year.

Inventory is the goods a business has available for resale.

Invoice is a document issued by the supplier of goods on credit showing details, quantities and prices of goods supplied.

Irrecoverable debt is an amount owing to a business which will not be paid by the credit customer.

Issued share capital is the amount of capital issued to the shareholders.

Journal is a book of prime entry used to record transactions which cannot be recorded in any other book of prime entry.

Liabilities represent anything owed by the business.

Limited company is a legal entity which has a separate identity from its shareholders, whose liability for the company's debts is limited.

Liquidity ratios measure the ability of the business to turn assets into cash to pay its short term debts.

Manufacturing account is part of the annual financial statements and is used to calculate the cost of goods produced.

Margin is the gross profit expressed as a percentage of the selling price.

Mark-up is the gross profit expressed as a percentage of cost price.

Matching principle means that the revenue of the accounting period is matched against the costs of the same period.

Materiality principle means that individual items which will not significantly affect either the profit or the assets of a business do not need to be recorded separately.

Money measurement principle means that only information which can be expressed in terms of money can be recorded in the accounting records.

Net book value of a non-current asset is the cost price minus the total depreciation to date.

Nominal (general) ledger the ledger where all the other accounts are maintained.

Non-current assets are assets which are obtained for use and not for resale, which help the business earn revenue.

Non-current liabilities are amounts owed which are not due for repayment within the next 12 months.

Non-trading organisation is an organisation formed to provide facilities and services for members. They are not formed with the aim of making a profit.

Paid up capital is that part of the called up share capital for which the company has received payment from shareholders.

Partnership is a business in which two or more people work together as owners with a view to making profits.

Partnership agreement is a document setting out the rules under which the partners will operate the business, including profit-sharing arrangements.

Glossary

Partnership appropriation account is part of the year-end financial statements. It shows the division of the profit or loss between the partners.

Petty cash book is used to record low-value cash payments.

Prepaid expense is an expense paid during the financial year which relates to a future accounting period.

Prepaid income is income received during the financial year which relates to a future accounting period.

Prime cost is the total of the direct materials, direct labour and direct expenses. It is the cost of the essentials necessary for production.

Principle of duality means that every transaction is recorded twice – once on the debit side and once on the credit side.

Profit for the year is the final profit after any other income has been added to the gross profit and the running expenses have been deducted.

Profitability ratios measure the performance of the business by comparing the profit to other figures in the same set of financial statements.

Provision for doubtful debts is an estimate of the amount which a business will lose in a financial year because of irrecoverable debts.

Prudence principle means that profits and assets should not be overstated and losses and liabilities should not be understated. However, the exercise of produce does not allow the deliberate understatement of assets or income, or the deliberate overstatement of liabilities or expenses. In short, produce does not permit bias.

Purchases journal shows a list of the names of businesses from which credit purchases have been made, the value of the goods purchased and the date on which the purchases were made.

Purchases ledger is a ledger in which the accounts of credit suppliers are maintained.

Purchases ledger control account is an account summarising all the accounts of the trade payables.

Purchases returns journal shows a list of the names of businesses to which goods, previously purchased on credit, have been returned, the value of the goods returned and the date on which the returns were made.

Rate of inventory turnover is the number of times a business replaces its inventory in a given period of time.

Realisation principle means that revenue is only regarded as being earned when the legal title to goods passes from the seller to the buyer.

Receipt is a written acknowledgement of money received and acts as proof of payment.

Receipts and payments account is a summary of the cash book which is prepared annually by a non-trading organisation.

Redeemable preference shares are those preference shares which must be bought back by the company at an agreed date and for an agreed price.

Reducing balance method of depreciation is where the depreciation charged each year decreases as it is calculated on the net book value rather than the cost.

Residual profit is the profit remaining after adjusting the profit for the year for interest on drawings, interest on capital and partners' salaries. It is divided between the partners in the agreed profit-sharing ratio.

Residual value is the value of a non-current asset at the end of its useful life.

Revaluation method of depreciation is where the opening and closing value of a non-current asset are compared (after adjusting for any additions during the year) to determine the depreciation for the year.

Revenue expenditure is money spent on running a business on a day-to-day basis.

Revenue receipt is money received by a business from normal trading activities.

Sales journal shows a list of the names of businesses to which credit sales have been made, the value of the goods sold and the date on which the sales were made.

Sales ledger is the ledger in which the accounts of credit customers are maintained.

Sales ledger control account is an account summarising all the accounts of the trade receivables.

Sales returns journal shows a list of the names of businesses which have returned goods previously sold on credit, the value of the goods returned and the date on which the returns were made.

Service business is one which provides a service.

Statement of account is a document issued by the seller of goods on credit to summarise the transactions for the month.

Statement of affairs is a summary of the financial position of a business on a certain date. It is prepared instead of a statement of financial position when double entry records have not been maintained.

Statement of financial position is a statement of the assets and liabilities of a business on a certain date.

Straight line method of depreciation is where the same amount of depreciation is charged each year.

Subscriptions are amounts members of an organisation pay, usually annually, to use the facilities provided by the club or society.

Surplus arises when the gains of a non-trading organisation exceed the expenses.

Suspense account is a temporary account opened in order to make the totals of a trial balance agree.

Trade discount is a reduction in the price of goods and the rate often increases according to quantity purchased.

Trade payables represent the amount the business owes to the credit suppliers of goods (the trade creditors).

Trade receivables represent the amount owed to the business by its credit customers (the trade debtors).

Trading business is one which buys and sells goods.

Trial balance is a list of balances on the accounts in the ledger at a certain date.

Work in progress is the goods which are partly completed at the end of the financial year.

Index

accounting, definition 3, 345
accounting entity principle 121
accounting equation 4–6
accounting ratios 313
accounting rules 121–9
accounting statements
    limitations 326–7
    users 325–6
accruals 133
accruals principle 123
accrued expenses 133–5, 345
accrued income 142–4, 345
accumulated depreciation 163
accumulated fund 267, 272–3, 345
adjustments, year-end 133, 297
analysis and interpretation
    inter-firm comparison 322–4
    limitations of accounting statements 326–7
    liquidity ratios 317–21, 346
    overview 313–14
    profitability ratios 315–17, 347
    users of accounting statements 325–6
analysis columns 54, 345
appropriation accounts 280, 347
asset accounts 159
assets
    definition 4, 345
    recorded in ledger accounts 13–14
    recorded in statements of affairs 242
    recorded in statements of financial position 111–12
    see also current assets; non-current assets

balances, opening 138–41, 147–9
balancing ledger accounts 17–18, 345
bank charges 196
bank interest 196
bank managers 325
bank overdrafts 43–4, 201–2, 345
bank reconciliation
    and overdrafts 201–2
    differences between records 195–6
    stages of 197–200
bank reconciliation statements 197, 345
bank statements 195–6, 345
boards of directors 303
book-keeping 3, 345
    see also double entry book-keeping
books of prime (original) entry 40, 79, 345
business entity principle 121, 345

called up capital 304, 345
capital
    definition 4, 112, 345
    employed 313
    of clubs and societies 267
    owned 313
    profit calculated by changes in 242–3
    working 313
capital accounts 17, 103–4, 242–3, 281
capital expenditure 126, 154, 345
capital receipts 126–7, 165, 345
carriage 23, 345
carriage inwards 23, 345
carriage outwards 23, 345
cash
    floats 53
    goods purchased for 18
    goods sold for 20
    not yet credited 195
cash books
    bank overdrafts in 43–4
    contra entries in 40–3
    errors in 196
    items not recorded in 196
    three column 44–5
    two column 40
    see also petty cash books
cash discount 44–5, 68, 252, 345
cheques
    dishonoured 45, 196, 346
    goods purchased for 18
    goods sold for 20
    not yet credited 195
    not yet presented 195
    payments by 73, 345
closing capital 242–3
closing work in progress 294
clubs and societies
    accounting terms used by 269
    as non-trading organisations 262
    calculation of accumulated fund 272–3
    calculation of sales and purchases 271–2
    members 326
    membership subscriptions 262, 270–1, 348
    preparation of income and expenditure accounts 265–7
    preparation of income statements 264
    preparation of receipts and payments accounts 262–3
    preparation of statements of financial position 267–9
combined expense accounts 141–2

commission, errors of 34, 218
comparability of financial statements 125
compensating errors 35, 218
complete reversal, errors of 34, 218
concepts (accounting principles) 121
conservatism (prudence principle) 124, 347
consistency principle 122, 345
contra entries
    in cash books 40–3, 345
    in control accounts 235–7, 345
control accounts
    advantages 229
    balances on both sides of 234–5
    contra entries 235–7, 345
    purchases ledger 232–3, 347
    purpose 229
    sales ledger 229–31, 347
conventions (accounting principles) 121
correction of errors 218–21
cost of production 292, 345
cost of sales 97
costs, historic 326
credit
    goods purchased on 18–19, 82
    goods sold on 20, 79
credit balances 234–5
credit cards 40
credit control 174
credit limits 174
credit notes 71–2, 345
credit purchases 249
credit sales 248
credit side of a ledger account 11
credit transfers 40, 196
creditors, trade 5, 19
creditors ledgers (purchases ledgers) 39, 347
current accounts 281–2
current assets 112, 136, 345
current liabilities 112, 133, 345
current ratio 317–18
customers 326

debentures 305, 345
debit balances 234–5
debit cards 40
debit notes 69–71, 345
debit side of a ledger account 11
debtors, trade 5, 20
debtors ledgers (sales ledgers) 39, 347
debts
    irrecoverable 172, 174, 346
    written off 172–4, 345

debts recovered accounts 172
deficits 265, 345
depletion of non-current assets 155
depreciation
    accumulated 163
    causes 154–5
    definition 154, 346
    in the financial statements 162–5
    in the ledger 159–62
    methods of calculating 155–8
depreciation to date 163
deterioration of non-current assets 154
direct debits 40, 196
direct expenses 291
direct labour costs 291
direct material costs 291, 292
direct wages 291
directors, boards of 303
discount
    cash 44–5, 68, 252, 345
    trade 68, 82, 85, 348
discount allowed 44–5
discount received 44–5
dishonoured cheques 45, 196, 346
disposal of non-current assets 165–7
dividends 303, 304–5, 306
double entry book-keeping
    advantages 242
    definition 3, 346
    principles 11–12
    see also ledger accounts
drawings 17, 346
drawings accounts 282
dual aspect principle 122, 347

economic reasons for depreciation 154
electronic payments 40
employees 326
equity 305, 346
errors
    compensating 35, 218
    correction of 218–21
    effects on profit 222–3
    effects on statements on financial position 223
    of commission 34, 218
    of complete reversal 34, 218
    of omission 34, 218
    of original entry 35, 218
    of principle 35, 218
excess of expenditure over income (deficit) 265, 345

excess of income over expenditure (surplus) 265, 348
expense accounts
    combined 141–2
    opening balances of 138–41
expenses
    accrued 133–5, 345
    in ledger accounts 14–16
    manufacturing 291
    prepaid 136–8
external users of accounting statements 325–6

factory overheads 291
financial statements 3, 125–6
financial year 7
fixed instalment method of depreciation (straight line method) 155–6, 159–62, 348
floats, cash 53
folio numbers 11
fundraising activities 265

general journals see journals (general journals)
general ledgers (nominal ledgers) 39, 346
going concern principle 122, 346
goods purchased for cash or cheque 18
goods purchased on credit 18–19, 82
goods returned 21–3, 83
goods sold for cash or cheque 20
goods sold on credit 20, 79
goodwill 112, 346
government departments 326
gross margin 315–16
gross profit 97, 254, 295, 346
gross profit as a percentage of turnover (gross margin) 315–16

historic cost principle 122, 154, 346
historic costs 326
horizontal format
    income statements 97, 99
    statements of financial position 113

imprest system 53, 346
income
    accrued 142–4
    in ledger accounts 14–16
    prepaid 144–6, 347
income accounts, opening balances of 147–9
income and expenditure accounts 265–7, 346

income statements
    definition 3, 95, 346
    horizontal and vertical formats 97–8, 99–100
    of clubs and societies 264
    of limited companies 305
    of service businesses 105–6
    profit and loss section of 99–101, 296–7
    recording accrued and prepaid expenses in 133–8
    recording accrued and prepaid income in 142–6
    recording depreciation in 162–3
    recording irrecoverable debts in 172
    recording provision for doubtful debts in 175–80
    trading section of 97–9, 264, 295–6
    transferring ledger account totals to 102–4
incomplete records 242–57
indirect factory expenses 291
intangible non-current assets 111–12
interest, bank 196
inter-firm comparison 322–4
inter-ledger transfers (contra entries) 235–7, 345
internal users of accounting statements 325
international accounting standards 125–6
interpretation see analysis and interpretation
inventory
    at the end of the year 103
    at the start of the year 103
    definition 5, 346
    manufacturing 294
    of stationery etc. 138
    turnover 255–6, 319, 347
    valuation 127–9
inventory accounts 18, 103
invoices 68–9, 346
irrecoverable debts 172, 174, 346
irrecoverable debts accounts 172
issued share capital 304, 346

journals (general journals)
    correction of errors 218–21
    definition 207, 346
    non-regular transactions 210–18
    opening entries 207–9
    purchase and sale of non-current assets 209–10

Index

labour costs 291
ledger accounts
   balancing 17–18
   in partnerships 281–4
   interpretation 25–6
   layout 11, 24–5
   recording assets and liabilities in 13–14
   recording carriage inwards and carriage outwards in 23
   recording drawings in 17
   recording expenses and income in 14–16
   recording sales, purchases and returns in 18–23
   transferring totals to income statements 102–4
   see also cash books; nominal ledgers (general ledgers); purchases ledgers; sales ledgers
ledgers, definition 11
lenders 325
liabilities
   current 112, 133, 345
   definition 4, 346
   non-current 112, 346
   recorded in ledger accounts 14–16
   recorded in statements of affairs 242
   recorded in statements of financial position 112–15
lifespan of non-current assets 154
limited companies
   debentures 305, 345
   definition 303, 346
   income statements 305
   nature of 303
   share capital 304–5
   statements of changes in equity 306–7
   statements of financial position 307–8
liquid (acid test) ratio 318
liquidity ratios 317–21, 346
loan notes (debentures) 305, 345
loans, from partners 278–9
loss for the year 99, 103–4

managers 325
manufacturing accounts
   adjustment for work in progress 294
   calculation of unit cost 295
   definition 291, 346
   preparation 292–3

manufacturing businesses
   elements of cost of manufacture 291
   preparation of profit and loss section of income statement 296–7
   preparation of statement of financial position 297
   preparation of trading section of income statement 295–6
   year-end adjustments 297
   see also manufacturing accounts
margin 254, 346
mark-up 254, 346
matching principle
   applied to expenses 133, 136
   applied to income 142, 144
   definition 123, 346
material costs 291, 292
materiality principle 123, 346
membership subscriptions 262, 270–1, 348
money measurement principle 124, 346
money paid 54
money received 54

narratives, in journals 207
net book value 154, 157, 346
net current assets 313
net purchases 97
net realisable value of inventory 127
nominal accounts 39
nominal ledgers (general ledgers) 39, 346
non-current assets
   capital expenditure on 126
   definition 346
   disposal of 165–7
   low-value items 123
   recording purchase and sale of 209–10
   tangible and intangible 111–12
   see also depreciation
non-current liabilities 112, 346
non-redeemable preference shares 305
non-regular transactions 210–18
non-trading organisations 262, 346
   see also clubs and societies

obsolescence of non-current assets 154
omission, errors of 34, 218
opening balances
   expense accounts 138–41
   income accounts 147–9
opening capital 242–3
opening journal entries 207–9
opening work in progress 294

ordinary shares 305
original entry, errors of 35, 218
'other payables' 135
'other receivables' 137
overdrafts, bank 43–4, 201–2, 345
overdue accounts 174
overheads, factory 291
owners, business 325
owner's equity (capital) *see* capital

paid up capital 304, 346
partnership agreements 279, 346
partnership appropriation accounts 280, 347
partnerships
   advantages and disadvantages 278
   agreements 279, 346
   definition 278, 346
   loans from partners 278–9
   partners' ledger accounts 281–4
   preparation of appropriation accounts 280–1
   preparation of statements of financial position 284–5
petty cash books
   definition 53, 347
   imprest system 53–4
   layout 54
   preparation 54–7
petty cash vouchers 53
physical deterioration of non-current assets 154
ploughing back profits 306
potential buyers of a business 325
preference shares 304–5
prepaid expenses 136–8, 347
prepaid income 144–6, 347
prepayments 136
prime cost 292, 347
prime entry, books of 40, 79, 345
principle, errors of 35, 218
principle of consistency 122, 345
principle of duality 122, 347
principle of prudence 124, 347
private limited companies 303
production, cost of 292, 345
profit
   calculated by changes in capital 242–3
   different definitions of 326
   effect of correcting errors 222–3
   for the year 99, 103, 347
   gross 97, 254, 295, 346
   margin 316–17
   ploughing back 306
   residual 280, 347

profit and loss section of income
    statements 99–101, 296–7
profit for the year 99, 103, 347
profit margin 316–17
profitability ratios 315–17, 347
provision for depreciation accounts
    159
provision for doubtful debts
    adjusting 177–80
    creating 175–6
    definition 174–5, 347
prudence principle 124, 347
public limited companies 303
purchases accounts 18–19
purchases journals (purchases books;
    purchases day books) 82, 347
purchases ledger control accounts
    232–3, 347
purchases ledgers 39, 347
purchases returns 21
purchases returns journals (purchases
    returns books) 83–5, 347

rate of inventory turnover 255–6, 319,
    347
raw materials 291, 292
realisation principle 124, 347
receipts 74, 347
receipts and payments accounts
    262–3, 347
reconciliation, bank *see* bank
    reconciliation
redeemable preference shares 305, 347
reducing balance method of
    depreciation 157, 347
relevance of financial statements 125
reliability of financial statements 125
residual profit 280, 347
residual value 156, 347
retained earnings 306
return on capital employed (ROCE) 315
returned goods 21–3, 83
returns inwards 21
returns inwards books (sales returns
    journals) 80–2, 347
returns outward 21
returns outward books (purchases
    returns journals) 83–5, 347
revaluation method of depreciation
    158, 162, 347
revenue 96
revenue expenditure 126, 347
revenue receipts 127, 347
ROCE (return on capital employed) 315
royalties 291

sales, cost of 97
sales accounts 20–1
sales journals (sales books; sales day
    books) 79, 347
sales ledger control accounts 229–31,
    347
sales ledgers 39, 347
sales returns 21
sales returns journals (sales returns
    books) 80–2, 347
service businesses 105–6, 347
set-offs (contra entries) 235–7, 345
share capital 304
shareholders 303
shares 303–5
societies *see* clubs and societies
sole traders 4, 95
standing orders 40, 196
statements of account 72–3, 348
statements of affairs 242–53, 348
statements of changes in equity 306–7
statements of financial position
    content 6–7
    definition 3, 111, 348
    effect of correcting errors 223
    horizontal and vertical formats
        113–14
    of clubs and societies 267–9
    of limited companies 307–8
    of manufacturing businesses 297
    of partnerships 284–5
    recording accrued and prepaid
        expenses in 133–5
    recording accrued and prepaid
        income in 142–6
    recording assets in 111–12
    recording depreciation in 163
    recording liabilities in 112–15
    recording provision for doubtful
        debts in 175–80
stationery, inventory of 138
straight line method of depreciation
    155–6, 159–62, 348
subscriptions, membership 262, 270–1,
    348
subscriptions accounts 270
subsidiary books (books of prime entry)
    40, 79, 345
surpluses 265, 348
suspense accounts 219, 348

'T' account format 24
tangible non-current assets 111
three column cash books 44–5
three column running balance
    accounts 24–5
time, depreciation over 297

timing differences
    and accounting statements 327
    and bank statements 195
total accounts *see* control accounts
total trade payables accounts
    (purchases ledger control accounts)
    232–3, 347
total trade receivables accounts (sales
    ledger control accounts) 229–31, 347
trade creditors 5, 19
trade debtors 5, 20
trade discount 68, 82, 85, 348
trade payables 5, 325, 348
trade payables ledgers (purchases
    ledgers) 39, 347
trade payables/purchases ratio 321
trade payables turnover 321
trade receivables 5, 348
trade receivables ledgers (sales ledgers)
    39, 347
trade receivables/sales ratio 320
trade receivables turnover 320
trade unions 326
trading businesses 105, 348
trading section of income statements
    97–9, 264, 295–6
treasurers of clubs and societies 262
trial balances
    and financial statements 95
    definition 30, 348
    errors affecting 219
    errors in 34–5
    errors not shown by 218
    preparation 30–3
    purpose 30
two column cash books 40

understandability of financial
    statements 125–6
unit cost 295

vertical format
    income statements 98, 100
    statements of financial position 114

wages 291
wear and tear on non-current assets 154
work in progress 294, 348
working capital 313
working capital ratio 317–18
written down value (net book value)
    154, 157, 346
written off debts 172–4, 345

year-end adjustments 133, 297